Natural Resources and Public Property under the Canadian Constitution

Natural Resources
and
Public Property
under the
Canadian Constitution

GERARD V. LA FOREST QC

University of Toronto Press

TO MARIE

1765746

Preface

This book largely reproduces a series of lectures given at the Faculté de droit of the Université de Montréal in the fall of 1962. The lectures were the outcome of the kind invitation of that faculty to give a course on a constitutional law subject of my choice to the doctoral students in the faculty's then recently inaugurated graduate programme. The book follows the lectures quite faithfully, though the treatment of certain topics, notably the more detailed sections of the British North America Act, 1930, has been considerably expanded, and other sections, particularly the chapter on offshore submarine resources, have been substantially rewritten in the light of recent developments. The lectures were originally given under the title, "The Constitution and Public Property." The name, though technically accurate, has been changed because the term "public property" ordinarily connotes a much more restricted subject than is here dealt with, for public property in the constitution includes all the natural resources comprised in the public domain.

The invitation to deliver these lectures was most welcome. Not only did it afford me the opportunity to delve into a relatively unexplored subject which, as I have tried to indicate in the Introduction, seems to me to be of fundamental importance; as well, I was able to observe at first hand the functioning of a civil law school that follows the French tradition of legal education. But perhaps most rewarding was the opportunity to savour the university atmosphere in Montreal during this most exciting period of French Canada's history, an experience all the more fascinating to a French Canadian from another province. One often hears of the "quiet revolution" now unfolding itself in Quebec, but it is often overlooked in other parts of Canada that one can equally well speak of a French-Canadian Renaissance. It is this blossoming of French culture and ideas that I found especially impressive. The remarkable progress of the Université de Montréal is one of the more striking aspects of this development. The Faculté de droit has shared fully in this movement; for example, the establishment of the Institut de recherche en droit public marks an important step in the development of juridical science in this country.

I am most grateful to the late Dean Maximilien Caron and the other members of the faculty, particularly Professor Jean Beetz, the former Director of the Institut, and now Dean of the faculty, for making my sojourn in Montreal so pleasant. I would also be remiss in my duty if I did not specially thank Dean William F. Ryan of the Faculty of Law of the University of New Brunswick who not only took over a part of my duties during my absence but whose friendship and encouragement were a constant help throughout my period at the University of New Brunswick. I am also grateful to the editor of the *Canadian Bar Review* for permission to reproduce that portion of chapter four dealing with public harbours which appeared, with variations, in the December 1963 issue of that publication (41 *Can. Bar Rev.* 519) under the title "The Meaning of 'Public Harbours' in the Third Schedule to the British North America Act, 1867."

Finally, I should like to express my appreciation to the Canada Council for a grant that ensured publication of the work, and to members of the editorial department of the University of Toronto Press for their assistance during its publication.

G. V. LA F.

Faculty of Law, University of Alberta
December 1968

Contents

Introduction

The public domain has always been, and continues to be of major importance in the workings of the Canadian constitution. In the early years of Canada, the British government could well ignore the wishes of the representatives of the people and govern through a governor and his council because many of the expenses of government were met without the help of the electorate. The Crown owned all the ungranted lands and many valuable rights of a semi-proprietary nature, the revenues from which could be used for the public service of the country. Power of the legislatures to appropriate these revenues was a necessary goal in the struggle for responsible government.

Under the Confederation arrangements, the revenues from public property remained subject to the appropriation of the provinces, except those arising out of certain properties (such as, for example, public harbours) that are closely associated with matters within the legislative competence of the federal parliament. The revenues from public property, it was thought, would be adequate or nearly adequate to meet the needs of the public service, and to this day they continue to provide a substantial portion of the revenues of the provinces. A different practice prevailed in the new provinces carved out of the vast territories comprising the former Rupert's Land and North-western territories. There the federal government retained ownership of the natural resources for many years, thereby ensuring substantial control of the development of the west. But this anomalous situation was removed in 1930 when the Resources Agreements transferred to the Prairie provinces the administration and control of their natural resources.

The early years of Confederation saw many cases dealing with the distribution of public property between the federal and provincial authorities, and today all major problems of ownership of the public domain have been settled except, in some provinces, the conflicting claims to offshore submarine resources. The partition of the public domain between the Dominion and the provinces constitutes the major part of this work. Generally the result is that all natural resources in the provinces, except those specifically transferred to the federal authorities, belong to the provinces, and those outside the limits of the provinces belong to the federal government.

The courts have stood firm against any use of federal legislative power amounting in substance to an exercise of proprietary rights over provincial property. This judicial attitude clearly coincides with the general approach of the Fathers of Confederation, for a reading of the British North America Act in the light of earlier history reveals with abundant clarity that the Fathers intended the bulk of the public domain to remain vested in the provinces. But while one may agree with the general result and its basic accord with the fundamental nature of Canadian federalism, judicial craftsmanship in this area (particularly by the Privy Council) leaves much to be desired. Though it was clearly necessary for the courts to safeguard this important source of provincial revenue against federal encroachment, the restrictive approach to federal rights, whether legislative or proprietary, whenever they came in contact with provincial proprietary interests, seems excessive. One has only to mention the interpretation given the items transferred by virtue of section 108 of the BNA Act to make the point. The artificial division of the foreshore of public harbours, for example, is surely out of place in constitutional interpretation; it is not even certain yet whether the federal interest in a public harbour includes the underlying minerals in the bed and foreshore. A similar approach was followed when federal legislative power conflicted with provincial property rights. Some cases indicate that the federal parliament may lack power to expropriate provincial lands for schemes falling squarely under such legislative heads as seacoast and inland fisheries and Indians, and that in expropriating such lands it is limited to the type of interest required to effect the particular purpose; for instance in expropriating for railway purposes, the federal government is constitutionally limited, according to some *dicta*, to surface rights. Reformulation of principles on broader lines seems clearly called for. The essential is the protection of provincial public property; any attempt at federal encroachment must be resisted, but this should not require fragmentation of ownership or artificial restrictions on federal legislative power.

The raising of a revenue is not the sole reason that public property is of fundamental importance to the provinces. It also provides them with a powerful instrument for the control of their economic and political destinies. By requiring that resources from public property be processed within its boundaries, a province can materially contribute towards the establishment of secondary industries there, and prevent the export of raw material to other countries. It can also encourage colonization and the development of industry by judicious grants of such property. It can further shape the economy by public ownership of industry and thereby dictate what class will control the economic sphere of society.

Ownership of public property also strengthens the position of the provinces in relation to the federal authorities. A province has wider legislative jurisdiction over its property than over private property, and this sometimes gives it some control in areas that would otherwise be wholly federal. The mere ownership of property gives the province considerable bargaining power when the federal government proposes schemes requiring the use of such property. Again, the ownership of property may be a means of diverting revenues from the federal to the provincial coffers. A provincially owned industry is constitutionally exempt from taxation by the federal parliament, so that revenues derived from taxes that would go to the federal government if an industry were privately owned remain as profits to the province, a matter of no inconsiderable importance having regard to the great demands made on the taxing powers of the provinces.

The federal government also uses its powers over public property as a means of fostering important schemes. In the early days of Confederation, grants of public property under the control of the federal government played no inconsiderable part in the construction of the railways and the colonization of the west. The federal government has long implemented policies within its sphere – notably in regard to railways, aeronautics, radio, and television – through public ownership, and in doing so it can and has created monopolistic tax-free enterprises. Moreover there is nothing to prevent it from acquiring or carrying on undertakings ordinarily falling within the provincial sphere and operating them free of provincial regulatory control by virtue of its exclusive legislative jurisdiction over its property. This head of power includes the federal "lending" and "spending" powers and so constitutes part of the basis for many important social service schemes such as family allowances and the many federal money-lending activities. Through conditional grants in aid the federal authorities also exercise considerable indirect control over many matters that would otherwise be within the provincial sphere. This is sometimes done with the co-operation of the provinces, but the desire of a province to share in benefits provided by the federal parliament may cause it to accept policies that it might not otherwise follow.

It might be added that the federal parliament has considerable powers in respect of provincial natural resources because, in legislating within its power, its authority is paramount. Thus if a province wishes to develop its fisheries or develop power or exploit minerals in navigable waters, it must comply with any applicable federal legislation. It is obvious, therefore, that much of Canada's resources cannot be developed without co-operation between federal and provincial authorities. But to do this intelligently, knowledge of their jurisdiction is highly desirable, if not absolutely necessary.

From the foregoing one would expect to find considerable literature on the constitutional position of natural resources and public property. Yet there is very little. Clement devoted an important chapter to Crown property in his *Canadian Constitution*, but that book is now over fifty years old. There are, too, Mr. Justice Laskin's paper for the Resources for Tomorrow Conference and several useful notes in his casebook; considerable work has also been done on the federal "spending power." But little else is available.

There is, therefore, a crying need for a general survey of the whole subject, and that is the purpose of this study. In making this examination, I have confined myself to the constitutional framework. True, considerable historical perspective is given, but this is done not for antiquarian reasons but to explain the present situation. No examination of the political implications of the law is made except, interstitially, to show the context in which the law exists. Nor is the whole of the constitutional law of natural resources and public property examined. The unwritten parts of the constitution borrowed from Great Britain are not, in general, studied in any detail. Thus such matters as the manner of issuing letters patent, the limitations present in a Crown grant and many other problems are dealt with, if at all, in relation to some special situation in the Canadian constitution. The study, in fact, is largely confined to the provisions of the BNA acts dealing specifically with natural resources and public property, and the position of the federal and provincial authorities under these. The application of other parts of the constitution to natural resources is not examined. Non-constitutional statutes affecting natural resources and public property are studied when they substantially alter the general constitutional position, but no attempt is made to canvass all statutes providing for local or minor variations.

Natural Resources and Public Property under the Canadian Constitution

CHAPTER ONE

Historical Background

IN ENGLAND

For a full understanding of the constitutional role of natural resources in Canada, it is necessary to resort to history. And, in common with most subjects on Canadian constitutional law, the beginnings of this history are to be found in England. It is, of course, beyond the scope of this study to deal in any detail with the English background, but enough must be said to explain the Canadian position.

Public property and public rights in property have played a central role in English constitutional law.[1] In feudal times the bulk of national services was paid out of territorial and casual revenues, most of which accrued from the king's property or his rights in the property of others. First, he obtained the rents from the ancient demesne, the unappropriated land which before the conquest was considered land of the nation that the king could use only with the consent of the wise but which after the conquest became *terra Regis* that he could use as he pleased. The king also was entitled to the rights arising out of feudal tenure, which supplied him with an army and many profitable incidents such as escheats. In addition he had numerous prerogative rights – rights arising out of his pre-eminence and legal dignity at common law – which provided him with further revenue. Thus the sovereign is entitled to all mines of gold and silver in the realm, whether situate in his own land or in that of a subject. And among other rights that might be named are *bona vacantia*, including waifs, wrecks, estrays, and treasure trove, *droits* of the Admiralty, fines, recognizances, legal fees, forfeitures, and such other oddities as royal fish, swans, and deodands. Some of these are still of practical importance[2] and those that have been discussed in Canadian cases will be examined later.[3]

These are by no means all the sources of revenue enuring to the king by

1/The following account is based in large measure on Sir Wm. Blackstone's *Commentaries on the Laws of England*, Book 1, c.8; F. W. Maitland, *The Constitutional History of England* (Cambridge, 1950), pp.92–6, 251, 430–8; Halsbury's *Laws of England* (3rd ed., London, 1954), VII: "Constitutional Law," at 450 *et seq.*
2/For a full discussion, see Halsbury, *ibid.*, at 453 *et seq.*
3/See *infra*, at 79–83.

virtue of his prerogative, but they are enough to indicate why the king in early times seldom had to call upon parliament for money to run the affairs of the country. His ordinary revenues, as they were called, were sufficiently large to support his needs for considerable periods without extraordinary revenues or, as we would say today, taxation. Consequently it was natural that the king should not be held accountable for the revenues so derived. They were his to spend as he pleased, and he was not responsible to parliament or any other body for the way he did it.

Even with the passing of feudalism the revenues of the king remained large. For one thing, when acts of parliament had the effect of depriving him of revenues, parliament granted him in return the proceeds from certain taxes and imposts. Thus, when military tenures were abolished at the Restoration, the king was compensated for the loss of the revenues therefrom by an excise on beer, cider, and spirits, a right that was to enure to himself, his heirs, and successors forever.[4] This and other taxes so granted became part of the king's ordinary and hereditary revenues.

But, while the king's income was large, it became less and less adequate to maintain national services and, increasingly, he had to resort to parliament for extraordinary revenues, or taxation. For a considerable time, parliament made no attempt to assign the uses to be made of this money. Once voted, revenues from taxation, like the king's ordinary and hereditary revenues, were his to spend as he saw fit. But in 1665 when a very large sum of money was granted to Charles II for the conduct of the Dutch War, a clause was inserted in the Act declaring that the money should be applied solely for the purposes of the war.[5] Similar appropriations were made during his reign, and after the Revolution the invariable practice of parliament when granting money was to appropriate it for particular purposes.

The king, however, still had the ordinary and hereditary revenues which were unappropriated by parliament and which, therefore, he could use as he saw fit. But in time these became inadequate to support even the expenses of the royal household, though it should not be overlooked that these expenses included many items that would now be considered as responsibilities of the state. Parliament took steps to remedy the situation in the reign of William and Mary when, to supplement the hereditary excise and the old hereditary revenues, it granted them a further excise for their lives.[6] This revenue was unappropriated and so uncontrolled by parliament. But in 1698 a measure of control was introduced. A new tax

4/(1660), 12 Car. II, c.24(Imp.).   5/17 Car. II, c.1(Imp.).
6/1 Wm. & M., c.3(Imp.).

was granted to William III for life, but it was provided that if the revenues from certain sources mentioned in the Act (including the Crown lands, many of the smaller prerogatives, and the hereditary excise) should exceed £700,000, then no more than that sum should be applied to any use or purpose without authority of parliament.[7] However, a different arrangement was made with him in 1700,[8] and on the accession of Anne certain sources of revenue (in the main those derived from the old prerogative rights, the Crown lands, and the hereditary excise and certain excise and customs granted to the Queen during her life) were again declared to be for the support of Her Majesty's household and the honour and dignity of the Crown.[9] However, an important restriction was made on the Queen's power of alienating Crown lands. Henceforth, she and her successors could not, in the absence of statute, grant land for a longer period than thirty-one years or three lives, and such leases were to be subject to the ancient rent or a reasonable rent. This was to prevent the lavish grants of Crown lands that had been made by several kings, including Anne's predecessor William III, which had resulted in increasing parliament's contribution to the royal household. But because no distinction was made between the sovereign in his public and private character this prevented him from conveying all lands held in his name, whether purchased from public funds or from his privy purse. To remedy the situation an act of 1800 empowered the king to hold land in a private capacity and to convey land purchased from his privy purse to the same extent as a subject.[10] The arrangement made with George I was similar to that made with Anne, but he was granted an extra £120,000.[11] A similar settlement was made with George II, but parliament promised him a revenue of £800,000.[12]

With the accession of George III, a new system, the civil list, was introduced. In return for surrendering the major portion of the hereditary revenues of the Crown into the consolidated revenue fund, he was promised a yearly sum of £800,000 from Parliament, to meet his expenses.[13] It should be noted that the expenditures for the royal household included items that were clearly national responsibilities, notably the salaries of judges, ambassadors, and commissioners of the treasury, and it is this that gives it its name of civil list: the money was voted to provide for civil government. This system continued under George IV, except that the king's income as such was clearly set out.[14] William IV gave up further

7/9 & 10 Wm. III, c.23(Imp.).   8/10 & 11 Wm. III, c.2(Imp.).
9/(1701), 1 Anne, stat. 1, c.7(Imp.).   10/39 & 40 Geo. III, c.88(Imp.).
11/(1714), 1 Geo. I, stat. 1, c.1.(Imp.).   12/(1727), 1 Geo. II, stat. 1, c.1(Imp.).
13/(1760), 1 Geo. III, c.1(Imp.).
14/(1820), 1 Geo. IV, c.1; (1821), 1 & 2 Geo. IV, c.31(Imp.).

hereditary revenues for an annual sum, and it was also provided that the salaries of judges and ambassadors were no longer payable by him.[15] The civil list system has continued with each sovereign since that time.[16] The king or queen on accession agrees that the ordinary and hereditary revenues of the Crown shall be paid into the consolidated revenue fund for his or her life and six months, in return for a fixed annual sum.

The result is that under modern English law the revenues collected by the state, whether arising out of the old territorial and casual revenues or taxation, are still the Queen's revenues, but by statute they are paid into the consolidated revenue fund and are used for the public purposes for which they may be appropriated by parliament. The Queen, however, now has her private income – her privy purse – in respect of which she has substantially the same rights as a private person has to his property.

IN PRE-CONFEDERATION CANADA

The relevance of the preceding discussion to Canada must now be examined. In so far as those portions of Canada that were formerly colonies settled by British settlers are concerned, the law is clear. To a settled colony the colonists bring such parts of the common law as are suitable to their situation and condition,[17] and the sovereign stands to possessions so acquired in a position analogous to his status in the United Kingdom.[18] Consequently in such colonies the sovereign owns all ungranted lands[19] and is entitled to the same territorial and casual revenues arising by prerogative right as in England.[20]

But Canada, of course, consists not only of settled colonies but also of colonies acquired from the French king by cession or conquest. This

15/(1831), 1 Wm. IV, c.25(Imp.).

16/(1837), 1 & 2 Vict., c.2; (1901), 1 Edw. VII, c.4; (1910), 10 Edw. VII & 1 Geo. V, c.28; (1937), 1 Edw. VIII & 1 Geo. VI, c.32; (1952), 15 & 16 Geo. VI & 1 Eliz. II, c.37(Imp.).

17/*Doe d. Hannington* v. *McFadden* (1836), 2 N.B.R. 153; *Doe d. Anderson* v. *Todd* (1846), 2 U.C.Q.B. 82; *Uniacke* v. *Dickson* (1848), 2 N.S.R. 287; *The Lauderdale Peerage* (1885), 10 A.C. 692, *per* Lord Blackburn, at 744 *et seq.*; *R.* v. *Bank of Nova Scotia* (1885), 11 S.C.R. 1, *per* Strong J., at 17–18.

18/*Anon.* (1722), 2 P. Wms. 75; 24 E.R. 646; *R.* v. *Bank of Nova Scotia* (1885), 11 S.C.R. 1, at 18; *Liquidators of Maritime Bank* v. *R.* (1888), 17 S.C.R. 657, *per* Ritchie C.J. and Strong J., at 661, 662, 668.

19/See *Mercer* v. *Attorney-General of Ontario* (1883), 5 S.C.R. 538. esp. *per* Ritchie C.J.; *St. Catherine's Milling and Lumber Co.* v. *R.* (1887), 13 S.C.R. 577; *Doe d. Burk* v. *Cormier* (1891), 30 N.B.R. 142.

20/*R.* v. *Bank of Nova Scotia* (1885), 11 S.C.R. 1, at 17–18; *Liquidators of Maritime Bank* v. *R.* (1888), 17 S.C.R. 657, at 661, 662, 668; *Liquidators of Maritime Bank* v. *Receiver-General of New Brunswick* (1888-89), 20 S.C.R. 295.

raises two problems. First, the law applicable to the prerogative rights to property in conquered countries is by no means clear. Secondly, there is difficulty in determining which parts of Canada are subject to the laws of settled colonies and which to conquered colonies. For clarity it seems best to begin the examination of the law respecting conquered colonies with Quebec as it existed at the conquest, for it clearly was governed by the law respecting conquered colonies.

Campbell v. *Hall*[21] makes it clear that a country conquered by British arms becomes a dominion of the king in the right of his Crown, that the laws of the conquered country remain in force until altered by the conqueror (and in this connection it should be noted that, with certain exceptions, an alteration of the laws may be made by the king by prerogative right until he has granted a legislative assembly to the colony), and that when the king takes the inhabitants under his protection they become British subjects. By the proclamation of 7 October 1763, the King duly took the inhabitants of the then province of Quebec under his protection and provided that courts be set up "for hearing and determining all Causes, as well Criminal as Civil, according to Law and Equity, and as near as may be agreeable to the Laws of England."[22] This having proved unsuitable to the French inhabitants, the Quebec Act[23] was passed providing, *inter alia*, "that in all Matters of Controversy relative to Property and Civil Rights, Resort shall be had to the Laws of *Canada*, as the Rule for Decision of the same." This re-introduced the Civil Law in Quebec.

Dissatisfaction now prevailed among the English inhabitants and so from the province of Quebec two separate provinces, Upper and Lower Canada, were created by the Constitutional Act of 1791.[24] The Act provided for the continuation of pre-existing laws,[25] but in 1792 a statute of Upper Canada provided that "in all matters of controversy relative to property and civil rights, resort shall be had to the laws of England as the rule for the decision of the same."[26] This distinction was continued when the united province of Canada was established,[27] and so was in effect when section 6 of the British North America Act, 1867, provided that what had formerly been Upper and Lower Canada should constitute Ontario and Quebec, respectively. Out of these facts arises a serious question whether in determining a matter concerning prerogative rights to property in Quebec or Ontario, one must look solely to the English law of prerogative or whether one must also look to the French law.

21/(1774), 1 Cowp. 204; 98 E.R. 1045.   22/See R.S.C., VI, 6127, at 6129.
23/(1774), 14 Geo. III, c.83, s.8(Imp.).   24/ 31 Geo. III, c.31(Imp.).
25/S.33.   26/32 Geo. III, c.1(U.C.).
27/(1840), 3 & 4 Vict., c.35(Imp.).

The Ontario Court of Common Pleas, in *Dixson* v. *Snetsinger*,[28] and four of five judges in the Supreme Court of Canada, in *In Re Provincial Fisheries*,[29] supported the view that by virtue of the cession of Canada by France to Great Britain, the British Crown acquired the rights and pre-rogatives previously belonging to the French king. These rights, they continue, were not taken away by either the proclamation of 1763 or the statute of Upper Canada making English law the rule of decision in that province. Strong C.J. and King and Girouard JJ. believed that this reasoning was applicable not only to Quebec and Ontario but to the Mari-time provinces as well, inasmuch as these territories were originally ceded by France to Great Britain. Strong C.J. and King J. also felt that it might apply to the province of Manitoba and the Northwest (then including what is now Saskatchewan and Alberta) so far at least as those portions of the territory of the Dominion were acquired under the tenth article of the Treaty of Utrecht by the description of "the bay and streights of Hudson, together with all lands, seas, seacoast, rivers and places situate in the said bay and streights, and what belong thereunto." And the later legislation adopting English law as the rule of decision in the Prairie provinces and the territories would not alter the situation any more than the Ontario statute.[30] They were clear, however, that the principle was inapplicable to British Columbia, and this would also appear to be true of Newfound-land, though even this province was once claimed by France.

While there is thus strong authority for asserting the acquisition by the English king of the prerogative rights of the French king on the cession of Canada, the question can hardly be regarded as settled. In the later case of *Attorney-General of Canada* v. *Attorney-General of Quebec*[31] the Privy Council pointed out that if the question had been necessary to decide it might have been "necessary to determine whether, on the cession of Canada to England in 1763, the French law as to the Royal Prerogative was abrogated and the law of England substituted for it." The reasoning in *Campbell* v. *Hall*[32] also seems inconsistent with this view. That case holds that a country conquered by the king's arms becomes a dominion of the king in right of his Crown, from which one would assume his pre-rogative rights are in force therein. True, the case also asserts that the local laws continue until the king alters them, but this must surely refer to laws regulating private rights, not the constitutional position of the sovereign.

28/(1872), 23 U.C.C.P. 235.
29/(1895), 26 S.C.R. 444.
30/This was originally done, so far as the Prairie provinces and the territories are concerned, by NWT Ord. of 1884, No. 26.
31/[1921] 1 A.C. 413, at 423. 32/(1774). 1 Cowp. 204; 98 E.R. 1045.

The case also adds that when conquered people are taken under the king's protection, they become his subjects, and their rights as British subjects may well be inconsistent with the prerogatives of the former sovereign. Furthermore, according to the reasoning in *In Re Provincial Fisheries*, the Maritime provinces would be subject to the rule of conquered countries, but the entire system of law in these provinces is based on the premise that they are settled, not conquered, colonies.[33]

For these reasons, it is submitted that prerogative rights under English law apply throughout Canada, subject to the qualifications to be made later regarding Quebec. Any other conclusion would be highly inconvenient. In controversies affecting Crown rights (not only in Quebec but in many other parts of Canada), it would often require an examination of the rights of the French king in the eighteenth century. And the courts would at times also have to undertake the impossible task of determining whether a particular area came within French or English jurisdiction before the cession. Thus the law regarding public rights in property would vary not only between provinces, but also between various parts of the same province. It would not, however, alter the rule that the Crown is the owner of all ungranted lands, because this was also the law of France at the conquest.[34]

This view does not involve any disagreement with the result of *Dixson* v. *Snetsinger*[35] or *In Re Provincial Fisheries*.[36] Those cases involved the question whether in a Crown grant of land adjoining a *de facto* navigable, but non-tidal, river (such as certain parts of the St. Lawrence) the grantee acquires the bed *ad medium filum*. Under the law of England, the grantee acquires the bed, but under French law the Crown retains the bed in trust for the public. The courts held the French rule applicable in Canada. Actually the same result could be reached by holding that the English rule is inapplicable to our situation and condition, and Strong C.J. in *In Re Provincial Fisheries*[37] also arrived at his conclusion by this route. And in *Fort George Lumber Co.* v. *Grand Trunk Pacific Ry.*,[38] Clement J. came to the same conclusion on the ground that the

33/*Doe d. Hannington* v. *McFadden* (1836), 2 N.B.R. 153; *Uniacke* v. *Dickson* (1848), 2 N.S.R. 287. In *R.* v. *Bank of Nova Scotia* (1885), 11 S.C.R. 1, at 18, Strong J. himself asserted that English law was the rule of decision in Prince Edward Island. Even in conquered countries there is authority that English settlers take English law with them: see *Terrell* v. *Secretary of State for the Colonies*, [1953] 2 All E.R. 490.
34/See *St. Catherine's Milling and Lumber Co.* v. *R.* (1887), 13 S.C.R. 577, *per* Taschereau J., at 644.
35/(1872), 23 U.C.C.P. 235.   36/(1895), 26 S.C.R. 444.
37/*Ibid.*, *per* Strong C.J. (King J. concurring) at 520–1, 528.
38/(1915), 24 D.L.R. 527.

Proclamation of 1763 (which has the force of statute) [39] by its invitation to settlers impliedly gave a public right to navigate streams, because settlement would otherwise have been impossible.

There is no doubt, however, that the sovereign's rights have been subjected to minor modifications in Quebec to adapt them to the needs of the civil law system. Thus in Quebec a Crown grant of land adjoining a non-tidal navigable or floatable river does not, in the absence of an express grant, include the bed, whatever the common law rule in Canada may be. [40] In this case, the principle benefits the Crown, but that is not always so. The Queen's priority over creditors of equal degree does not apply to Quebec; there Crown priority extends only against assets of a debtor who is a Crown officer liable to account for public moneys collected or held by him. [41] An explanation of the displacement of the English by the French prerogative appears in *Monk* v. *Ouimet* [42] where Dorion C.J. expressed the view that the higher prerogatives which form part of public law are in force throughout the Empire, whereas minor prerogatives not essential to the supremacy of the Crown, such as the right of preference over creditors, are not in effect in Quebec but are governed by the civil law, the maintenance of which was guaranteed by treaty. The reliance on a treaty seems foreign to English law but the statement seems otherwise sound. Strong J., in the Supreme Court of Canada, arrived at a similar conclusion in *R.* v. *Bank of Nova Scotia* [43] when he stated that "even in colonies not governed by English law, and which, having been acquired to the Crown of Great Britain by cession or conquest, have been allowed to remain under the government of their original foreign laws, all prerogative rights of the Crown are in force, except such minor prerogatives as may conflict with the local law." In *Exchange Bank of Canada* v. *The Queen*, [44] the Privy Council appears to have been of the view that such modifications

39/See *Campbell* v. *Hall* (1774), 1 Cowp. 204; 98 E.R. 1045; *St. Catherine's Milling and Lumber Co.* v. *R.* (1888), 13 S.C.R. 577; *R.* v. *McMaster*, [1926] Ex.CR. 68; *Attorney-General of Canada* v. *George* (1964), 45 D.L.R. (2d) 709; reversed on other grounds: *R.* v. *George*, [1966] S.C.R. 267; *R.* v. *White and Bob* (1963), 50 D.L.R. (2d) 613, *per* Norris J.A.
40/ *Hurdman* v. *Thompson* (1895), 14 Que. Q.B. 409; *Attorney-General of Quebec* v. *Fraser* (1906), 37 S.C.R. 577; *Wyatt* v. *Attorney-General of Quebec*, [1911] A.C. 489; *Leamy* v. *R.* (1916), 54 S.C.R. 143.
41/*Attorney-General* v. *Black* (1828), Stu.K.B. 324; (1884) 7 L.N. 324; *Monk* v. *Ouimet* (1874), 19 L.C.J. 71; *Attorney-General* v. *Judah* (1884), 7 L.N. 147; *R.* v. *Exchange Bank* (1885), M.L.R. 1 Q.B. 302 (and on appeal, *sub nom; Exchange Bank of Canada* v. *R.* (1886), 11 A.C. 157); *Colonial Piano Ltd. and Lamarre Trustee* v. *Minister of Customs and Excise* (1927), 65 Que. S.C. 316; *Re La Chaussure Crescent* (1926), 8 C.B.R. 92; *Re D. Moore Co. Ltd.*, [1928] 1 D.L.R. 383; *Re Mendelsohn* (1960), 22 D.L.R. (2d) 748. For a discussion of the point, see p. 145–6.
42/(1874), 19 L.C.J. 71; see also *R.* v. *Exchange Bank* (1885), M.L.R. 1 Q.B. 302.
43/(1885), 11 S.C.R. 1, at 18.
44/(1886), 11 A.C. 157.

resulted from a proper interpretation of the clause in the Quebec Act re-introducing French law in Quebec. It is true that the sovereign is generally not bound by statute,[45] but a statute bestowing a system of law on a colony is hardly an ordinary piece of legislation and it must be taken to allow minor adaptations of Crown rights so as to give full effect to the grant. Even if it might at one time have been open to doubt that prerogative rights are subject to modification in Quebec, there has now been a uniform current of decisions to this effect extending for too long a period to be upset.[46]

As already seen, in Canada the sovereign owned all ungranted lands and (subject to certain qualifications in Quebec) had prerogative rights and privileges similar to those in England, and owned any revenues derived therefrom. However, it would appear that in practice the Crown held and disposed of these lands and the proceeds and revenues thereof for the benefit of the colonies in which they were situate.[47] Still, these revenues were not within the control of the local assemblies. The king retained an unfettered discretion to spend them for a much longer time than in England. The act of Anne,[48] which had restricted alienation by the Queen and her successors, expressly applied only to England and Wales and the town of Berwick-on-Tweed, and no similar Act affecting the property accruing in the colonies to the sovereign *jure coronae* had been passed.[49] Until the accession of William IV no express mention was made in the English civil lists acts of casual and hereditary revenues arising in the colonies, and it is an open question whether the language of 39 and 40 George III, chapter 88 and the statutes amending it, extending as they did to "all cases in which his Majesty, his heirs or successors, hath or shall in right of his Crown become entitled by escheat, &c." was sufficient to include revenues in the colonies.[50] But 1 William IV, chapter 25 makes it clear that not only the casual and heredity revenues in England, but also

45/See, *inter alia, Théberge* v. *Landry* (1876–77), 2 A.C. 102; *Mercer* v. *Attorney-General of Ontario* (1883), 5 S.C.R. 538, at 665–6, *per* Henry J.
46/See *Exchange Bank of Canada* v. *R.* (1886), 11 A.C. 157.
47/See *per* Ritchie C.J. in *Mercer* v. *Attorney-General of Ontario* (1883), 5 S.C.R. 538, at 632; see also preamble to (1852), 15 & 16 Vict., c.39(Imp.); see also Instructions to Governor Wilmot of Nova Scotia, dated 16 March 1764, Art. 28 in Cartwright's *Cases Decided on the British North America Act, 1867* (Toronto, 1887), vol. III, 555, at 566; Cf. *In re Natural Resources (Saskatchewan)*, [1932] A.C. 28, at 38.
48/(1701), 1 Anne, stat. 1, c.7(Imp.).
49/See *per* Gwynne, J., in *Mercer* v. *Attorney-General of Ontario* (1883), 5 S.C.R. 538, at 682. See also *Attorney-General of Canada* v. *Higbie*, [1945] S.C.R. 385, *per* Rinfret C.J. and Taschereau J., at 409, but see *per* Kerwin, Hudson, and Rand JJ., at 424, 432.
50/See *per* Gwynne, J., in *Mercer* v. *Attorney-General of Ontario, ibid.*, at 683 on whose judgment most of the material in this section is based; see also *per* Ritchie C.J., in the same case.

those in the colonies were to be made part of the consolidated revenue fund of Great Britain in exchange for the civil list. And the same was done at the accession of Queen Victoria to the throne.[51]

While the sovereign no longer had unfettered discretion over the hereditary revenues in the colonies, it was not the colonies that had the appropriation thereof, but the British parliament. The first change took place in New Brunswick in 1837, when the Imperial government decided to surrender these revenues to the province. The Governor of the province was much opposed to the bill and, among other arguments, raised a doubt whether His Majesty could surrender such rights to a colony; the law officers of the Crown answered in the affirmative.[52] Accordingly in 1837 an act, prepared in England and modelled on 1 William IV, chapter 25, was passed by the New Brunswick legislature[53] whereby, after reciting that "his most gracious Majesty had been pleased to signify to his faithful Commons of New Brunswick, that His Majesty will surrender up to their control and disposal the proceeds of all His Majesty's hereditary, territorial and casual revenues, and of all His Majesty's woods, mines and royalties ... on a sufficient sum being secured to His Majesty, his heirs and successors, for the support of the Civil Government in this Province," it was enacted that the proceeds of the above should be paid to the provincial treasurer, who was authorized to receive the same for the use of the provinces. The Act then granted a civil list of £14,500 per annum for ten years, from 31 December 1836, when the Act should expire. The provisions of this Act were re-enacted and made perpetual in the Revised Statutes of 1854.[54] It is interesting to note that, while in England the heredity revenues are only surrendered by each sovereign for his reign and six months, here the surrender was perpetual, a device also employed in the BNA Act.

The next province to obtain control of the Crown's casual and hereditary revenues was Canada, on its creation from the old provinces of Upper and Lower Canada in 1840. By section 5 of the Union Act[55] a consolidated revenue fund was created for the province and sections 52 and 54 provide for a civil list. Under section 52, the provinces were to pay, out of the consolidated revenue fund, an annual sum of £45,000 for defraying the salaries of the governor, lieutenant governor, and judges, and the further sum of £30,000 for the life of Her Majesty and five years afterwards, for defraying the salaries of government officials. In return for this, Her Majesty surrendered forever three-fifths of her territorial and other

51/(1837), 1 & 2 Vict., c.2(Imp.).
52/See *Mercer* v. *Attorney-General of Ontario* (1883), 5 S.C.R. 538, at 630–2, 686–7.
53/(1837), 8 Wm. IV, c.1(N.B.).
54/R.S.N.B. 1854, title 3, c.5.
55/(1840), 3 & 4 Vict., c.35(Imp.).

revenues arising in the province, and two-fifths of such revenues during her life and five years, the whole to be payable into the consolidated revenue fund of the province.

The Legislative Assembly of Canada was not satisfied with these provisions because they violated the principle that the colonial legislature should have the same control over territorial and casual revenues arising in the province as the Imperial parliament exercised over like revenues arising within the United Kingdom. Accordingly, in 1846 the legislature passed a bill which, after reciting that "the granting of a [provincial] Civil List constitutionally belongs to your Majesty's faithful Canadian people in their Provincial Parliament," made provisions of a similar nature to sections 51, 52, and 54 of the Union Act, except that they varied the amounts payable to Her Majesty by way of civil list and altered some of the salaries. The bill was reserved for the royal assent and transmitted to England for the purpose of being laid before both houses of parliament. Following this a British statute[56] was passed authorizing Her Majesty, with the assent of the Privy Council, to assent to the provincial bill, and it was further enacted that if Her Majesty should assent thereto, sections 50 to 57 of the Union Act should be repealed from the coming into force of the provincial Act. The bill was subsequently assented to and became law.[57] The province had thus achieved recognition of the principle that it should have the same control over provincial territorial and casual revenues as the British parliament exercised in England.

Nova Scotia was next to achieve control of the territorial and casual revenues arising in the province. This was effected by an act of 1849.[58]

Though, as we have seen, the English civil lists acts covering the reigns of William IV and Victoria expressly included hereditary and casual revenues arising in the colonies, provincial lands had been granted, and moneys arising from such grants had been appropriated, by authority of the Crown as well as by authority of colonial statutes as if those acts had not been passed. This raised doubts whether the colonial revenues did not fall within the English acts, and whether these revenues might lawfully be appropriated to the public purposes of the colony. Consequently an Imperial act[59] was passed in 1852 providing that the civil lists acts of William IV and Victoria should not be deemed ever to have extended to moneys arising from the disposition of Crown lands in the colonies, nor to invalidate any grant or other disposition already made or to be made. It was further provided that any appropriation made by the Crown for the public purposes of the province which would have been valid but for these statutes should not be invalidated by them.

56/(1847), 10 & 11 Vict., c.71(Imp.).   57/(1846), 9 Vict., c.114(Can.).
58/(1849), 12 & 13 Vict., c.1(N.S.).   59/(1852), 15 & 16 Vict., c.39(Imp.).

This, then, was the situation at Confederation in the provinces originally uniting to form the Dominion of Canada. The entire control, management, and disposition of the Crown lands, and the proceeds of the provincial public domain and casual revenues arising in these provinces were confided to the executive administration of the provincial governments and to the legislative action of the provincial legislatures so that Crown lands, though standing in the name of the Queen, were, with their accessories and incidents, to all intents and purposes the public property of the respective provinces in which they were situate.[60] These revenues were quite substantial and the Fathers of Confederation thought that, along with the subsidies granted to the provinces and the absorption by Canada of a substantial part of the provincial debts and the power of direct taxation, they should prove adequate to provide them with an adequate revenue for performing their limited functions. This was made clear by Galt during the Confederation Debates where he said: "We may, however, place just confidence in the development of our resources, and repose in the belief that we shall find in our territorial domain, our valuable mines and our fertile lands, additional sources of revenue far beyond the requirement of the public service."[61]

Only such public works and property as were related to the jurisdiction of the federal government were assigned to the Dominion.

60/See *per* Ritchie C.J. in *Mercer* v. *Attorney-General of Ontario* (1883), 5 S.C.R. 538, at 633.
61/*Confederation Debates* (1865), 68.

CHAPTER TWO

Distribution of Resources
at Confederation

The distribution of resources between the Dominion and the provinces at Confederation was effected largely by part VIII of the British North America Act, 1867.[1] The resemblance between this part and the old civil lists acts is readily apparent. It distributes Crown property and imposes certain charges, including the salary of the governor general, on the federal consolidated revenue fund which it creates. The sections distributing property read as follows:

102 All Duties and Revenues over which the respective Legislatures of Canada, Nova Scotia, and New Brunswick before and at the Union had and have Power of Appropriation, except such Portions thereof as are by this Act reserved to the respective Legislatures of the Provinces, or are raised by them in accordance with the special Powers conferred on them by this Act, shall form One Consolidated Revenue Fund, to be appropriated for the Public Service of Canada in the Manner and subject to the Charges in this Act provided.

107 All Stocks, Cash, Banker's Balances, and Securities for Money belonging to each Province at the Time of the Union, except as in this Act mentioned, shall be the Property of Canada, and shall be taken in Reduction of the Amount of the respective Debts of the Provinces at the Union.

108 The Public Works and Property of each Province, enumerated in the Third Schedule to this Act, shall be the Property of Canada.[2]

109 All Lands, Mines, Minerals, and Royalties belonging to the several Provinces of Canada, Nova Scotia, and New Brunswick at the Union, and all Sums then due or payable for such Lands, Mines, Minerals, or Royalties, shall belong to the several Provinces of Ontario, Quebec, Nova Scotia, and New Brunswick in which the same are situate or arise, subject to any Trusts existing in respect thereof, and to any Interest other than that of the Province in the same.

110 All Assets connected with such Portions of the Public Debt of each Province as are assumed by that Province shall belong to the Province.

113 The Assets enumerated in the Fourth Schedule to this Act belonging at the Union to the Province of Canada shall be the Property of Ontario and Quebec conjointly.[3]

1/30 & 31 Vict., c.3 (Imp.).
2/The third schedule is reproduced and fully dealt with in chapter four.
3/The fourth schedule is reproduced in Appendix A.

117 The several Provinces shall retain all their respective Public Property not otherwise disposed of in this Act, subject to the Right of Canada to assume any Lands or Public Property required for Fortifications or for the Defence of the Country.

126 Such Portions of the Duties and Revenues over which the respective Legislatures of Canada, Nova Scotia, and New Brunswick had before the Union Power of Appropriation as are by this Act reserved to the respective Governments or Legislatures of the Provinces, and all Duties and Revenues raised by them in accordance with the special Powers conferred upon them by this Act, shall in each Province form One Consolidated Revenue Fund to be appropriated for the Public Service of the Province.

It should be noted that the public property sought to be distributed was property over which the provinces had power of appropriation at the union. In some provinces certain Crown property was, at union, under the administration of the Imperial government, not the provinces, and consequently was not affected by the BNA Act. This can be exemplified by *Attorney-General of British Columbia* v. *Attorney-General of Canada*.[4] In 1859 the Governor of British Columbia who, under his commission, had autocratic power in the colony and could act on behalf of the colony or the Empire, had reserved a piece of land called Deadman's Island. In 1884, after British Columbia had entered into Confederation, the Imperial government purported to transfer the land to the Dominion government, but the British Columbia government claimed the land on the ground that it had been appropriated for the benefit of the province and had remained vested in the province by virtue of section 117 of the BNA Act. The Dominion claimed the land either by virtue of the transfer or by section 108 of that Act. The Privy Council held on the evidence that the land had been reserved by the Governor for military purposes which was then under the direction of the Imperial parliament. The land was, therefore, under the control of the Imperial parliament and had not been appropriated for the benefit of the province. Consequently it did not pass to the Dominion under section 108 or to the province under section 117 but remained under the administration of the British government until its transfer to the Dominion in 1884.

THE NATURE OF PUBLIC PROPERTY

It will be observed that what is distributed by sections 102 and 126 are the "Duties and Revenues over which the respective Legislatures of

4/[1906] A.C. 552; the Dominion's title to the land concerned was also recognized in *Attorney-General of Canada* v. *Gonzalves*, [1926] 1 D.L.R. 51 and in *Attorney-General of Canada* v. *Cummings*, [1926] 1 D.L.R. 52.

Canada, Nova Scotia, and New Brunswick had before the Union Power of Appropriation." Under section 102 all revenues and duties assigned to Canada form a consolidated revenue fund to be appropriated for the public service of Canada. Similarly, the duties and revenues assigned to each province are to form a provincial consolidated revenue fund to be appropriated to the public service of the province. Yet sections 107, 108, 109, 113, and 117 purport to deal with "property belonging to" or "the Property of" the provinces or the Dominion, or "their Public Property," and similar expressions appear in sections 92(5) and 125. The truth of the matter is that in speaking of property as "belonging to" or as "the Property" or "Public Property" of Canada or the provinces, we are using the words in a special sense. More accurately this property is vested in the Queen. But by pre-Confederation civil lists acts these properties were made subject to the appropriation of the provincial legislatures for the benefit of the provinces. Thus, while title to the property remained vested in the Queen, the duties and revenues therefrom were to be used before Confederation for the benefit of the various provinces, and since that time for the benefit of the Dominion or the provinces in accordance with the provisions of the sections of the BNA Act we are now examining. The point was thus made by Lord Watson in *St. Catherine's Milling and Lumber Co.* v. *R.*:

By an Imperial statute passed in the year 1840 (3 & 4 Vict. c. 35), the provinces of Ontario and Quebec, then known as Upper and Lower Canada, were united under the name of the Province of Canada, and it was, inter alia, enacted that, in consideration of certain annual payments which Her Majesty had agreed to accept by way of civil list, the produce of all territorial and other revenues at the disposal of the Crown arising in either of the united Provinces should be paid into the consolidated fund of the new Province. There was no transfer to the Province of any legal estate in the Crown lands, which continued to be vested in the Sovereign; but all moneys realized by sales or in any other manner became the property of the Province. In other words, all beneficial interest in such lands within the provincial boundaries belonging to the Queen, and either producing or capable of producing revenue, passed to the Province, the title still remaining in the Crown. That continued to be the right of the Province until the passing of the British North America Act, 1867 ...[5]

In construing these enactments, it must always be kept in view that, wherever public land with its incidents is described as "the property of" or as "belonging to" the Dominion or a Province, these expressions merely import that the right to its beneficial use, or to its proceeds, has been appropriated to the Dominion or the Province, as the case may be, and is subject to the control of its legislature, the land itself being vested in the Crown.[6]

5/(1888), 14 A.C. 46, at 55.
6/*Ibid.*, at 56; the same principle is expressed in numerous other cases; see, *inter alia, Attorney-General of British Columbia* v. *Attorney-General of Canada* (1889),

Provincial or Dominion control over public property is not limited to the legislative control over the revenues referred to by Lord Watson in the last sentence. There is also an executive aspect. The mere surrender of the revenues from Crown lands to the legislature did not divest Her Majesty of power of administration and control thereof, including the power to dispose of it by grant, lease, or other conveyance.[7] In Canada this power is exercised subject to the advice of the government of the Dominion or a province. That is why in *Ontario Mining Co.* v. *Seybold*[8] Lord Davey, after citing the last passage above quoted, felt it advisable to remark:

> Their Lordships think that it should be added that the right of disposing of the land can only be exercised by the Crown under the advice of the Ministers of the Dominion or province, as the case may be, to which the beneficial use of the land or its proceeds has been appropriated, and by an instrument under the seal of the Dominion or the province.

From this it can be seen that the reference to public property as "belonging" to the Dominion or the province is most appropriate. Nowhere is this made more apparent than in the comments of Ritchie C.J. in *Mercer* v. *Attorney-General of Ontario*[9] on the situation existing in the provinces immediately before Confederation:

> Thus we see, that at the time of the union the entire control, management, and disposition of the crown lands, and the proceeds of the provincial public domain and casual revenues, were confided to the executive administration of the provincial government as representing the Crown, and to the legislative action of the provincial legislatures, so that the crown lands, though standing in the name of the Queen, were with their accessories and incidents, to all intents and purposes the public property of the respective provinces in which they were situate ... and was ... grantable by the Lieutenant Governor under the great seal of the province when the same should be disposed of by the provincial authorities in the interest of the province.

Still the special nature of public ownership must steadily be kept in mind. It is a power of the provincial (or Dominion) authorities to administer and control for the provincial (or Dominion) benefit property vested in the Queen. Consequently when it is desired to transfer public property

14 A.C. 295, at 303 and *Liquidators of Maritime Bank* v. *Receiver General of New Brunswick*, [1892] A.C. 437, at p. 444; *Attorney-General of Canada* v. *Higbie*, [1945] S.C.R. 385.

7/This is most clearly brought out in *Attorney-General of Canada* v. *Higbie*, [1945] S.C.R. 385 but is recognized in many other cases; see, *inter alia, Mercer* v. *Attorney-General of Ontario* (1881), 5 S.C.R. 538, at 633; *Farwell* v. *R.* (1893–94), 22 S.C.R. 553, at 561; *Ontario Mining Co.* v. *Seybold*, [1903] A.C. 73, at 79.

8/[1903] A.C. 73, at 79; see also the cases cited *ibid*.

9/(1881), 5 S.C.R. 538, at 633.

from a province to the Dominion, or the contrary, the appropriate means of doing so is not by an ordinary conveyance but by an order in council; it is not a conveyance of property but the transfer of the administration of the Queen's property from one government to another.[10] Newcombe J. in *Re Saskatchewan Natural Resources*[11] put it this way:

It is objected that, although the Territories were made part of the Dominion and became subject to its legislative control, there was no grant or conveyance of the lands by the Imperial Crown to the Dominion; but that was not requisite, nor was it the proper method of effecting the transaction. It is not by grant *inter partes* that Crown lands are passed from one branch to another of the King's government; the transfer takes effect, in the absence of special provision, sometimes by Order in Council, sometimes by despatch. There is only one Crown, and the lands belonging to the Crown are and remain vested in it, notwithstanding that the administration of them and the exercise of their beneficial use may, from time to time, as competently authorized, be regulated upon the advice of different Ministers charged with the appropriate service.

It goes without saying that the legislature could by statute convey land or permit its transfer by ordinary conveyance.[12]

A word must be said of the relationship between the executive and legislative power over public property. In England the Queen's power of disposition has been restricted by the statute of Anne,[13] and in Canada there are provincial statutes regulating the disposition of Crown lands.[14] But the state of the law in Canada apart from statute is not completely settled. In *Attorney-General of Canada* v. *Higbie*[15] it was argued that while power of disposition is in the Crown, this power can only be exercised by statutory authorization. Considerable reliance was placed on the fact that Lord Watson in the statement previously quoted had spoken of the province's right to public lands as "subject to the control of its legislature" but, as was pointed out by several of the judges, these words, if

---

10/*Attorney-General of British Columbia* v. *Attorney-General of Canada* (1889), 14 A.C. 295, at 301; *Burrard Power Co.* v. *R.*, [1911] A.C. 87, at 95; *Esquimalt and Nanaimo Ry. Co.* v. *Treat*, [1919] 3 W.W.R. 356; *Re Saskatchewan Natural Resources*, [1931] S.C.R. 263, at 275; *Attorney-General of Canada* v. *Higbie*, [1945] S.C.R. 385.
11/[1931] S.C.R. 263, at 275; the judgment was expressly approved by the Privy Council; see [1932] A.C. 28, at 40; see also *Attorney-General of Canada* v. *Higbie* [1945] S.C.R. 385.
12/See, *inter alia*, *Attorney-General of British Columbia* v. *Attorney-General of Canada* (1889), 14 A.C. 295, at 301; *Burrard Power Co.* v. *R.*, [1911] A.C. 87; *Re Armstrong and Van Der Weyden*; *Re Armstrong and Blancher* (1965), 46 D.L.R. (2d) 629.
13/(1701), 1 Anne. Stat.1, c.7.
14/See, for example, the New Brunswick Crown Lands Act, R.S.N.B. 1952, c.53.
15/[1945] S.C.R. 385; the point is also discussed by Duff J., (*diss.*) in *Cunard* v. *R.* (1910), 43 S.C.R. 88.

anything more than *obiter*, "might be taken as referring to that control which a provincial legislature may undoubtedly exercise and not that it is the sole branch of a Provincial Government to act under all circumstances."[16] Kerwin and Hudson JJ. found it unnecessary to express an opinion on the matter, and it is not entirely clear what the view of Rand J. was.[17] But Rinfret C.J. and Taschereau J. were clear that, in the absence of a restrictive statute, the Crown was free to convey Crown lands on the advice of the appropriate executive. They relied heavily on the fact that at common law the Crown had a right to transfer its lands by virtue of the prerogative, and in the absence of express terms, a statute should not be construed as interfering with Crown rights; there was nothing in the BNA Act affecting this right. They also relied on statements indicating that transfers of property by the Crown are made on the advice of the appropriate ministers but, as the other judges pointed out, these are not conclusive because they may have been meant only to describe the manner of making transfers, not to assert that the power existed in the absence of statute.

With respect, the view of Rinfret C.J. and Taschereau J. seems to be correct. The Crown has from time immemorial had the power to control and manage its land and other property, including the power of disposing of it. The surrender of revenues by the pre-Confederation civil lists acts created an obligation on the part of the Crown to pay any revenues from its public lands and other hereditary sources of revenue into the provincial treasury for the use of the provinces, but this did not interfere with the Crown's power of administering the lands (including their sale). When it was thought advisable to limit the power of sale, this was expressly done.[18] Nor did the BNA Act alter the situation beyond dividing the revenues previously appropriated for the provinces between the Dominion and the provinces.

The point squarely in question in the *Higbie* case was somewhat more difficult: whether a province could transfer land to the Dominion in the absence of statute. Rinfret C.J. and Taschereau J. were of the opinion that their views regarding transfers to individuals applied *a fortiori* to this situation, which, they explained, was merely a transfer by His Majesty of the administration of his public property from his provincial to his Dominion government. Rand J., however, took the view that a provincial

16/*Ibid.*, *per* Kerwin J. (Hudson J. concurring), at 425; see also *per* Rinfret C.J. (Taschereau J. concurring) in *ibid.*, at 405.
17/*Ibid.*, at 434–35, he seems to throw doubt on it, but at 431–32 he seems to recognize it and at the bottom of 432 he states that such a power may exist.
18/Note the limitations imposed by the New Brunswick Civil List Act, R.S.N.B., 1854, Title 3, c.5.

government could not, in the absence of legislation transfer the right to administer public property to the Dominion, for the following reasons:

But it is put as within the general power to alienate and it is argued that, if the Crown can transfer title to a subject, a fortiori can it effect a transfer to the administrative control of another group of constitutional advisers. But the argument, in my opinion, is unsound. The power of the provincial executive must obviously be looked upon as being fundamentally in relation to provincial administration and correspondingly that of the Dominion. This is necessarily involved in a federal distribution of plenary powers. The provincial function is exercised under provincial legislative control and I am unable to see how that authority, in the absence of legislation, can extend to an act merely of transferring its own proper subject-matter to another executive and legislative administration. That is rather a surrender than an exercise of function and I cannot agree that it is within the scope of the powers to which the statute gives rise, or the division of which it effects.[19]

Kerwin and Hudson JJ., as we have seen, found it unnecessary to express an opinion on the question so the point is unsettled, but the view of Rinfret C.J. and Taschereau J. seems preferable. Rand J. relies on the fact that in transferring land to the Dominion the province incidentally loses legislative power, but, with respect, this argument is not convincing. For even on a transfer of land to an individual the province loses some measure of legislative control over it,[20] and there is no doubt that the Crown in right of the federal government can accept surrender of the Indian's usufructuary title in a reserve, even though the effect is that the administration and legislative power over the land then vests in the provincial government and legislature.[21]

INTER-RELATION OF THE SECTIONS

We must now turn our attention to a general consideration of the meaning of each section and its relation to the others.

Section 102 was first discussed in *Attorney-General of Ontario* v. *Mercer*.[22] There it was argued that escheats fell within the "revenues" over which the provinces had at the union power of appropriation and so "belonged" to the Dominion by virtue of the section. The Privy Council agreed that the word "revenues" was apt to cover territorial as well as other revenues, including escheats, unless they fell within the exceptions set forth in that section as reserved to the provinces. Those exceptions, their Lordships pointed out, were of two kinds: (1) such of the duties and revenues appropriated to the provinces before the union and "reserved to

19/[1945] S.C.R. 385, at 433. 20/See pp. 168–9.
21/See pp. 112–14. 22/(1882–83), 8 A.C. 767.

the respective legislatures of the provinces" by this Act, which their Lord-ships averred had reference to section 109; and (2) revenues "raised by them [the provinces] in accordance with the special powers conferred on them by this Act," that is, under section 92 of the BNA Act. Their Lord-ships then went on to say that escheats fell within section 109 (for reasons to be discussed later) [23] and so fell within the first exception in section 102. Their Lordships took a similar view in the *St. Catherine's Milling* case,[24] but they observed that the first exception in section 102 might have refer-ence to section 117 as well as to section 109, although they seemed to feel that section 117 was merely another way of expressing what was contained in section 109, and they further specified that section 92(5) was referred to in the second exception. Actually the first exception would also appear to refer to section 110, and the second to revenues collected under section 92(15) as well as section 92(5). The only other case dealing with section 102 that should be looked at is *R. v. Attorney-General of British Colum-bia*.[25] There it was argued that the result of giving an extensive meaning to the word "royalties" in section 109 would be to give the words "Lands, Mines, Minerals, and Royalties" a meaning co-extensive with "Duties and Revenues" in section 102, and thus the exceptions in that section would be as wide as the grant. To this their Lordships replied that, while formally the argument had some weight, there was no doubt that Crown lands and minerals, forests, and precious minerals belong to the province under section 109, so that any other revenue derived from royalties would have relatively slight importance. Their Lordships, therefore, gave the word "royalties" a wide meaning, but nonetheless refused to decide that the reservation in section 109 was exhaustive of the grant in section 102.

In the above cases the Board dealt with section 102 as if it had the effect of distributing property to the Dominion, but in no case has it been held that property was distributed by the section,[26] and while the possi-bility that it does was kept open in *R. v. Attorney-General of British Columbia* it is difficult to imagine a situation where this could happen, having regard to the wide interpretation given to section 109. With respect, it is suggested that section 102 was never intended as a provision for distributing assets and that their Lordships were misled into looking at it in that light by the nature of the arguments before them. The true purpose of section 102, it is submitted, is to set up a consolidated revenue

23/See p. 79.
24/(1888), 14 A.C. 46.   25/[1924] A.C. 213.
26/In *In re International and Interprovincial Ferries* (1905), 36 S.C.R. 206, Tasche-reau C.J. stated that the section conveyed to the Dominion the revenues derived from licensing ferries but he seemed to believe that the right flowed from the legislative power over that subject matter.

fund for Canada into which all duties and revenues from assets otherwise assigned to or leviable by the Dominion under the Act are to be paid and appropriated for the public service of Canada. This explains why section 109 appears to leave no room for the operation of the supposed words of grant in section 102. Section 102 is merely the counterpart for the Dominion of section 126 which provides for the payment of the revenues of the provinces into their respective consolidated revenue funds. Whatever assets were conveyed to the Dominion had consequently to be handled by substantive provisions. While it does not afford a legal argument for the view, it is interesting to note that the Fathers of Confederation did not consider provisions similar to sections 102 and 126 either in their deliberations[27] or in the Quebec Resolutions,[28] though they had clearly provided for the division of property set forth in the other sections of the BNA Act. Indeed it is not until the third draft of the Act that the counterparts of sections 102 and 126 appear.[29] They seem to have been written in by the draftsman simply to ensure that consolidated revenue funds were created and that casual and hereditary revenues from properties assigned to the Dominion or the provinces, which at common law belonged beneficially as well as legally to the Queen, should be paid therein and be held for the beneficial interest of Canada or the provinces.

The provisions under which property formerly appropriated for the benefit of the provinces is assigned to the Dominion are sections 107, 108, and, possibly, 117. Section 107 conveys all cash, stocks, and other liquid assets belonging to the provinces at the union to the Dominion, and provides that they are to be taken in reduction of the public debts of the provinces. However, it is only to operate "except as in this Act mentioned," which presumably refers to the assignment of sums owing in respect of lands, mines, minerals and royalties, which by section 109 are assigned to the provinces. The section seems of so little practical importance today as to require no further elaboration.

Section 108 is the most important section conveying property to the Dominion. It provides that the public works and properties enumerated in the third schedule to the Act shall be the property of Canada. This section is discussed in detail in chapter four. For the moment, it is sufficient to say that the onus of proving that property belongs to the Dominion under this section, rather than to the province under the residuary sections 109 and 117, is upon those who allege it.[30]

27/See Joseph Pope's *Confederation Documents* (Toronto, 1895), at 25.
28/See *ibid.*, at 49–50.
29/*Ibid.*, at 170; cf. with rough draft, *ibid.*, at 135–36. No property provisions appear in the first draft, these having been reserved for further consideration: *ibid.*, at 157.
30/*R.* v. *Jalbert*, [1938] 1 D.L.R. 721; see also pp. 49, 61–2.

Finally, section 117, which provides for the retention by the provinces of their public property not otherwise disposed of is made "subject to the Right of Canada to assume any Lands or Public Property required for Fortifications or for the Defence of the Country." The nature of the Dominion's right under this section was briefly examined in *Attorney-General of Quebec* v. *Nipissing Central Ry. and Attorney-General of Canada*,[31] where it was argued that since special provision was made for the Dominion to take provincial public property for military purposes, provincial public property could not be expropriated by the Dominion for other purposes. The Board rejected the argument, stating that the reservation for the Dominion in section 117 referred to executive, not legislative, action. From this it would appear that the purpose of the enactment is to enable the federal executive to exercise the common law power to take all necessary steps, including the assumption of private property, without the aid of legislation to maintain order in cases of civil insurrection or the defence of the realm, even where this involves the assumption of property appropriated for provincial purposes.[32] Such a power could be given the Dominion executive under the Dominion power to legislate respecting defence or other heads of power, but it should be remembered that there was no Emergency Powers Act in 1867.

The provisions distributing assets to the provinces are sections 109, 110, and 117. Of these, section 110 (which assigns assets connected with any portion of the public debt assumed by a province to that province), may be disposed of by saying that it never appears to have raised any problem in court. Section 109 provides that all lands, mines, minerals, and royalties belonging to the provinces of Canada, Nova Scotia, and New Brunswick at the union, as well as any sum then due or payable therefor, shall belong to the provinces of Ontario, Quebec, Nova Scotia, and New Brunswick in which they are situate or arise, but this assignment is made subject to any trust in respect thereof or any interest other than that of the province therein. The section has frequently come up for judicial examination and will be discussed in more detail later.[33] Here it is sufficient to make the following comments. The section, though it makes no reference to the legislatures, is concerned with provincial public property, not to lands held as private property within the province. This is pointed out in *Attorney-General of Ontario* v. *Mercer*[34] where the court indicated that this was made clear by the language of section 125 (which exempts pro-

31/[1926] A.C. 715, esp. at 723.
32/The power is discussed under the title "Martial Law" in Wade and Phillips, *Constitutional Law* (7th ed., London, 1965), at 402, *et seq.*
33/See chap. five.
34/(1882–83), 8 A.C. 767, at 775–76.

vincial and federal property from taxation) and section 117. Section 125 clearly applies only to public property but like section 109 it refers simply to "lands or property *belonging to* Canada, or any province," and section 117 refers to the property retained by the province as "public property." The second point to be made about section 109 is that it has been interpreted as a residuary clause disposing of the natural resources and prerogative revenues belonging to the provinces before Confederation; unless such property is otherwise specifically dealt with in some other section, it falls within section 109.[35]

Section 117 is also a residuary section and in the original scheme of the Fathers of Confederation it was the sole residuary section, there being no equivalent to section 109.[36] But it has been referred to by the Earl of Selborne in *Attorney-General of Ontario* v. *Mercer*[37] as not very material except in illustrating the fact that "property belonging to the provinces" in section 109 referred to public property of the provinces. And in the *St. Catherine's Milling Co.* case,[38] it was treated as little more than a different method of expressing what is contained in section 109 and as a declaration that provincial public property retained by the provinces is subject to the right of Canada to assume such property for fortifications or the defence of Canada. Still it is certainly apt to describe any personal property owned by the province at the union and not otherwise transferred, and this is not covered by section 109. The Supreme Court of Canada has quite frequently relied on the section as disposing of the residue of pre-Confederation provincial property.[39]

Whatever the exact interrelation of sections 109 and 117 may be, the general picture is clear that only that portion of the property belonging to the provinces at Confederation specifically listed in sections 107 and 108 and possibly, 117 is assigned to the federal government; the provinces are assigned the residue. This is made clear by the following statement of Lord Herschell in the *Fisheries* case:[40] "The Dominion of Canada was called into existence by the British North America Act, 1867. Whatever proprietary rights were at the time of the passing of that Act possessed by the provinces remain vested in them except such as are by any of its express enactments transferred to the Dominion of Canada." What is

---

35/See *R.* v. *Jalbert*, [1938] 1 D.L.R. 721.
36/See Joseph Pope's *Confederation Documents* (Toronto, 1895), pp. 25–26; the relevant passage is quoted *infra*, at p. 26.
37/(1882–3), 8 A.C. 767, at 776.
38/(1888), 14 A.C. 46, at 57.
39/See, *inter alia*, *R.* v. *Robertson* (1882), 6 S.C.R. 52, *per* Ritchie C.J., at 122; *Holman* v. *Green* (1881), 6 S.C.R. 707, *per* Strong J., at 716; *Mercer* v. *Attorney-General of Ontario* (1881), 5 S.C.R. 538, *per* Ritchie C.J., at 644.
40/[1898] A.C. 700, at 709.

more, the onus of proving that any property transferred by the Act falls under any other section lies on those who allege it.[41] That this mirrors the views of the Fathers of Confederation is evident from the motion carried on 22 October 1864, at the Quebec Conference. It reads as follows:

It was moved by the Honourable Mr. Galt:–
1. That the Confederation shall be vested at the time of the union with all cash, bankers' balances, and other cash securities of each Province.
2. That the Confederation shall be vested with the public works and property of each Province, to wit:– [Here follow most of items listed in the third schedule.]
3. The several Provinces shall remain each vested with all public property therein, except such as is hereinbefore vested in the Confederation, subject to the right of the Confederation to assume any lands or public property required for fortifications or the defence of the country.[42]

Finally, provision is made by section 113 for the property listed in the fourth schedule to belong to Ontario and Quebec conjointly. It should also be noted that section 142 provides that the division and adjustment of the debts, credits, liabilities, properties, and assets of Upper and Lower Canada shall be referred to three arbitrators, one chosen by the government of Ontario, one by the government of Quebec, and one by the government of Canada. Difficulties arose in implementing the section[43] but statutory arrangements were made between the Dominion and the provinces for the arbitration and settlement of the accounts between them[44] and the contemplated adjustments were made pursuant to several arbitral awards.[45]

41/R. v. Jalbert, [1938] 1 D.L.R. 721.
42/Joseph Pope's Confederation Documents, pp. 25–26; the terminology of the Quebec Resolutions more closely resembles the act as enacted; see ibid., at 49–50.
43/In In re Ontario and Quebec Arbitration (1878), 6 L.J.N.S. 212; 4 Cartw. Cases 712, the Privy Council held that no appointment once made under this provision could be revoked and that a majority of the arbitrators could make a valid award notwithstanding the absence of the third arbitrator who had affected to resign and an attempted revocation of his appointment by the government that had appointed him.
44/(1891), 54 & 55 Vict., c.6(Can.); (1891), 54 Vict., c.2(Ont.); (1890), 54 Vict., c.4(P.Q.).
45/See Attorney-General of Canada v. Attorney-General of Ontario, [1897] A.C. 199; Province of Quebec v. Dominion of Canada (1898), 30 S.C.R. 151; Attorney-General of Ontario v. Attorney-General of Quebec, [1903] A.C. 39; Attorney-General of Ontario v. Attorney-General of Canada (1907) S.C.R. 14; Attorney-General of Quebec v. Attorney-General of Ontario, [1910] A.C. 627. The provision is now spent: see the Public Accounts, 1902–3, at 11–12.

CHAPTER THREE

Post-Confederation Distribution
of Resources

RUPERT'S LAND AND THE
NORTHWEST TERRITORIES

The British North America Act, 1867, of course, originally applied only to the provinces of Ontario, Quebec, Nova Scotia, and New Brunswick, but provision was made by section 146 for the admission of Newfoundland, Prince Edward Island, and British Columbia on addresses of the Houses of Parliament of Canada and the appropriate legislature, and for the admission of Rupert's Land and the North-western Territories on address of the Houses of Parliament of Canada. Such admissions were to be made on such terms and conditions in the addresses as might be approved by Her Majesty, subject to the provisions of the BNA Act.

The first action under this section was the admission of Rupert's Land and the North-western Territories into Canada.[1] Before this could be done, however, several steps had to be taken. By a charter granted by Charles II, the Hudson's Bay Company had been granted a vast extent of land which was not well defined but was assumed to cover the whole of what was later known as Rupert's Land. The company also exercised governmental authority over the North-western Territories, but the beneficial interest to the land therein does not appear to have been assigned to anyone and consequently remained in the Crown. Before Rupert's Land could become part of Canada, therefore, an arrangement had to be made with the Hudson's Bay Company. Accordingly the Imperial parliament passed the Rupert's Land Act, 1868,[2] enabling Her Majesty to accept a surrender of all lands held or claimed as Rupert's Land from the company upon such terms and conditions as might be agreed upon by Her Majesty and the company and for admitting such lands into the Dominion. The surrender was duly made, and an order in council,[3] dated 23 June 1870,

---

1/The following account is based largely on that appearing in *In re Natural Resources (Saskatchewan)*, [1932] A.C. 28; for a full discussion, see Chester Martin, *"Dominion Lands" Policy* (Toronto, 1938).
2/31 & 32 Vict., c.105(Imp.).   3/See R.S.C. 1952, VI, 6237.

was passed pursuant to section 146 of the BNA Act and section 5 of the Rupert's Land Act, 1868, admitting Rupert's Land and the North-western Territories into the union. Under the terms of union the Hudson's Bay Company was paid £300,000 and retained certain proprietary interests.[4]

It was generally supposed that not only legislative and administrative power but, except as regards the property reserved to the company, proprietary rights as well, had passed to Canada under the order in council, but in 1930 when the natural resources of Manitoba, Saskatchewan, and Alberta were surrendered,[5] Saskatchewan questioned the point; accordingly in the terms of the agreement providing for the surrender of the resources to that province, paragraph 23 appears providing for the submission to the Supreme Court of Canada of questions for determining the rights of Canada and the province to the lands, mines, and minerals now lying within the province before the province was established in 1905, and to the rights and liabilities arising from the alienation by Canada before that time of any of those assets or royalties incident thereto. The case was duly referred to the Supreme Court[6] which upheld the proprietary right of the Dominion to the land until the transfer in 1930. From this judgment the province appealed to the Privy Council.[7] The province's argument was that the order in council never transferred the land to Canada but that it was held by the Crown for the benefit of the settlers of the area and not for the benefit of Canada as a whole; that even if the proprietary rights did pass to Canada, it held them for the benefit of the inhabitants of the area only. The argument was thus summarized by the Privy Council:

The argument of the Attorney-General for the Province may be summarized as follows. There was a well-established Imperial policy as to colonies that they should enjoy, for the benefit of the inhabitants, the revenues of lands in the colony vested in the Crown. This did not depend upon the colony being self-governing. This area was a colony before 1867, and though as to a large part of it the land was vested in the Hudson's Bay Company, yet on the surrender by that Company of its charter the colony was restored to its appropriate position of enjoying proprietary rights in the land. It therefore was in the same position as the original colonies, whose rights to the land were maintained as a fundamental principle of the British North America Act. On the true construction of the Order in Council and the legislation giving effect to

4/Though the Act speaks of the retention of this property, the Privy Council held in substance that it was a transfer and consequently that the company had not retained the precious metals that belonged to it before the transfer; see *Hudson's Bay Co.* v. *Attorney-General of Canada*, [1929] A.C. 285; for further obligations under the surrender, see pp. 123, 187.
5/Pursuant to agreements confirmed by, and appearing in the schedule to the BNA Act, 1930 (21 Geo. V, c.26(Imp.)).
6/*Re Saskatchewan Natural Resources*, [1931] S.C.R. 263.
7/*In re Natural Resources (Saskatchewan)*, [1932] A.C. 28.

the admission of the area into the Confederacy, the Dominion Government and Dominion Legislature were intended to administer the land revenues for the beneficial use of the inhabitants only of the area in question. Upon the establishment of the Province it must be taken to have attained its majority, and was entitled to go back to 1870 and have an account of the use of its resources during that time.[8]

While their Lordships found it difficult to understand how Saskatchewan could possibly lay claim to resources before its existence as a separate entity, they nevertheless tackled the argument. They questioned the proposition that there was an invariable rule that the Crown placed its beneficial interest in land at the disposal of a particular colony; this appeared to be a question of fact in each case. In this particular case, the Crown had parted with its interest in Rupert's Land to the Hudson's Bay Company, and it is doubtful that the North-western Territories were sufficiently settled to bring in the supposed rule alleged by Saskatchewan. But their Lordships found it unnecessary to decide the case on this point. Even assuming these propositions were established, they pointed out, it was clear that the Rupert's Land Act, the order in council, and the addresses of the Houses clearly envisaged that the resources of the area would pass to Canada to be administered for the benefit of the whole country. The case, therefore, makes it clear that when Rupert's Land and the North-western Territories were transferred to Canada, Canada acquired full beneficial rights over all the resources of the area, except such lands and property retained by the Hudson's Bay Company under the terms of union. This continues to apply to the Yukon and Northwest Territories today.

MANITOBA

In anticipation of the admission of Rupert's Land and the North-western Territories as part of Canada, the parliament of Canada passed the Manitoba Act, 1870,[9] establishing Manitoba as a new province; whatever doubts may have existed concerning Canada's power to do so were removed by the BNA Act, 1871.[10] The general application of the BNA Act, 1867, to Manitoba is provided for in section 2 which reads as follows:

> **2**   On, from and after the said day on which the Order of the Queen in Council shall take effect as aforesaid, the provisions of the British North America Act, 1867, shall, except those parts thereof which are in terms

8/*Ibid.*, at 37–38.   9/32 & 33 Vict., c.3(Can.).
10/34 & 35 Vict., c.28(Imp.). That Act and the Rupert's Land Act, 1868, 31 & 32 Vict., c.105(Imp.) make it clear that the Canadian parliament, in creating new provinces, may provide for variations from the powers given to other provinces: see *Reference re s. 17 of The Alberta Act*, [1927] S.C.R. 364; *Attorney-General of Saskatchewan* v. *Canadian Pacific Ry. Co.*, [1953] A.C. 594.

made, or, by reasonable intendment, may be held to be specially applicable to, or only to affect one or more, but not the whole of the Provinces
now composing the Dominion, and except so far as the same may be
varied by this Act, be applicable to the Province of Manitoba, in the
same way, and to the like extent as they apply to the several Provinces
of Canada, and as if the Province of Manitoba had been one of the
Provinces originally united by the said Act.

In so far as the public domain is concerned, however, this provision
must be read in the light of section 30 of the same Act which provides
that:

30   All ungranted or waste lands in the Province shall be, from and after the
date of the said transfer, vested in the Crown, and administered by the
Government of Canada for the purposes of the Dominion. ...

At first sight, section 2 would appear to apply the property provisions
of the BNA Act, 1867, to Manitoba, subject, of course, to the important
exception in section 30. This, however, raises several difficulties. In the
first place, one of the key provisions of that Act, section 109, refers
specifically to the provinces of Ontario, Quebec, Nova Scotia, and New
Brunswick. This difficulty, however, has now been removed, for the Privy
Council has held that in applying the section to other provinces it should
be read as if those provinces were enumerated in the section.[11] A second
problem is more general. The property sections of the BNA Act purport
to distribute between the Dominion and the provinces property already
belonging to the provinces, but Manitoba did not own any property before
union. The point was raised in *Attorney-General of Alberta* v. *Attorney-
General of Canada*[12] in connection with a similar provision in the Alberta
Act, but was rejected by the Privy Council. Their Lordships pointed out
that section 21 of the Act (which is similar to section 30 of the Manitoba
Act) is meaningless unless it is assumed that the property reserved by that
section would otherwise be transferred to the province. Thus section 2,
standing by itself, would effect a division of property similar to that made
in the BNA Act.

But section 30 makes a fundamental change from the situation in the
other provinces. It provides that the ungranted and waste lands shall be
retained by the Dominion. This would clearly include base mines and
minerals,[13] and water rights,[14] though not the right to precious minerals

11/*Attorney-General of British Columbia* v. *Attorney-General of Canada* (1889),
14 A.C. 295, at 304; see also *Holman* v. *Green* (1881), 6 S.C.R. 707.
12/[1928] AC. 475.
13/*Attorney-General of British Columbia* v. *Attorney-General of Canada* (1889),
14 A.C. 295.
14/*Burrard Power Co. Ltd.* v. *R.*, [1911] A.C. 87.

and other sources of revenue comprised in the word "royalties" in section 109.[15] It would appear, therefore, that only the royalties arising in the province were transferred to Manitoba by section 2. This situation was made applicable to the territories added to the province when its boundaries were extended in 1881[16] and in 1912.[17] Some minor exceptions were made; thus, certain roads, trails, road allowances, and highways,[18] and for a time the swamp lands,[19] were transferred to the province. But it was not until 1930 that the bulk of Manitoba's natural resources were transferred to it by agreement validated by the BNA Act, 1930.[20] The background and effect of this Act will be discussed later.[21]

BRITISH COLUMBIA

British Columbia was admitted into the union on 16 May 1871 by order in council under section 146 of the BNA Act.[22] The provisions of the Act were made applicable to it by paragraph 10 of the terms of union which is almost identical with section 2 of the Manitoba Act except that it does not state expressly the time from which it is to operate.[23] One of the effects of this section is to apply the property sections of the BNA Act to British Columbia[24] as of the day of its entrance into Confederation,[25] whether or not the hereditary revenues had been surrendered to it before Confederation.[26] But paragraph 11 provided that British Columbia would convey to the Dominion government a tract of land twenty miles in breadth on each side of a railway connecting the British Columbia seaboard to the railway

15/*Attorney-General of British Columbia* v. *Attorney-General of Canada* (1889), 14 A.C. 295.
16/44 Vict., c.14(Can.); see s.2.   17/2 Geo. 5. c.32(Can.); see s.6.
18/(1895), 58 & 59 Vict., c.30(Can.).
19/(1885), 48 & 49 Vict., c.50, s.1; but see (1912), 2 Geo. V, c.32, s.2(Can.).
20/21 Geo. V, c.26(Imp.).   21/See pp. 35–45.
22/See R.S.C. 1952, VI, 6259.
23/Though the order in council does set the day of entry; see *ibid.*, at 6259.
24/*Attorney-General of British Columbia* v. *Attorney-General of Canada* (1889), 14 A.C. 295; *Re: Offshore Mineral Rights of British Columbia*, [1967]. S.C.R. 792; see also *Holman* v. *Green* (1881), 6 S.C.R. 707.
25/*Attorney-General of Canada* v. *Ritchie Contracting Co.*, [1919] A.C. 999; this is also assumed in *Attorney-General of British Columbia* v. *Attorney-General of Canada* (1889), 14 A.C. 295, at 304; see also *Holman* v. *Green* (1881), 6 S.C.R. 707; *Western Counties Ry. Co.* v. *Windsor and Annapolis Ry. Co.* (1882), 7 A.C. 178.
26/Though it does not appear that the sovereign ever formally surrendered the territorial and casual revenues to British Columbia before Confederation as occurred in the older provinces, it has been assumed by the highest authority that this was the case: *Attorney-General of British Columbia* v. *Attorney-General of Canada* (1889), 14 A.C. 295; *Attorney-General of British Columbia* v. *Canadian Pacific Ry.*, [1906] A.C. 204; *Attorney-General of Canada* v. *R. and Rithet* (1922), 63 S.C.R. 622;

system of Canada which the Dominion undertook to build. Because of engineering and other difficulties the line of railway contemplated by article 11 was not constructed for a considerable time and differences arose between the governments of British Columbia and Canada.[27] These were settled by an agreement which was subsequently ratified by the legislatures of Canada and the province. The agreement, *inter alia*, modified article 11 to this extent. The government of Canada agreed to convey the public lands along the railway, wherever it might be finally located, to a width of 20 miles on either side of the line (subsequently called the Railway Belt) and, in addition, to convey 3½ million acres of land in the Peace River District, in one rectangular block east of the Rocky Mountains, and joining the Northwest Territories (subsequently called the Peace River block). On the other hand, the Dominion undertook with all convenient speed to offer the lands for sale on liberal terms to actual settlers, and to give to persons who had squatted there a right of preemption to lands improved at the rates charged settlers generally. In accordance with this agreement, the lands forming the Railway Belt and the Peace River block were granted to the Dominion government by a British Columbia statute.[28]

The relation of the provisions respecting the Railway Belt and the Peace River block to section 109 of the BNA Act came up in *Attorney-General of British Columbia* v. *Attorney-General of Canada*.[29] About

---

Attorney-General of Canada v. *Higbie*, [1945] S.C.R. 385; *Re: Offshore Mineral Rights of British Columbia*, [1967] S.C.R. 792. Cassels J., in *R.* v. *Rithet* (1918), 17 Ex. C.R. 109, held that the effect of (1852), 15 & 16 Vict., c.39 s.2(Imp.) (which was passed to make British civil lists acts inapplicable to the colonies; see p. 13) was to vest in British Columbia the territorial and casual revenues other than *droits* of the Crown and *droits* of the admiralty. (These *droits* would not in any case appear to belong to the provinces, being subject to the Dominion's legislative power over navigation and shipping; see in this connection *Toronto* v. *R.*, [1932] A.C. 98). The judgment was reversed on other grounds in the Supreme Court of Canada: *Attorney-General of British Columbia* v. *R. and Rithet* (1922), 63 S.C.R. 622, but Idington J. expresses the same view. In the Privy Council the Board found it unnecessary to express an opinion on the point: *R.* v. *Attorney-General of British Columbia*. [1924] A.C. 213, at 220–21. Assuming, however. that these revenues were not surrendered, *Attorney-General of Alberta* v. *Attorney-General of Canada*, [1928] A.C. 475 makes it clear that British Columbia is in the same position as the other provinces.

27/For a brief history of the Railway Belt, see *Attorney-General of British Columbia* v. *Attorney-General of Canada* (1889), 14 A.C. 295.

28/47 Vict., c.14, s.2(B.C.); this by no means ended the differences between Canada and the province regarding the matter; see, for example, *McGregor* v. *Esquimalt and Nanaimo Ry. Co.*, [1907] A.C. 462; *Esquimalt and Nanaimo Ry. Co.* v. *Treat*, [1919] 3 W.W.R. 356; *Wilson* v. *Esquimalt and Nanaimo Ry. Co.*, [1922] 1 A.C. 202.

29/(1889), 14 A.C. 295; see also *Esquimalt and Nanaimo Ry.* v. *Bainbridge*, [1896] A.C. 561.

1884 a considerable quantity of gold was found in the Railway Belt and a controversy arose whether it belonged to the Dominion or the province. The province argued that by section 109 lands, mines, minerals, and royalties were assigned to the province, that precious metals such as gold fell within the term "royalties," and that, consequently, unless the province expressly conveyed them, they belonged to the province. Article 11 merely purported to convey the land within the Railway Belt and while this would include the base metals it could not convey the precious metals. The Dominion, on the other hand, argued that while the royalties would have been reserved had the conveyance been one by deed to a private citizen, this consideration was inapplicable to a transfer of the administration of Crown property from the province to the Dominion. The Privy Council accepted the submission of the province. It interpreted article 11 as an exception to section 109. Section 109 retained to the provinces all lands, mines, minerals, and royalties subject to the appropriation of the province before union. Article 11 excepted from this enactment the "public lands" in the Railway Belt, and, while this term would include the base metals as accessories, *jura regalia* or royalties had never been considered as accessories to land and so were not transferred to the Dominion. Consistently with this reasoning, a later case held that the water rights on the land belonged to the Dominion by virtue of its ownership of the land.[30] The subsequent disposition of the Railway Belt and the Peace River block will be examined later in connection with the BNA Act, 1930.

PRINCE EDWARD ISLAND

The next province to enter Confederation was Prince Edward Island in 1873. In the terms of union it was provided that the provisions of the BNA Act should apply except in so far as they are especially applicable to one province.[31] This, we saw, includes the property provisions of that act,[32] and there was here no problem such as occurred in *Attorney-General of Alberta* v. *Attorney-General of Canada*,[33] for in 1851 Prince Edward Island had been granted control of its territorial and casual revenues arising in the province.[34]

There were some minor provisions regarding the distribution of public property in the terms of union. The railways under contract and in the

30/*Burrard Power Co.* v. *R.*, [1911] A.C. 87.
31/Order in council under section 146 of the BNA Act, dated 26 June 1873: reproduced in R.S.C. 1952, VI, 6271.
32/See the discussion of this section in connection with Manitoba, at 29–30.
33/[1928] A.C. 475; see p. 30.
34/Vict., c.3 (P.E.I.). The government of Prince Edward Island did not in fact hold any land from the Crown and was given a special subsidy; see the terms of union in R.S.C. 1952, VI, 6271, at 6273.

course of construction were expressly transferred to the Dominion, though this was probably covered by the third schedule to the BNA Act. This would seem to be equally true of the transfer to the Dominion of the new building housing the law courts and registry office together with the land adjoining it and the steam dredge boat then in course of construction, but these were probably added because the Dominion paid consideration for them. Finally, the operation of the third schedule is slightly qualified by the provision that the provincial government's steam ferryboat is to remain the property of the Island.

OTHER TERRITORIES

Until 1878 there were still some British territories and islands in North America (apart from Newfoundland) that had not been made part of Canada but, following an address by the Senate and House of Commons of Canada of 3 May 1878, all such territories and islands, with the exception of Newfoundland and its dependencies, were annexed to Canada by an order of the Queen in council of 31 July 1880.[35] While no special mention is made of the proprietary rights to land and royalties in the area, there can be no doubt from the language of the order and the general intention of the transfer that the Queen now holds these lands for the general benefit of Canada.

ALBERTA AND SASKATCHEWAN

In 1905, under the BNA Act, 1871,[36] Canada created the provinces of Alberta[37] and Saskatchewan.[38] As in the case of the other provinces entering the union after 1867 there was enacted a provision (section 3 in both Acts) applying the BNA Act to the provinces, but distribution of property under the provision was very restricted, for section 21 of both Acts retained to the Dominion all lands, mines, minerals, and royalties incident thereto, subject to the provisions of that section. The section reads as follows:

> **21**   All Crown lands, mines and minerals and royalties incident thereto, and the interest of the Crown in the waters within the province under The Northwest Irrigation Act, 1898, shall continue to be vested in the Crown and administered by the Government of Canada for the purposes of Canada, subject to the provisions of any Act of the Parliament of

35/See R.S.C. 1952, VI, p. 6281.
36/34 & 35 Vict., c.28, s.2(Imp.).
37/The Alberta Act, 4 & 5 Edw. VII, c.3(Can.).
38/The Saskatchewan Act, 4 & 5 Edw. VII, c.42(Can.).

Canada with respect to road allowances and roads or trails in force immediately before the coming into force of this Act, which shall apply to the said province with the substitution therein of the said province for the Northwest Territories.

In lieu of these assets section 20 of each Act provides for an annual payment to be made to each province. As we have seen, sections 3 and 21 were discussed in *Attorney-General of Alberta* v. *Attorney-General of Canada*[39] where it was held that their combined effect was to retain for the Dominion all lands, mines, minerals, and royalties incident thereto, including escheats, and to transfer royalties not incident to lands, mines, and minerals, such as *bona vacantia*, to the province. Section 22 of both acts provides for an equal division of property and assets and debts and liabilities of the Northwest Territories and for a settlement of any differences arising out of the division to be made by three arbitrators, one to be appointed by each province and one by the Dominion.

1765746

THE BRITISH NORTH AMERICA ACT, 1930

It will be observed that in all the Prairie provinces the natural resources belonged to the Dominion, whereas in the other provinces they belonged to the provinces. This policy was continued even when the boundaries of the provinces were extended. Thus, when the boundaries of Quebec and Ontario were extended to Hudson Bay[40] these provinces automatically obtained proprietary rights to the resources in the area.[41] But it was made clear that Manitoba did not assume control of the resources within its area when its boundaries were extended.[42] It is not surprising that the Prairie provinces should have found this difference in treatment irksome and they protested against it constantly.[43] Finally in 1929 and 1930 Canada entered into agreements with Manitoba, Saskatchewan, and Alberta on the express understanding that these three provinces should be placed on a footing of equality with the other provinces; the agreements were later confirmed pursuant to their terms by federal and provincial statutes and

---

39/[1928] A.C. 475; the case is discussed in more detail at p. 30.
40/By the Quebec Boundaries Extension Act, 1912, 2 Geo. V, c.45(Can.), and the Ontario Boundaries Extension Act, 1912, 2 Geo. V, c.40(Can.).
41/S.2 of these Acts speaks simply of extending the limits of these provinces, but the obvious intention was to convey property as well as jurisdiction, as is evident from other sections and the express provision in the Manitoba Act passed in the same session.
42/(1884), 44 Vict., c.14, s.2(Can.); (1912), 2 Geo. V, c.26, s.6(Can.).
43/For a brief discussion, see *In re Natural Resources (Saskatchewan)*, [1932] A.C. 28. For a full account, see Chester Martin, "*Dominion Lands*" *Policy* (Toronto, 1938).

the BNA Act, 1930.[44] The agreements not only provide for the distribution of public property but also contain many provisions respecting legislative jurisdiction over such property. The latter will be examined later;[45] here we are primarily concerned with the distribution of property, though some mention will be made of some administrative and transitional provisions.

Each agreement with the Prairie provinces provides for the transfer to the province of the type of assets that were transferred to other provinces by virtue of section 109 of the BNA Act, 1867, subject to the same exceptions as are mentioned in that section. Because of the importance of this provision it must be quoted at length:

1   In order that the Province may be in the same position as the original Provinces of Confederation are in virtue of section one hundred and nine of the British North America Act, 1867, the interest of the Crown in all Crown lands, mines, minerals (precious and base) and royalties derived therefrom within the Province, and all sums due or payable for such lands, mines, minerals or royalties, shall, from and after the coming into force of this agreement, and subject as therein otherwise provided, belong to the Province, subject to any trusts existing in respect thereof, and to any interest other than that of the Crown in the same, and the said lands, mines, minerals and royalties shall be administered by the Province for the purposes thereof, subject, until the Legislature of the Province otherwise provides, to the provisions of any Act of the Parliament of Canada relating to such administration; any payment received by Canada in respect of any such lands, mines, minerals or royalties before the coming into force of this agreement shall continue to belong to Canada whether paid in advance or otherwise, it being the intention that, except as herein otherwise specially provided, Canada shall not be liable to account to the Province for any payment made in respect of any of the said lands, mines, minerals or royalties before the coming into force of this agreement, and that the Province shall not be liable to account to Canada for any such payment made thereafter.[46]

It will be observed that unlike section 109 the only royalties transferred by this paragraph are those derived from lands, mines, and minerals. That is because all other royalties had already been conveyed to the Prairie provinces. Another difference is that the paragraph expressly conveys the precious metals, but this must have been added *abundante cautela* because precious metals are clearly comprised in the term "royalties."[47]

44/(1930), 20 & 21 Geo. V (1st sess.), cc.3, 29, 41(Can.); (1930), 20 Geo. V, c.30(Man.); (1930), 20 Geo. V, c.87(Sask.); (1930), 20 Geo. V, c.21(Alta.); (1930), 21 Geo. V, c.26(Imp.).
45/See pp. 180–9.
46/For a brief discussion, see *Prudential Trust Co. Ltd.* v. *Registrar, Humboldt*, [1957] S.C.R. 656.
47/*Attorney-General of British Columbia* v. *Attorney-General of Canada* (1889), 14 A.C. 295; see also *Esquimalt and Nanaimo Ry.* v. *Bainbridge*, [1896] A.C. 561 and *Hudson's Bay Co.* v. *Attorney-General of Canada*, [1929] A.C. 285.

To avoid accounting difficulties, all sums paid to Canada before the commencement of the agreement in respect of these lands, mines, minerals, and royalties are to continue to belong to it and the provinces are entitled to keep all payments made thereafter.[48]

Apart from this paragraph, there are several others expressly conveying property from the Dominion to the Prairie provinces. Thus each of these provinces is assigned the money and securities constituting that portion of the school lands fund derived from the disposition of any school lands within the province or within those parts of the Northwest Territories and – in the case of Manitoba – the District of Keewatin, that are now within the province.[49] The fund was established under provisions of the Dominion Lands Act enacted in 1872 and 1879.[50] Under the 1872 statute two sections of land were set aside in each township in Manitoba and the then Northwest Territories as an endowment for education. The 1879 statute provided for the manner of sale of these lands, for investing the proceeds from such sales and other revenues from the lands in government securities and the payment of the interest thereon, after expenses of management, to the province or territory to support public schools as the province or territory should deem expedient. In the 1930 agreement, however, a limitation was imposed on the province's power of administering this fund and the school lands (which like other public lands had been transferred by paragraph 1); it was provided that this fund and lands should be administered by the province in accordance with sections 37 to 40 of the Dominion Lands Act.[51] This limitation was somewhat relaxed in Saskatchewan in 1948,[52] and another modification was made in all three provinces in 1951,[53] but it was not until 1961 that this exception to the equalization policy of the 1930 agreements was removed by an amendment which provided that the school lands and school lands fund should be administered or disposed of in such manner as the provinces may determine.[54]

The agreements also provide that all rights of fishery shall belong to and be administered by the province and that the province shall have the

48/Para. 2, British Columbia Railway Belt and Peace River block agreement, validated by the BNA Act, 1930, 21 Geo. V, c.26, contains a similar provision.
49/Para. 6 of each agreement.
50/(1872), 35 Vict., c.23, s.22; (1879), 31 Vict., c.31, ss.22, 23(Can.). For an account of the matter, see *Debates of the House of Commons*, 1960–61, at 8499–500.
51/Para. 7 of each agreement.
52/(1947–48), 11 & 12 Geo. VI, c.69(Can.); (1949), 13 Geo. VI, c.12(Sask.).
53/(1951), 15 Geo. VI (1st sess.), cc.37, 53, 60(Can.); (1952), 16 Geo. VI & 1 Eliz. II (1st sess.), c.44(Man.); (1951), 15 Geo. VI, c.18(Sask.); (1951), 15 Geo. VI. c.3(Alta.).
54/(1960–61), 9 & 10 Eliz. II, c.62(Can.); (1963), 12 Eliz. II, c.53; (1962), 11 Eliz. II, c.33(Sask.); (1962), 11 Eliz. II, c.57(Alta.).

right to dispose thereof by sale, licence, or otherwise, subject to Canada's legislative jurisdiction over seacoast and inland fisheries.[55] The provision is discussed later.[56]

It was also intended by paragraph 1 of the agreement to transfer all water rights to the province[57] and there is a paragraph in each agreement providing that the provision in section 4 of the Dominion Power Act declaring that every undertaking in that Act is a work for the general advantage of Canada should stand repealed in so far as it applies to these provinces, though the right of the Canadian parliament to make a similar declaration in the future was preserved.[58] It was doubted, however, whether these paragraphs were sufficient to transfer the water rights under the Dominion Water Power Act and Irrigation Act,[59] so paragraph 1 was amended in 1938 to provide for the transfer to the provinces of the interest of the Crown in the waters and water powers under those Acts and all sums due or payable in respect thereof, and the amendment was made effective as of the commencement of the Resources Agreements.[60]

Other provisions of the agreements provide that Canada is to retain the types of property that in other provinces would be vested in it. Thus it retained all its interests in, and administrative power over, Crown lands upon the security of which any advance had been made under the Soldier Settlement Act.[61] Again, every lien upon an interest in any unpatented land passing to the province under the agreement that was then held by Canada, as security for an advance made by Canada for seed grain, fodder, or other relief, continues to be vested in Canada, but the province undertook to collect the sums due (except so far as they may be agreed to be uncollectable) and pay them to Canada after deducting such expenses as might be agreed upon between the appropriate federal and provincial ministers; upon payment of the advance, any document required to discharge it may be executed by such provincial officer as may be authorized to do so under the law of the province.[62]

The agreements also retain for the Dominion the beneficial interest in, and administration of, certain lands therein described to be used as

55/Para. 10 in the Manitoba agreement; para. 9, Saskatchewan and Alberta agreements.
56/See pp. 166–7.
57/See *Debates of the House of Commons*, 1930, at 1600.
58/Para. 9, Manitoba agreement; para. 8, Saskatchewan and Alberta agreements.
59/*Debates of the House of Commons*, 1930, at 1539–41, 1577, 1600, 1701.
60/Validated by (1938), 2 Geo. VI, c.36(Can); (1937–38), 1 & 2 Geo. VI. c.27(Man.); (1938), 2 Geo. VI, c.14(Sask.); (1938), 2 Geo. VI (1st sess.), c.14(Alta.).
61/Para. 14, Manitoba agreement; para. 13, Saskatchewan and Alberta agreements; para. 21, Railway Belt and Peace River block agreement with British Columbia, is identical.
62/Para. 17, Manitoba and Alberta agreements; para. 18, Saskatchewan agreement.

national parks, including the mines and minerals (precious and base) therein and royalties incident thereto, but on a declaration by the parliament of Canada that any such lands, mines, minerals, or royalties are no longer required for the purpose, they shall forthwith belong to the province.[63] In addition, by paragraph 16 of the Alberta agreement the Dominion government undertook to introduce legislation to exclude from the parks certain areas agreed upon by the Dominion and the province that were of substantial commercial value, in return for certain undertakings by the province. These undertakings relate to legislative power and will be examined in that connection along with other provisions dealing with legislation respecting national parks.[64] Finally, in the Saskatchewan agreement paragraph 17 provides that if it is hereafter agreed between Canada and the province that any further lands should be set aside as national parks, the provisions of the agreement relating to parks shall apply thereto unless otherwise agreed.[65]

Indian reserves in the Prairie provinces are also retained by the Dominion and it is provided that each of these provinces will set aside further Crown lands for reserves whenever necessary to enable Canada to fulfil its obligation under the Indian treaties.[66] Two other provisions relating to Indians – one adopting with modifications an agreement with Ontario respecting reserves, and another assuring the Indians hunting and fishing rights on lands surrendered by them – affect Dominion and provincial property rights but will be discussed in detail in other contexts.[67]

Finally, in paragraph 18 of the Manitoba and Alberta agreements and paragraph 19 of the Saskatchewan agreement there is a general reservation to the Dominion of lands for which Crown grants had been made and registered under the Real Property Act of Manitoba or the Land Titles Act of Saskatchewan or Alberta and of which the Dominion was, or was entitled to become, registered owner at the commencement of the agreement, and any ungranted lands of the Crown upon which public money of Canada had been expended or which were, at the commencement of the agreement, in use or reserved by Canada for federal administration. Paragraph 19 of the Saskatchewan agreement came up for consideration before Davis J. of the Queen's Bench Division of the Saskatchewan

---

63/Para. 15, Manitoba agreement; para. 14, Saskatchewan and Alberta agreements; paras. 14, 15, and 19. The British Columbia Railway Belt and Peace River block agreement contains substantially similar provisions, see p. 44; for the legislative aspects of these provisions, see pp. 187–9.

64/See pp. 187–9.

65/Para. 20, British Columbia Railway Belt and Peace River block agreement, is identical.

66/Para. 11. Manitoba agreement; para. 10, Saskatchewan and Alberta agreements.

67/Paras. 12 and 13, Manitoba agreement; paras. 11 and 12, Saskatchewan and Alberta agreements; see pp. 130, 180–2.

Supreme Court in *Attorney-General of Canada* v. *Toth*.[68] There certain lands originally belonging to the Dominion were set aside as an Indian reserve, but the Indians subsequently surrendered their usufructuary title to the Crown in return for a money payment. Later the land was transferred to the Soldier Settlement Board (a federal agency). The Board then granted the land to an individual but reserved the minerals. The court had to determine whether, under these circumstances, the land vested in the province under paragraph 1 of the Resources Agreement or was retained by the Dominion under paragraph 19. For the Dominion it was urged that public money of Canada had been expended both on the survey of the reserve and also in payment for the surrender of the Indians' usufructuary title. But the court rejected both branches of the argument. If the expenses of a survey were included as an expenditure of federal money under paragraph 19, then paragraph 1 effecting a general transfer to the provinces would be meaningless for, at the date of the agreement, practically all land in the province had been surveyed at the expense of the Dominion. Nor was the payment to the Indians an expenditure on the land, but rather payment for the surrender of the right to the use and occupation of the land. The "reference to the expenditure of public money meant money paid out for such improvements as buildings, dams, waterways, drainage, air fields and things of a like nature by which the land was substantially benefited."[69] But the Dominion succeeded on another ground. When the land was transferred to the Soldier Settlement Board, it was then reserved for the purposes of federal administration. When the Board conveyed the land it reserved, as it was bound to do under section 57 of the Soldier Settlement Act, the minerals in the land. It must be inferred that the minerals were reserved for the same administrative purpose as that for which the Act was passed. This was confirmed by the fact that in 1949 the Crown decided to accord to purchasers under the Act the privilege of applying for the mineral rights. If, however, the minerals had been reserved by the Crown upon the transference of the land to the Board, then they would not have been reserved for the purposes of federal administration, and would have been transferred to the province under paragraph 1 of the agreement.

The equalization policy was rounded out by several financial terms. The subsidies payable to the provinces were adjusted to take into account the transfer of the natural resources,[70] and it was provided that the federal

68/(1959), 17 D.L.R. (2d) 273.
69/*Ibid.*, at 278.
70/Paras. 20 and 21, Manitoba and Alberta agreements; paras. 21 and 22, Saskatchewan agreement.

government should pay the provinces such further consideration as was necessary to place the provinces in a position of equality with the other provinces with respect to the administration and control of their natural resources as from their entry into Confederation in 1905; these amounts were decided by joint commissions.[71] Saskatchewan was not satisfied with being placed in an equal position as of 1905, but claimed to be legally entitled to the beneficial interest in the resources within its boundaries from the time their administration had been transferred to Canada under section 146 of the BNA Act, 1867, and the Rupert's Land Act. As a result, paragraph 23 of the agreement with that province provided for referring the matter to the Supreme Court of Canada, and the province signed the agreement subject to the reservation that neither the agreement nor any statute confirming it should prejudice its right to question the legislative competence of Canada to pass certain sections of the Saskatchewan Act and the Dominion Lands Act.[72] Section 2 of the BNA Act, 1930, placed Alberta in the same position.[73] As has been seen, however, the Supreme Court of Canada and the Privy Council rejected the claim of Saskatchewan.[74]

In one case the payment to attain equality flows from a province to the Dominion. Under an agreement with Ontario and Manitoba, a convention and protocol with the United States relating to the Lake of the Woods and the Lac Seul Conservation Act, 1928, Canada had expended and was responsible for further expenditures for the development of power and navigation on the Winnipeg River in Manitoba. The expenditure for navigation was, of course, a federal matter but that for the development of water power enures to the benefit of the province. Consequently, by paragraph 8 of the Manitoba agreement, it is provided that the province will make fifty equal annual payments covering the proportionate part chargeable to the power development and interest at the rate of five per cent.

A few provisions establish administrative procedures for giving effect to the transfer. Paragraph 3 of each agreement provides that any power or right which, by any contract, lease, or other arrangement or any federal Act or regulation relating to the property transferred is reserved to the

71/Para. 22, Manitoba and Alberta agreements; para. 24, Saskatchewan agreement. In Manitoba the commission had already sat and determined the amounts. In Saskatchewan and Alberta, the commissions sat later and the exact amounts were settled by agreements: see (1947), 11 Geo. VI, c.77(Can.); (1948), 12 Geo. VI, c.16(Sask.); (1947), 11 Geo. VI, c.5(Alta.).
72/Para. 27.
73/21 Geo. V, c.26(Imp.).
74/*In re Saskatchewan Natural Resources*, [1931] S.C.R. 263; [1932] A.C. 28; see pp. 28–9.

governor general in council or the minister of the interior or any federal officer, may be exercised by the appropriate provincial officer;[75] it also applies to any portion of a national park that may be transferred to the provinces in the future.[76] The paragraph was discussed in *Huggard Assets Ltd.* v. *Attorney-General of Alberta.*[77] In 1913 the Crown in right of Canada, and pursuant to the Dominion Lands Act, granted to the plaintiff's predecessor in title a certain area subject to payment to the Crown of such royalties for any petroleum derived therefrom as might from time to time be prescribed by regulations of the governor in council. The Board held that this gave the Dominion power to impose and vary the royalties at any time after the grant, but the Dominion had never imposed any royalty in respect of the area. After the transfer of resources, however, Alberta purported to levy a royalty in respect of petroleum and natural gas derived from the area under provincial orders in council. The Privy Council held that the province was justified in doing so; the right to levy royalties under the grant was a "right" reserved to the Crown by a "contract ... or arrangement" within the meaning of paragraph 3.

In order that the provinces may be in a position to deal adequately with their property another paragraph provides that Canada will deliver originals or complete copies of all records of dealings relating exclusively to the property transferred, give the provinces access to all other documents relating to such dealings and permit the province to have copied any document required for effective administration of the property.[78]

The agreement with Manitoba came into effect on 15 July 1930.[79] Those with Saskatchewan and Alberta were to come into effect on 1 August 1930,[80] but they were later amended so that the rights and powers of each party should continue unchanged until 1 October 1930.[81] The agreements

75/By para. 15, Manitoba agreement, para. 14, Saskatchewan and Alberta agreements, para. 3 applies to national parks lands conveyed under those paragraphs; para. 4, British Columbia Railway Belt and Peace River block agreement, is substantially the same as para. 3; for national parks lands, see British Columbia agreement, para. 19.
76/Para. 15, Manitoba agreements; para. 14, Saskatchewan and Alberta agreements; para. 19, British Columbia Railway Belt and Peace River block agreement, has similar effect.
77/[1953] A.C. 420; cf., *Attorney-General of Alberta* v. *Majestic Mines Ltd.,* [1942] S.C.R. 402.
78/Para. 23, Manitoba and Alberta agreements; para. 25, Saskatchewan agreement; para. 25, British Columbia Railway Belt and Peace River block agreement, is identical.
79/Para. 25, Manitoba agreement.
80/Para. 28, Saskatchewan agreement; para. 25, Alberta agreement; para. 27, British Columbia Railway Belt and Peace River block agreement is identical.
81/(1931), 21 & 22 Geo. V, cc.15, 51(Can.); (1931), 21 Geo. V, c.5(Alta.); (1931), 21 Geo. V, c. 85(Sask.).

may be amended by complementary legislation of the federal parliament and the provincial legislature concerned,[82] and this novel method of constitutional amendment has been exercised on several occasions.[83]

The Prairie provinces were not alone in being dissatisfied with the property arrangements with the Dominion. From the beginning, conflicts had arisen between British Columbia and the Dominion regarding the Railway Belt and the Peace River block.[84] Finally, in 1927, a commissioner was appointed to enquire into the province's claim for a reconveyance of these lands. The commissioner reported that the province had no legal claim to the lands, but that its request should be considered from the standpoint of fairness and justice and he recommended that the lands should be restored to the province. Accordingly the Dominion agreed to retransfer the land by agreement of 20 February 1930, later validated in accordance with its terms by federal and provincial statutes[85] and the BNA Act, 1930.[86] The major term of the agreement reads as follows:

1   Subject as hereinafter provided, all and every interest of Canada in the lands granted by the Province to Canada as hereinbefore recited are hereby re-transferred by Canada to the Province and shall, from and after the date of the coming into force of this agreement, be subject to the laws of the Province then in force relating to the administration of Crown lands therein.

Though the terminology of this paragraph differs markedly from the general paragraphs transferring property to the Prairie provinces, its result on the lands concerned is very similar. The lands referred to are, of course, the portions of the Railway Belt and Peace River block that had not been

82/Para. 24, Manitoba and Alberta agreements; para. 26, Saskatchewan agreement; para. 26, British Columbia Columbia Railway Belt and Peace River block agreement, is identical.
83/(1931), 21 & 22 Geo. VI, c.15(Can.); (1931), 21 Geo. V, c.5(Alta.); (1931), 21 & 22 Geo. VI, c. 51(Can.); (1931), 21 Geo. V, c.85(Sask.); (1938), 2 Geo. VI, c.36(Can.); (1937–38), 1 & 2 Geo. VI, c.27(Man.); (1938), 2 Geo. VI, c.14(Sask.); (1938), 2 Geo. VI (1st sess.), c.14(Alta.); (1941), 4 & 5 Geo. VI, c.22(Can.); (1941), 5 Geo. VI, c.72(Alta.); (1945), 9 & 10 Geo. VI, c.10(Can.); (1946). 11 Geo. V, c.2(Alta.); (1947), 11 Geo. VI, c.45(Can.); (1947), 11 Geo. VI, c.17(Sask.); (1947–48), 11 & 12 Geo. VI, c.60(Can.); (1948), 12 Geo. VI, c.1(Man.); (1947–48), 11 & 12 Geo. VI, c.69(Can.); (1949), 13 Geo. VI, c.12 (Sask.); (1951), 15 Geo. VI (1st sess), c.53(Can.); (1952), 16 Geo. VI & 1 Eliz. II (1st sess.), c.44(Man.); (1951), 15 Geo. VI (1st sess.), c.60(Can.); (1951), 15 Geo. VI, c.18(Sask.); (1951), 15 Geo. VI (1st sess.), c.37(Can.); (1951), 15 Geo. VI, c.3(Alta.); (1960–61), 9 & 10 Eliz. II, c. 62(Can.); (1963), 12 Eliz. II, c.53(Man.); (1962), 11 Eliz. II, c.33(Sask.); (1962), 11 Eliz. II, c.57(Alta.).
84/For a short account of the matter, see the preamble to the Railway Belt and Peace River block agreement, validated by the BNA Act, 1930, 21 Geo. V, c.26(Imp.).
85/(1930), 21 & 22 Geo. V, c.37(Can.); (1930), 20 Geo. V. c.60(B.C.).
86/21 Geo. V, c.26(Imp.).

alienated. This includes the base mines and minerals[87] and water rights[88] in the land; the precious metals and other royalties related to land had never been transferred to the Dominion.[89] Consequently the provision puts the province in substantially the same position in relation to these lands as to its other public lands, except as modified by other terms of the agreement. As in the agreements with the Prairie provinces, paragraph 2 provides that payments made to Canada before the commencement of the agreement in respect of such lands are to continue to belong to Canada and the province is entitled to retain any payments made thereafter.

Many of the provisions of the agreement are similar to those in the agreements with the Prairie provinces.[90] Thus, paragraphs 21, 25, and 26 respecting Soldier Settlement Lands, records, and amendments to the agreement, respectively, are identical with those of the Prairie provinces. The same is virtually true of paragraph 23 which make a general reservation of lands obtained by Canada from private owners and lands on which it has expended moneys or has used or reserved for federal administration and paragraph 4 authorizing provincial officers to exercise powers formerly exercisable by federal officers. It also contains similar provisions – paragraphs 14, 15, and 19 – reserving national parks (together with all rights therein to lands, mines, and minerals, precious and base, and the royalties incident thereto) and for the revesting in the province of parks no longer required for national parks. As in Saskatchewan there is a provision (paragraph 20) providing that other parks may be set aside on mutual agreement, subject to similar terms except as otherwise agreed. The agreement also contains a few extra provisions relating to national parks. Water rights therein are expressly reserved for the Dominion by paragraph 18. Further, paragraph 17 provides that on the termination of any interest then outstanding in any person in land included within an area set aside for a national park, the land shall vest in, and be administered by, Canada as part of the park.

A number of provisions in the British Columbia agreement have no counterparts in the agreements with the Prairie provinces. The first concerns ordnance and admiralty land, which for many years had been disputed between the province and the Dominion. Paragraph 6 provides that ordnance and admiralty lands in the Railway Belt that have been or hereafter are transferred by Great Britain to Canada shall not be affected

87/*Attorney-General of British Columbia* v. *Attorney-General of Canada* (1889), 14 A.C. 295; *Esquimalt and Nanaimo Ry.* v. *Bainbridge*, [1896] A. C. 561.
88/*Burrard Power Co.* v. *R.*, [1911] A.C. 87.
89/*Attorney-General of British Columbia* v. *Attorney-General of Canada* (1889), 14 A.C. 295; *Esquimalt and Nanaimo Ry.* v. *Bainbridge*, [1896] A.C. 561.
90/See pp. 35–43.

by the agreement; consequently they belong to Canada. In addition, paragraph 7 provides that ordnance and admiralty property, within or outside the Railway Belt, that have been set aside as such before 16 May 1871 and have been or are hereafter transferred to Canada by Great Britain shall continue to be vested in and administered by the federal government for the purposes of Canada, but Canada agreed to recognize and confirm any previous alienations of such lands and to execute any obligation of the province respecting the land by virtue of any provincial agreement, statute, order in council, or regulation. Finally, paragraph 8 provides for the settlement of the location and boundaries of these lands by arbitration.

Paragraph 9 provides that Canada is to retain the wharves and wharf sites in the Railway Belt specified in schedule one to the agreement together with the adjacent lands required for their convenient use, the boundaries of which were to be ascertained by mutual agreement. But paragraph 10 provides that when any such land is no longer required for use as a wharf site it is to become the property of the province. Similarly, by paragraph 11 the foreshores and beds of harbours already established within the Railway Belt, as well as the foreshores and beds of the Fraser River and the Pitt River lying above the eastern boundaries of New Westminster Harbour and below lines to be ascertained and defined by agreement at the junction of Kanaka Creek with the Fraser River and at a point of the exit of the Pitt River from Pitt Lake. By paragraph 13, the Indian reserves in the Railway Belt and Peace River also continue to belong to Canada, but they are to be held in trust for the Indians in accordance with an order in council of 3 February 1930.[91]

By virtue of paragraph 27 the agreement came into effect on 1 August 1930.

NEWFOUNDLAND

Newfoundland became a province by virtue of the BNA Act, 1949,[92] giving effect to terms of union agreed upon on 11 December 1948. While there is a provision (term 3) like that for other provinces joining the union after 1867, providing for the general application of the BNA Acts to the province, terms 33, 34, 35, and 37 deal expressly with the distribution of public property and there is little if any room left for term 3 to operate in relation to property. Term 33 transfers the following public works and property to Canada when the service concerned is taken over by Canada:

> (a) the Newfoundland Railway, including rights of way, wharves, drydocks, and other real property, rolling stock, equipment, ships, and other personal property;

91/See pp. 131–3.   92/12 & 13 Geo. VI, c.22(Imp.).

(b) the Newfoundland Airport at Gander, including buildings and equipment, together with any other property used for the operation of the Airport;
(c) the Newfoundland Hotel and equipment;
(d) public harbours, wharves, break-waters, and aids to navigation;
(e) bait depots and the motor vessel *Malakoff*;
(f) military and naval property, stores, and equipment;
(g) public dredges and vessels except those used for services that remain the responsibility of Newfoundland and except the nine motor vessels known as the Clarenville boats;
(h) the public telecommunication system, including rights of way, land lines, cables, telephones, radio stations, and other real and personal property;
(i) real and personal property of the Broadcasting Corporation of Newfoundland; and
(j) subject to the provisions of Term thirty-four, customs houses, and post-offices and generally all public works and property, real and personal used primarily for services taken over by Canada.

These items, it will be noted, resemble the property listed in the third schedule to the BNA Act, 1867, except that they comprise additional property relating to modern activities of the federal government, such as the airport at Gander, the Newfoundland Hotel, the public telecommunication system, and the Broadcasting Corporation of Newfoundland. The property so transferred is made subject to any trusts in respect thereof and to any interest other than that of the province in the same. Term 34 makes elaborate provisions for the division of public buildings, included in paragraph (j) of term 33, which are used partly for services taken over by Canada and partly for services of the province. In such a case, the building belongs to whichever government uses more than half the floor space but the other government is entitled to rent the space used for its services on such terms as may be mutually agreed upon. The division is to be settled by agreement and if the division under the term results in either Canada or Newfoundland having an ownership substantially out of proportion to the total floor space used for its services an adjustment is to be made by agreement. Term 35 retains for the province all public works and property not transferred to the Dominion. Term 37 is modelled on section 109 of the BNA Act, 1867. It retains for the province all lands, mines, minerals, and royalties belonging to the province at union and all sums then due for the same, subject to any trusts existing in respect thereof and to any interest other than that of the province in the same. The term transfers the Crown lands and all the territorial and casual revenues appropriated for the use of the province before the union.[93] It would appear that some of the casual

93/See pp. 17, 75–84.

revenues may not have been formally transferred to the province before union;[94] if there was such an omission, term 3 would operate to put the province on the same footing as the other provinces.[95]

Paragraph (a) and (j) of term 33 were recently dealt with by Puddester J. of the Newfoundland Supreme Court in *Re Reid and Marsh*.[96] There the plaintiff, claiming under a lease from the province, sought possession of land leased to the defendant from the Dominion. The land in question originally belonged to the Newfoundland Railway but in 1934 the railway and all its property was vested in the Crown by statute. The province, as it had by statute a right to do, ceased operating the line of railway with which the land in question was connected in 1939 and constructed a highway on part of the territory occupied by this line. The land in question, however, was not used for the highway. The plaintiff argued that since the railway line had been abandoned it could have been leased by the province and so did not constitute railway lands at the union. The court agreed that the province might have appropriated the lands for other purposes before the union, but it held that since it had not done so the land passed to Canada by virtue of term 33(a) even though it was not then used for railway purposes. The Plaintiff further argued that the meaning of term 33(a) was cut down by term 33(j) which transferred to Canada "all property ... used primarily for services taken over by Canada." But the court held that these words were in the nature of catch-all and supplemented rather than cut down the words of paragraphs (a) and (i).

94/R.S.N. 1872, Title XIII, c.45, s.16 provides that: "16. The whole of the general and casual revenues derived from and out of the sale and rentals of all crown land and ships' room within this colony or its dependencies shall be annually accounted and paid to the Receiver General for the use of the colony." There are, however, casual revenues, such as *bona vacantia*, not derived from lands or ships' room. "Ships' room" was land on the sea coast set aside for fishing ships; See *R.* v. *Cuddihy* (1831), 2 Nfld. L.R. 8; affirmed: *Attorney-General* v. *Cuddihy* (1836), 1 Moo. P.C. 82; 12 E.R. 742; *R.* v. *Ryan* (1831), 2 Nfld. L.R. 47; affirmed: *Attorney-General* v. *Ryan* (1836), 1 Moo. P.C. 87; 12 E.R. 744.

95/*Attorney-General of Alberta* v. *Attorney-General of Canada*, [1928] A.C. 475. For a discussion of the case, see pp. 30, 35. In any event, the courts would probably assume that such a transfer took place: See *supra* note 26.

96/(1965), 51 D.L.R. (2d) 186.

CHAPTER FOUR

Section 108 of the British North America Act, 1867

Section 108 of the British North America Act, 1867, has received closer judicial examination than any other constitutional provision transferring property to the Dominion. It transfers the property described in the third schedule to the BNA Act, 1867, to the Dominion. That schedule reads as follows:

THE THIRD SCHEDULE

Provincial Public Works and Property to be the Property of Canada

1   Canals, with Lands and Water Power connected therewith
2   Public Harbours
3   Lighthouses and Piers, and Sable Island
4   Steamboats, Dredges, and Public Vessels
5   Rivers and Lake Improvements
6   Railways and Railway Stocks, Mortgages, and other Debts due by Railway Companies
7   Military Roads
8   Custom Houses, Post Offices, and all other Public Buildings, except such as the Government of Canada appropriate for the Use of the Provincial Legislatures and Governments
9   Property transferred by the Imperial Government, and known as Ordnance Property
10 Armouries, Drill Sheds, Military Clothing, and Munitions of War, and Lands set apart for general Public Purposes

Though the section originally applied only to property belonging to New Brunswick, Nova Scotia, Quebec, and Ontario, it was later extended to property of Prince Edward Island and British Columbia.[1] And though the remaining provinces have other provisions governing the transfer of certain of their property to the Dominion,[2] the decisions under section 108 may well be looked to as a guide for a general approach to those provisions and to the interpretation of expressions appearing in both section 108 and those provisions.

The first point to note about the section is that, the residue of public

1/See pp. 31, 33.   2/See pp. 35–47.

property being vested in the province, the onus of proving that a particular piece of property falls within the third schedule lies upon the person who alleges it.[3] Secondly, the relevant day for determining whether property fell within an item in that schedule is the day the particular province entered the union; thus the question whether river improvements in Quebec were transferred to the Dominion or not depends on whether they were river improvements on 1 July 1867, and whether a harbour in British Columbia has passed to the Dominion depends on whether it was a public harbour on 7 July 1870.[4] Finally, only such interest passed to the Dominion as was possessed by the province. This can be seen from *Western Counties Ry. Co.* v.*Windsor and Annapolis Ry. Co.*[5] where it was held that, while section 108 and the third schedule had the effect of transferring all railways belonging to Nova Scotia on 1 July 1867, they did not transfer any other or larger interest than was possessed by the province at the time. Accordingly, the Dominion took the Windsor Branch Railway subject to the same obligation as the provincial government, that is, to enter into a traffic arrangement with the respondent company in terms of an agreement confirmed by a pre-Confederation provincial statute.

PUBLIC HARBOURS

Item 2, "Public Harbours," has been subjected to greater judicial scrutiny than any other expression in the third schedule to the BNA Act. Oddly enough, questions on the matter arise more often in actions between private individuals than in actions between the Crown and private individuals. This usually occurs in cases where the plaintiff's action depends on a title derived from the provincial Crown and the defendant pleads that title is vested in the Crown in right of the federal government by virtue of section 108 of the BNA Act.

It is by no means easy to describe with precision what constitutes a public harbour, and, indeed, the Privy Council has repeatedly warned that it is neither convenient nor desirable to attempt an exact definition.[6] But, as Duff J. pointed out in *Attorney-General of Canada* v. *Ritchie Contracting and Supply Co.*,[7] one must have formed some idea of the attributes

3/*Attorney-General of Canada* v. *Higbie*, [1945] S.C.R. 385; *R.* v. *Jalbert*, [1938] 1 D.L.R. 721.
4/*Western Counties Ry. Co.* v. *Windsor and Annapolis Ry. Co.* (1882), 7 A.C. 178; *Holman* v. *Green* (1881), 6 S.C.R. 707, *per* Gwynne J.; *Attorney-General of Canada* v. *Ritchie Contracting and Supply Co.*, [1919] A.C. 999.
5/(1882), 7 A.C. 178; see also *Kennedy* v. *City of Toronto* (1886), 12 O.R. 211.
6/See, *inter alia*, *Attorney-General of Canada* v. *Attorney-General of Ontario*, [1898] A.C. 700; *R.* v. *Jalbert* [1938] 1 D.L.R. 721.
7/(1915), 52 S.C.R. 78, at 103.

of public harbours before entering into a consideration of whether or not a given body of water is a public harbour.

i   The Nature of a Harbour

The first problem to determine is the nature of a harbour, whether public or private. Some judges have cited the definition of Coulson and Forbes,[8] which derives from Hale's *De Portibus Maris*,[9] that a harbour is synonymous with a haven and is nothing more than "a place naturally or artificially made for the safe riding of ships."[10] The test, according to this, is not whether an inlet or arm of the sea is used for commercial purposes, but whether it is capable of sheltering ships from the violence of the sea. But the definition given in Stroud's[11] and derived from Lord Esher's judgment in *R.* v. *Hannam*[12] which stresses commercial use, has been preferred.[18] It reads: "A harbour, in its ordinary sense, is a place to shelter ships from the violence of the sea, and where ships are brought for commercial purposes to load and unload goods. The quays are a necessary part of a harbour."

We need not tarry over this possible conflict because the term "public harbour" has been held to connote public commercial user,[14] and we need concern ourselves for the moment solely with the degree of shelter that a body of water must afford to warrant its being called a harbour. Certainly it is not sufficient that an arm of the sea or a portion of a river may afford shelter in certain states of the wind, for any part of the shore may afford shelter from storms blowing off the land.[15] Thus in *McDonald* v. *Lake*

8/*The Law of Waters* (6th ed., London, 1952), at 83.

9/C.2.

10/See *per* Tuck, J., in *Nash* v. *Newton* (1891), 30 N.B.R. 610; Macdonald J., at the trial in *Attorney-General of Canada* v. *Ritchie Contracting and Supply Co.* (1914), 20 B.C.R. 333, makes use of the definition but prefers the one discussed *infra*.

11/Stroud's *Judicial Dictionary* (3rd ed., London, 1952), vol. 2, at 849.

12/(1886), 2 T.L.R. 234.

13/See Macdonald J., in *Attorney-General of Canada* v. *Ritchie Contracting and Supply Co.* (1914), 20 B.C.R. 333 and Duff J. in the same case in the Supreme Court of Canada (1915), 52 S.C.R. 78, at 103; *Re Dominion Coal Co. and County of Cape Breton* (1963), 40 D.L.R. (2d) 593, *per* Patterson J., at 646. See also *R.* v. *Jalbert*, [1938] 1 D.L.R. 721 where the Privy Council expressed the view that Hale's definition was of little help.

14/See p. 53.

15/*McDonald* v. *Lake Simcoe Ice and Cold Storage Co.* (1899), 26 O.A.R. 411 (reversed on other grounds: (1901), 31 S.C.R. 130); *Perry* v. *Clergue* (1903), 5 O.L.R. 357; *Pickels* v. *R.* (1912), 14 Ex.C.R. 379; *Attorney-General of Canada* v. *Ritchie Contracting and Supply Co.* (1914), 20 B.C.R. 333, in the British Columbia Court of Appeal, and *per* Duff J., in the Supreme Court of Canada: (1915), 52 S.C.R. 78; *R.* v. *Jalbert*, [1938] 1 D.L.R. 721.

Simcoe Ice and Cold Storage Co.[16] the Ontario Court of Appeal had to consider whether a small bay on Lake Simcoe, roughly semi-circular or semi-elliptical in form, about 308 yards wide at the mouth and 132 yards across at the centre, was a public harbour. The bay was equipped with a few private wharves and afforded protection to ships in certain directions of the wind, but when the wind was in another direction it afforded no shelter; on the contrary there was very great danger of a ship running ashore and, once in, great difficulty in getting out. The court could not declare this a public harbour, unless, as MacLellan J.A. put it, it was prepared to hold that every little indentation of the shore of the sea or of the inland lakes is a public harbour within the BNA Act.[17] Similarly, stretches of open riverfront where some protection might be afforded in certain directions of the wind by private wharves were considered not to constitute harbours in *Perry* v. *Clergue*;[18] in *R.* v. *Jalbert*[19] the Privy Council, while not expressly deciding the question, appeared to be of the same opinion. A harbour must, then, to some extent be an enclosure.[20] At the same time a bay does not require to be landlocked to be a natural harbour, and it is evident that no harbour provides absolute safety from the winds and sea at all velocities of the wind from all quarters and at all stages of the tide, and what may "be safe anchorage for one ship might mean disaster to another."[21] It is a question of degree.[22] The dividing line between what is and what is not a harbour is not easy to define, but the remarks of Irving J.A. respecting English Bay in *Attorney-General of Canada* v. *Ritchie Contracting and Supply Co.*[23] are helpful. English Bay, within the limits called in question in the action, is three miles wide at its entrance and maintains that breadth for nearly its entire length to the eastward, a distance of four miles. Here is what Irving J.A. said about it: "The facts established beyond question are that English Bay has many of the requisites of a good harbour, *viz.*: protection from wave and wind from many directions; good holding ground with plenty of depth, and freedom from rocks and shoals. Yet, in my opinion, it is not a harbour. The width of its mouth, having regard to its area, prevents its falling within the defini-

16/(1899), 260 A.R. 411.
17/*Ibid.*, at 422.
18/(1905), 5 O.L.R. 357.
19/[1938] 1 D.L.R. 721; see also in the Supreme Court of Canada [1937] 2 D.L.R. 291.
20/*Re Dominion Coal Co. and County of Cape Breton* (1963), 40 D.L.R. 593, *per* Patterson J., at 646.
21/See *Attorney-General of Canada* v. *Ritchie Contracting and Supply Co.* (1914), 20 B.C.R. 333, *per* Macdonald J., at 342.
22/See *ibid.*, *per* Macdonald J., at 342, and Martin J.A., at 344–5.
23/(1914), 20 B.C.R. 333.

tion of harbour. I would describe it as a roadstead."[24] The decision was later upheld by the Privy Council.[25]

ii   Characteristics of a Public Harbour

Assuming the existence of a harbour, what attributes characterize it as a public harbour within the meaning of the BNA Act? Certainly mere user by the public is not enough; it must have been public property of the province. Thus Saint John harbour, which was granted to the City of Saint John in its charter of 1784, remained vested in the city after Confederation.[26] On the other hand, a harbour is not a public harbour merely because it belonged to a province at union.[27] This contention was first advanced in *R*. v. *Bradburn*[28] where it was argued that the term "public harbour" had been used to distinguish such harbours from privately owned harbours. But the argument was rejected because the heading of the third schedule makes it clear that it deals only with provincially owned property, and there must have been some reason for adding the word "public."

What "public" was meant to describe first came up in the case of *Holman* v. *Green*[29] in the Supreme Court of Canada. There it was argued that, to constitute a public harbour, public money must have been expended in constructing or improving it, but Ritchie C.J. and Strong J. rejected the contention and were later upheld by the Privy Council in the *Fisheries* case.[30] Both judges agreed that the words should be construed in their full grammatical sense, and Strong J. stated that they simply meant "harbors which the public have a right to use."[31] The *Fisheries* case goes into more detail. In examining the question whether the foreshore of a harbour should be considered part of a public harbour, their Lordships stated that if "it had actually been used for harbour purposes, such as anchoring ships or landing goods, it would, no doubt, form part of the harbour."[32] The remarks of the Privy Council were directed solely at the

24/*Ibid.*, at 349.
25/*Attorney-General of Canada* v. *Ritchie Contracting and Supply Co.*, [1919] A.C. 999.
26/*R.* v. *St. John Gas Light Co.* (1895), 4 Ex. C.R. 326. It was later granted to the Dominion; see (1931), 21 Geo. V, c.68(N.B.).
27/*Attorney-General of Canada* v. *Ritchie Contracting and Supply Co.*, [1919] A.C. 999.
28/*R.* v. *Bradburn* (1913), 14 Ex. C.R. 419; affirmed by the Supreme Court of Canada (unreported: see *Maxwell* v. *R.* (1917), 17 Ex. C.R. 97, at 99.
29/(1881), 6 S.C.R. 707.
30/*Attorney-General of Canada* v. *Attorney-General of Ontario*, [1898] A.C. 700, at 711.
31/*Holman* v. *Green* (1881), 6 S.C.R. 707, at 716.
32/*Attorney-General of Canada* v. *Attorney-General of Ontario*, [1898] A.C. 700, at 712.

foreshore, but in the later case of *Attorney-General of Canada* v. *Ritchie Contracting and Supply Co.*[33] Duff C.J. took the view that the reference to loading and unloading applied to the solum as well and that these activities were not to be looked upon as a test but as illustrations of the types of user required to be shown to establish that a harbour was a public harbour. From this analysis it would appear that a public harbour is one that the public had a right to use, and did use, as a public harbour. The point was thus made by Lord Dunedin in *Attorney-General of Canada* v. *Ritchie Contracting and Supply Co.*:[34]

... the extreme view ... that every indentation of the coast to which the public have right of access, and which by nature is so sheltered as to admit of a ship lying there, is a public harbour, has been argued by the appellants in this case and rightly, as their Lordships think, rejected by all the learned judges in the courts below. Potentiality is not sufficient; the harbour must be, so to speak, a going concern. "Public harbour" means not merely a place suited by its physical characteristics for use as a harbour, but a place to which on the relevant date the public had access as a harbour, and which they had actually used for that purpose. In this connection the actual user of the site both in its character and extent is material.

Several points must now be made about what is meant by "use for harbour purposes." In the first place it may on occasion be difficult to say whether a use by the public may be described as one for harbour purposes. Thus in *R.* v. *Attorney-General of Ontario and Forrest*,[35] Duff C.J. left open the question whether the use of a harbour by fishermen for wintering boats would be evidence that it was part of a public harbour. Secondly, while most judges have not been explicit on the point, Duff C.J. and Rand J. have made it clear that the use by the public means use for commercial purposes as distinguished from purposes of navigation merely.[36] But mere commercial enterprise in relation to private wharves does not appear to be sufficient; "public" connotes governmental activity. Thus in *R.* v. *Jalbert*,[37] the Privy Council considered whether Chicoutimi had been a public harbour in 1867. What was claimed to have been a harbour was a stretch of river two miles in length, at each end of which was a private wharf with another private wharf situated in between. A good many coasting and

33/(1915), 52 S.C.R. 78, at 105–6; see also *R.* v. *Attorney-General of Ontario and Forrest*, [1934] S.C.R. 133.
34/[1919] A.C. 999, at 1003–4.
35/[1934] S.C.R. 133.
36/*Attorney-General of Canada* v. *Ritchie Contracting and Supply Co.* (1915), 52 S.C.R. 78, *per* Duff J.; *R.* v. *Attorney-General of Ontario and Forrest*, [1934] S.C.R. 133, *per* Duff C.J.; *Attorney-General of Canada* v. *Higbie*, [1945] S.C.R. 385, *per* Rand J. See Clement's *Canadian Constitution* (3rd ed., Toronto, 1916), at 612.
37/[1938] 1 D.L.R. 721; see also *McDonald* v. *Lake Simcoe Ice and Cold Storage Co.* (1899), 26 O.A.R. 411 (reversed on other grounds: (1901), 31 S.C.R. 130); *Perry* v. *Clergue* (1905), 5 O.L.R. 357.

ocean-going vessels came there to load and unload timber, small coastal steamers occasionally stopped to pick up passengers, the stream was publicly used by ships to anchor and lie in, and generally there was a considerable trade for the time and place. But the Privy Council, though it studiously refrained from deciding the question, expressed great doubt that Chicoutimi was a harbour in 1867, since there were no public wharves and consequently no public right of access until 1873. Still, a harbour may, in certain circumstances, be public though operated by a private individual. This can be seen from *R.* v. *Attorney-General of Ontario and Forrest*.[38] There the province of Ontario had, before Confederation, leased certain lands to an individual largely in consideration of his improving the harbour, Goderich Harbour, in the River Maitland. The lessee did improve the harbour and it was capable of use, and was actually used as a harbour in the commercial sense before Confederation. Tolls were charged by the lessee but they were fixed by the Crown. Rinfret J. (giving the judgment of all the judges except Duff C.J.) held that the harbour having been constructed with the encouragement of the Crown on land to which it held at least the reversion was a public harbour. Duff C.J. left the question open, because, before section 108 can apply, a harbour must have been part of the public works or property of the province at the union, whereas in this case a private person held a lease of the land.

While use of a publicly owned harbour by the public at union is the most common test for determining whether a harbour is a public harbour within section 108, it is not the only one. Duff J. in *Attorney-General of Canada* v. *Ritchie Contracting and Supply Co.*[39] mentioned two other situations that would tend to show that a harbour was a public harbour. One was evidence of recognition by competent public authority that the locality in controversy was a harbour in a commercial sense. He pointed out that a British Columbia ordinance in force at the union in 1871 provided for proclamations of ports, inland places, and waters as public harbours. If a harbour had been proclaimed under this ordinance it would have had great weight in showing that the harbour was a public harbour; conversely if some harbours were proclaimed thereunder and others were not, it would be strong evidence that those not proclaimed were not public harbours. In fact there was no evidence that a proclamation had ever been issued under the ordinance. The view is supported by *Rickey* v. *City of Toronto*[40] where it was held that no evidence of public use of Toronto harbour was necessary because it had been designated by a pre-Confederation statute as a public harbour.

38/[1934] S.C.R. 133; see also *Nash* v. *Newton* (1891), 30 N.B.R. 610.
39/(1916), 52 S.C.R. 78.
40/(1914), 30 O.L.R. 523. The statute in question is (1834), 5 Wm. IV, c.23(U.C.).

Another circumstance that Duff J., in the *Ritchie* case, considered of importance in determining whether a harbour was a public harbour is whether or not there had been expenditure of public money in connection with it. This may be exemplified by *Nash* v. *Newton*.[41] There a small fresh-water lake called Dark Harbour was, until 1846, separated from the Bay of Fundy by a sea wall consisting of boulders and sand. Seawater perco-lated to the lake whose waters were brackish and raised and lowered with the tide. Largely at the expense of the provincial government, which was authorized by special statutes, the adjoining owner dug a channel through the sea wall and thereafter the tide ebbed and flowed in Dark Harbour, fish came in, and the harbour was used for both shelter and commercial purposes by the adjoining owner. It seems doubtful from the *Jalbert*[42] case that had this been a natural harbour, the commercial user by the owner in the course of his business would have sufficed to make the harbour a public harbour. But the Supreme Court of New Brunswick had no diffi-culty in deciding that under the circumstances Dark Harbour was a public harbour and passed to the Dominion under section 108. Further support may be found in the judgment of Fournier J. in *Holman* v. *Green*;[43] in holding that Summerside harbour was a public harbour, he relied in part upon the fact (as he thought) that public moneys had been expended in developing it.

The foregoing gives the general tests for determining whether a harbour is a public harbour. The next matter to consider is the time at which these tests are to be applied. Does the term "public harbour" apply to (1) any public harbour whether created before or after Confederation, or (2) only to those in existence at Confederation? At one time a few judges accepted the former view. Thus in *Attorney-General of British Columbia* v. *Cana-dian Pacific Railway Co.*[44] Hunter C.J.B.C. expressed the view that jurisdiction over public harbours is latent, and attaches to any inlet or harbour as soon as it becomes a public harbour, and is not confined to such public harbours as existed at the time of union. But the impracticability of this view is evident from the remarks of Duff J. in *Attorney-General of Canada* v. *Ritchie Contracting and Supply Co.*[45] in the Supreme Court of Canada. He pointed out that if this construction were adopted in con-nection with public harbours, it would have to be applied to other items in

41/(1891), 30 N.B.R. 610.
42/[1938] 1 D.L.R. 721; see also *McDonald* v. *Lake Simcoe Ice and Cold Storage Co.* (1899), 26 O.A.R. 411 (reversed on other grounds: (1901), 31 S.C.R. 130). *Perry* v. *Clergue* (1905), 5 O.L.R. 357.
43/(1881), 6 S.C.R. 707.
44/(1904), 11 B.C.R. 289, at 296; see also *Kennelly* v. *Dominion Coal Co.* (1903–4), 36 N.S.R. 495.
45/(1915), 52 S.C.R. 78.

the schedule, including railways, and it could hardly have been contemplated that the roadbed of a provincial railway built by a province after Confederation should pass to the Dominion as soon as it was completed. This view was accepted by the Privy Council on appeal,[46] so that it is now settled that the harbours that passed to the Dominion under section 108 were those that fell within the description of public harbours on the day the particular province entered Confederation.

From what has been said, section 108 does not appear to have been intended to apply to obscure harbours, but rather to those publicly known or officially recognized by the provinces at union. For one of the important reasons for vesting public harbours in the Dominion was that, being charged with exclusive jurisdiction over such matters as navigation and shipping, seacoast and inland fisheries, lighthouses and buoys, it was no doubt expected that it would assume the burden of conservancy of harbours, and of maintaining navigation and harbour works.[47] It is also interesting to note that, when the words "public harbours" were used in other British statutes passed about the same time as the BNA Act, it meant those harbours that were going concerns, not any natural harbour capable of being used as a harbour.[48] Among the harbours that have been held to be public harbours within the third schedule are those of Summerside,[49] Sydney,[50] Halifax,[51] Montreal,[52] Toronto,[53] Vancouver,[54] Quebec,[55]; a number of harbours of lesser importance in New Brunswick[56] and Nova Scotia[57] have also been so considered. Among others not transferred by

---

46/[1919] A.C. 999; see also *Western Counties Ry.* v. *Windsor and Annapolis Ry. Co.* (1882), 7 A.C. 178, discussed at p. 49.

47/See *per* Duff C.J. in *R.* v. *Attorney-General of Ontario and Forrest*, [1934] S.C.R. 133; and McPhillips J.A. in *Attorney-General of Canada* v. *Ritchie Contracting and Supply Co.* (1914), 20 B.C.R. 333.

48/See *per* McPhillips J.A. in *Attorney-General of Canada* v. *Ritchie Contracting and Supply Co.* (1914), 20 B.C.R. 333, at 359.

49/*Holman* v. *Green* (1881), 6 S.C.R. 707.

50/*Kennelly* v. *Dominion Coal Co.* (1903–4), 36 N.S.R. 495.

51/*Maxwell* v. *R.* (1917), 17 Ex. C.R. 97; *Sisters of Charity* v. *R.* (1919), 18 Ex. C.R. 385.

52/*Montreal* v. *Montreal Harbour Comm.*, [1926] A.C. 299.

53/*Rickey* v. *City of Toronto* (1914), 30 O.L.R. 523.

54/*Attorney-General of British Columbia* v. *Canadian Pacific Ry. Co.*, [1906] A.C. 204; *Attorney-General of Canada* v. *Ritchie Contracting and Supply Co.*, [1919] A.C. 999; *Attorney-General of Canada* v. *Higbie*, [1945] S.C.R. 385.

55/*Samson* v. *R.* (1888), 2 Ex. C.R. 30; *Power* v. *R.* (1918), 56 S.C.R. 499.

56/Dark Harbour, Grand Manan: *Nash* v. *Newton* (1891), 30 N.B.R. 610; Newcastle: *Attorney-General of New Brunswick* v. *Town of Newcastle and Flett* (1947), 19 M.P.R. 365. In *Lunt* v. *Lloyd* (1881), 21 N.B.R. 203, Bathurst is spoken of as a public harbour though there is no holding to this effect.

57/St. Margaret's Bay: *Fader* v. *Smith* (1885), 18 N.S.R. 433; *Sword* v. *Sydney Coal Co.* (1891), 23 N.S.R. 214; aff'd: 21 S.C.R. 152; *Young* v. *Harnish* (1904), 37 N.S.R. 213; Getson's Cove, La Have River: *Zwicker* v. *La Have Steamship Co.*

section 108 is Saint John.[58] The status of Chicoutimi[59] and Annapolis[60] harbours is doubtful.

Finally it may be mentioned that Lefroy[61] has suggested that the word "public" might have been intended to indicate harbours which had been so declared by the Crown in exercise of its prerogative right to establish ports and grant port franchises, but as Clement[62] points out there is nothing in the cases to support this and it is very doubtful if there were or could be any such ports in Canada at Confederation.

iii   Nature of Dominion Interest

Having now examined the characteristics of public harbours, we must now look into the nature of the interest that passed to the Dominion. Was it a mere franchise, or was it a proprietary right? The point came up in *Holman* v. *Green*,[63] the first case on public harbours after Confederation. Holman had been granted a part of the foreshore of Summerside harbour under letters patent issued under the Great Seal of Prince Edward Island in 1877, three years after its entry into Confederation. At the time of the action Green was in possession of the land and had erected a wharf thereon. Holman brought an action of ejectment to recover possession of the land. Green raised the point, *inter alia*, that Summerside was a public harbour belonging to the government of Canada by virtue of section 108 of the BNA Act, and consequently that Holman had acquired no title under the letters patent. Green denied that section 108 had this effect and, even if it did, he averred, the Dominion acquired only a franchise, not a proprietary interest. The Supreme Court of Canada, however, held that the harbour had become vested in a proprietary sense in Canada by virtue of section 108. As Strong J. put it, there would have been no point in granting a mere franchise by section 108 because the Dominion might have assumed this jurisdiction under its legislative power over navigation and shipping. In any case the Dominion could not properly perform the duty of conservancy without owning the bed.

The Dominion could, however, perform its duty of conservancy without owning the fisheries or the underlying minerals, but in *Holman* v.

(1911), 9 E.L.R. 144; Barrington Passage: *Anderson* v. *R.* (1919), 59 S.C.R. 379. Most of these were not considered decisions on this point.
58/*R.* v. *St. John Gas Light Co.* (1895), 4 Ex. C.R. 326; the harbour was later transferred to the Dominion; see (1931), 21 Geo. V, c.68(N.B.).
59/*R.* v. *Jalbert*, [1938] 1 D.L.R. 721.
60/*Pickels* v. *R.* (1912), 14 Ex. C.R. 379.
61/Lefroy, *Canada's Federal System* (Toronto, 1913), at 691; see also *Nash* v. *Newton* (1891), 30 N.B.R. 610.
62/Clement, *Canadian Constitution* (3rd ed., Toronto, 1961) at 609.
63/(1881), 6 S.C.R. 707; see also *Attorney-General of Canada* v. *Keefer* (1889), 1 B.C.R. (pt. 2) 368.

Green[64] Strong and Fournier JJ. clearly thought these also belonged to the Dominion. Certainly the fisheries would appear to belong to the Dominion under the principle that the right to fish is an incident to the ownership of the bed;[65] this was the view of the Quebec Court of Queen's Bench, Appeal Side, in *Re Quebec Fisheries*.[66] However, there is authority the other way; in *Young* v. *Harnish*[67] the Supreme Court of Nova Scotia expressed the view that the fisheries do not necessarily constitute a part of the harbour. The ownership of minerals was specifically raised in *Attorney-General of British Columbia* v. *Esquimalt and Nanaimo Railway*[68] before the Supreme Court of British Columbia, where it was argued that only such property was conferred to the Dominion as was necessary to control the harbour. Only Martin J.A. found it necessary to deal with the point and, relying on *Holman* v. *Green*, he decided that minerals in harbours belonged to the Dominion. Against this may be placed the contrary opinion of Hunter C.J. of the same court in *Attorney-General of British Columbia* v. *Canadian Pacific Railway*.[69] Furthermore, the authority of *Holman* v. *Green* was considerably shaken by the restrictive interpretation of public harbours given by the Privy Council in the *Fisheries*[70] and subsequent cases; in view of the attitude of the Supreme Court of Canada to harbour works in *R.* v. *Attorney-General of Ontario and Forrest*[71] this restrictive approach may not be limited to the question of ownership of the foreshore. Especially is this so since the courts have recognized that the purpose of transferring public harbours to the Dominion was to assist it in the performance of its functions in relation to navigation and kindred powers.[72] Still, this fragmentation of ownership seems out of place in constitutional interpretation and the courts will probably follow the approach of *Holman* v. *Green* in this matter; most of the cases dealing with the ownership of the harbour beds are in accord with this approach.[73]

Even if ordinary minerals in public harbours were transferred to the Dominion by virtue of section 108, this does not necessarily include pre-

64/(1881), 6 S.C.R. 707. 65/See p. 77.
66/(1917), 35 D.L.R. 1. 67/(1904), 37 N.S.R. 213.
68/(1889), 7 B.C.R. 221.
69/(1904–5), 11 B.C.R. 289; see also *Re Dominion Coal Co. and County of Cape Breton* (1963), 40 D.L.R. (2d) 593, *per* Currie J.
70/*Attorney-General of Canada* v. *Attorney-General of Ontario*, [1898] A.C. 700; for this and the other cases alluded to in the text, see pp. 60–3.
71/[1934] S.C.R. 133. Cf. also the restrictive character of the federal power of expropriation according to Duff J. in *Reference re Waters and Water Powers*, [1929] S.C.R. 200; see p. 154.
72/See *Attorney-General of Canada* v. *Ritchie Contracting and Supply Co.* (1914), 20 B.C.R. 333, *per* McPhillips J.A.; *R.* v. *Attorney-General of Ontario and Forrest*, [1934] S.C.R. 133, *per* Duff C.J.
73/See pp. 63–4.

cious metals, for these belong to the Crown by prerogative right and such rights or royalties were expressly transferred to the province by section 109 of the BNA Act. *Holman* v. *Green*,[74] however, indicates that the Dominion's interest in public harbours is not limited to ordinary property rights but includes prerogative rights as well. Strong J. stated that the harbours in the widest sense of the word were transferred by section 108, "including all proprietary as well as prerogative rights,"[75] and Fournier J. agreed that after the transfer the provinces ceased to have any interest in the harbours.[76] These statements, however, must now be read in the light of the *Precious Metals* case.[77] There it was held that the transfer by British Columbia to the Dominion of "public lands" in the Railway Belt did not include the precious metals because the right to such metals was a royalty; that is, they belonged to the Crown by prerogative right and were not incident to land. The Privy Council there treated the grant of "public lands" as an exception to section 109 of the BNA Act, 1867, which transfers "Lands, Mines, Minerals, and Royalties" to the provinces. Similarly the grant under section 108 has been treated as an exception to the residuary transfer effected by section 109,[78] so precious metals in a public harbour should belong to the province. Any other result would be highly inconvenient. For royalties continue notwithstanding that the property concerned has passed to individuals and they include such other rights as escheats and *bona vacantia*[79]. Consequently, if the Dominion owns the royalties in public harbours and other lands and property described in the third schedule, and if it then conveys part of such lands to a private individual and he, or his successor, dies intestate without heirs, the land would escheat to the Crown in right of the Dominion rather than the province. This could lead to unnecessary litigation between the two governments that could only be decided by reference to whether or not the Dominion or the province owned the land at union, a problem that would become more difficult of solution with the passing years. Similar problems would arise in connection with precious metals found on lands conveyed by the Dominion to private individuals.

A few cases have arisen where the Crown in right of the province at Confederation owned not the fee simple to a harbour but merely some type of reversionary interest. In *Samson* v. *R.*[80] the Crown as represented by the Dominion authorities expropriated a water-lot at Lévis in the harbour of Quebec, and the owner claimed compensation. His title was

---

74/(1881), 6 S.C.R. 707.   75/*Ibid.*, at 719.   76/*Ibid.*, at 721–2.
77/*Attorney-General of British Columbia* v. *Attorney-General of Canada* (1889), 14 A.C. 295.
78/See p. 25.   79/See pp. 79–83.   80/(1888), 2 Ex. C.R. 30.

based on a pre-Confederation Crown grant by the lieutenant governor of
Quebec which contained a provision that upon giving the grantee twelve
months' notice, and paying a reasonable sum for improvements, the Crown
might resume possession of the lot for the purpose of public improvement.
It was held that, the property being situated in a public harbour, the power
would be exercisable by the Crown represented by the Dominion. Since,
however, the Crown had not exercised the power but had proceeded by
expropriation, it had to pay the fair value of the land at the time of expropriation, but this fair value must be determined by the nature of the title.
The case was subsequently followed by the Supreme Court of Canada in
Power v. *R.*[81] A related situation arose in *R.* v. *Attorney-General of
Ontario and Forrest*[82] where the Crown had leased harbour property.
The majority of the Supreme Court of Canada were of the opinion that the
reversion belonged to the Crown in right of Canada, but Duff C.J.
reserved the question.

iv   Extent of Harbour: the Foreshore

In *Holman* v. *Green*,[83] the Supreme Court of Canada held that the foreshore of a public harbour, that is, the land between high and low water
mark, was comprised in and formed part of the harbour, and so was transferred to the Dominion by section 108. This opinion, however, was
disapproved by the Privy Council in the *Fisheries*[84] case. Their Lordships
stated that it did not follow that because the foreshore on the margin of a
harbour was Crown property, it necessarily formed part of the harbour.
It would depend on the circumstances. If, for example, the foreshore had
actually been used for harbour purposes, such as anchoring ships or loading goods, it would form part of the harbour. But there were other cases in
which it would be equally clear that it did not form part of the harbour.
What falls within the description "public harbour" cannot be answered in
the abstract, but must depend upon the circumstances of each particular
harbour.

The decision has given rise to many problems. For the effect is that not
only must it be proved as a fact that the harbour was used as a public
harbour at the time of union; it must further be established as a fact that
the piece of foreshore in question was used for harbour purposes. This can

81/(1918), 56 S.C.R. 499.
82/[1934] S.C.R. 133.
83/(1881), 6 S.C.R. 707.
84/*Attorney-General of Canada* v. *Attorney-General of Ontario*, [1898] A. C. 700;
see also *Attorney-General of Canada* v. *Ritchie Contracting and Supply Co.*, [1919]
A.C. 999.

be illustrated by *Montreal* v. *Montreal Harbour Commissioners*[85] where the Privy Council held that only that part of Montreal harbour as it existed in 1867 vested in the Dominion under section 108, the rest of the bed and foreshore remained vested in the Crown in right of the province, and though a Dominion statute extending the harbour was valid, it was not effective to enlarge the property rights of the Dominion or enable it to take the land without compensation. As is evident from the case, a finding that a portion of the foreshore was part of a public harbour at Confederation does not mean that every part of the foreshore was transferred to the Dominion; it is necessary to prove that each particular piece that comes into question has been so used.[86] As it has been put, a portion of the foreshore may have been within the ambit of a public harbour, but that is not sufficient; it must have been used for harbour purposes.[87] It is true that Duff C.J. in *R.* v. *Attorney-General of Ontario and Forrest*[88] and Rand J. in *Attorney-General of Canada* v. *Higbie*[89] have indicated that this rule should be broadly construed, but this does not materially simplify the matter.

The onus of proof that a harbour is a public harbour within section 108 and that a part of the foreshore of a public harbour forms part of the harbour is on the person who alleges it.[90] Since this demands proof of facts existing before the province in question entered Confederation, it is obvious that obtaining evidence for these purposes is no easy matter. Witnesses are usually out of the question and so courts must rely on such evidence as plans, photographs, pilot's books and charts, to say nothing of descriptions contained in books.[91] In *Attorney-General of Canada* v. *Higbie*,[92] for example, use was even made of descriptions contained in "A Voyage of Discovery to the North Pacific Ocean and Round the World" by Captain Vancouver. Questions might well arise regarding the admissibility of such evidence, though in the *Higbie* case they were

---

85/[1926] A.C. 299; see also *R.* v. *Jalbert*, [1938] 1 D.L.R. 721; *Attorney-General of Canada* v. *Higbie*, [1945] S.C.R. 385; *Attorney-General of New Brunswick* v. *Town of Newcastle and Flett* (1947), 19 M.P.R. 365; *Re Dominion Coal Co. and County of Cape Breton* (1963), 40 D.L.R. (2d) 593, *per* MacDonald J.

86/*Ibid.* Cf. the approach in *Kennelly* v. *Dominion Coal Co.* (1903–4), 36 N.S.R. 495, which must no longer be considered as authority on this point: see *Pickels* v. *R.* (1912), 14 Ex.C.R. 379 and *Attorney-General of Canada* v. *Ritchie Contracting and Supply Co.* (1914), 20 B.C.R. 333, *per* Martin J.A., at 352.

87/*R.* v. *Jalbert*, [1938] 1 D.L.R. 721.

88/[1934] S.C.R. 133.

89/[1945] S.C.R. 385.

90/*Ibid.*; *R.* v. *Jalbert*, [1938] 1 D.L.R. 721.

91/*Ibid.*; See also *Maxwell* v. *R.* (1917), 17 Ex.C.R. 97; *Attorney-General of New Brunswick* v. *Town of Newcastle and Flett* (1947), 19 M.P.R. 365.

92/[1945] S.C.R. 385.

regarded as admissible because they were the best available[93] and because no objection to their production had been made at the trial. Similarly, in *Attorney-General of British Columbia* v. *Canadian Pacific Railway Co.*,[94] the Privy Council accepted somewhat "scanty" evidence as establishing that a portion of Vancouver harbour was a public harbour at the time of British Columbia's union with Canada. As their Lordships put it, "it was perhaps as good as could reasonably be expected with respect to a time so far back, and a time when the harbour was in so early a stage of its commercial development."[95] This statement was made in 1906; it is obvious that the difficulty of producing the required evidence nowadays would be vastly increased.

Once it has been determined that a particular portion of the foreshore of a public harbour formed part of a harbour, will that be binding in subsequent litigation against persons who were not parties to the original action? The point arose in *Attorney-General of Canada* v. *Higbie*.[96] There it was argued that a portion of the foreshore of Burrard Inlet was part of Vancouver harbour and reliance was placed on the finding of Duff J. in *Attorney-General of British Columbia* v. *Canadian Pacific Railway Co.*[97] that the whole area between the First and Second Narrows (within which the land in question in the *Higbie* case was situate) was a public harbour. Rinfret C.J. and Taschereau J. held that the facts as found by Duff J. should be held to be definitely settled as against the whole world.[98] But Kerwin and Hudson JJ. left the question open. They pointed out that even if such a finding were acceptable in a subsequent action, it would only apply to the particular area in reference to which the finding was made. Though the judgment of Duff J. stated that the whole of the vast area between the First and Second Narrows was a public harbour, this was unnecessary to the decision and his finding should be limited to the actual locality in question in the case before him.[99]

The unsatisfactory state of the law is evident from the following quotation from the judgment of Rand J. in the *Higbie* case:

Disregarding any question of the nature or extent of ownership below low water mark, logically it would be necessary to traverse the whole shore bordering on such a body of water as Burrard Inlet and to establish in fact for each segment the required use. Precise limits or boundaries from such a use are out of the question. Unless characterized in its practical application by broad

93/Citing *R.* v. *Ship "Emma"*, [1936] S.C.R. 256.
94/[1906] A.C. 204.   95/*Ibid.*, at 209–10.
96/[1945] S.C.R. 385.   97/(1904), 11 B.C.R. 289.
98/See also the dissenting judgment of McPhillips J.A., in *Hadden* v. *Corp. of North Vancouver* (1922), 30 B.C.R. 497.
99/Approving the majority decision in *ibid.*

considerations of convenience, as undoubtedly the decisions mentioned contemplate, this rule might work out of a patchwork of ownership both inconvenient and embarrassing ...

And with the property in a public harbour below low water mark generally in the Dominion, the Provincial and Dominion ownership of sections of foreshore, isolated from upland, with occasional private ownership annexed to upland, presents a mosaic which I will not further complicate by suggesting a possible parcelling of ownership of the harbour bed itself.[100]

v Extent of Harbour: the Bed

The question of ownership of the beds of public harbours has yet to be squarely raised, but with the increase in underwater mining developments the point may well arise. It would appear from the passage just quoted that Rand J. was unwilling to parcel out the harbour bed itself, but would hold that it belonged to the Dominion without requiring proof that the particular part of the bed was used for harbour purposes at union. While they do not expressly deal with the point, *Samson* v. *R.*[101] and *Power* v. *R.*[102] (the latter, in the Supreme Court of Canada) are only explicable on this hypothesis. There, it will be remembered, the court held that reservations, in Crown grants of a water lot within the ambit of a public harbour, under which the Crown might retake the land if ever required for public improvement were held to have passed to the federal government. If the lots had formed part of the foreshore it would have been necessary to show their use as public harbours before Confederation,[103] but this was not the case here because they were private property. In *Fader* v. *Smith*,[104] the Supreme Court of Nova Scotia held in effect that a small creek or cove capable of navigation that abutted a public harbour was part of the harbour notwithstanding that it did not have the name or character of a harbour and had not been so used except in two exceptional instances which the court did not consider material. Most of the cases dealing with ownership of the harbour beds, then, seem to be inspired by the approach in *Holman* v. *Green*[105] rather than that of the *Fisheries*[106] case. But one judge, Macdonald C.J.A., in *Attorney-General of Canada* v. *Ritchie Contracting and Supply Co.*,[107] appears to have taken the view that the same principles applied to the bed as to the foreshore. However, the inconvenience of this view is so great that judges should be slow to accept it.

100/*Attorney-General of Canada* v. *Higbie*, [1945] S.C.R. 385, at 430–1.
101/(1888), 2 Ex.C.R. 30.   102/(1918), 56 S.C.R. 499.
103/See pp. 60–1.   104/(1885), 18 N.S.R. 433.
105/(1881), 6 S.C.R. 707; see esp. at 719, 721–2.
106/*Attorney-General of Canada* v. *Attorney-General of Ontario*, [1898] A.C. 700.
107/(1914), 20 B.C.R. 333, at 347–8.

Even if the beds of public harbours are held to belong to the Crown in right of the Dominion, this does not solve all problems respecting ownership of underwater resources in connection with public harbours. For, as was pointed out by Macdonald C.J.A. in the *Ritchie* case,[108] "There must be some point at which the bed of the sea changes its character from seabed to harbour bed." In areas where the seabed belongs to the province, drawing the line may be no easy problem. And if the view of Macdonald C.J.A., that the principles applicable to the foreshore apply to the bed, is upheld, the situation would be even more complex for on that basis he considered it "conceivable that there could be several harbours within English Bay, which has an area of twelve square miles."[109] Nomenclature may be deceiving the other way. For example, in *Maxwell* v. *R.*,[110] Cassels J. pointed out that various parts of Halifax harbour were called by separate names. Finally it may be mentioned that the extent of a public harbour raises no problem if it was defined by statute before Confederation. Toronto harbour is an example.[111]

vi   Harbour Works

The extent of the Dominion's rights in harbour works in existence before Confederation was discussed in *R.* v. *Attorney-General of Ontario and Forrest*.[112] The work there in question was a cribwork allegedly erected in the harbour of Goderich on Ship Island in the River Maitland to improve the resistance against the impact of ice and flood of an ice-breaker placed across a branch of the river between the island and the mainland. The work could probably be regarded as a harbour work or a river improvement, either of which would be transferred to the Dominion under section 108. It was not necessary to come to any decision on the matter because it was not proved that the cribwork was ever built, but all the judges expressed views on the matter. All were agreed that the cribwork alone would be transferred under section 108, not the whole island, but there were differences of views concerning the interest that would pass in the lands on which the cribwork was erected. Rinfret J. speaking for himself and the other puisne judges, doubted whether any more than an easement on Ship Island would pass, but Duff C.J. thought the Dominion acquired title to at least as much of the site and of the subsoil as might be regarded as reasonably necessary to give the Dominion free scope for the

108/*Ibid.*, at 348.
109/*Ibid.*, at 348.
110/(1917), 17 Ex.C.R. 97, at 101.
111/*Rickey* v. *City of Toronto* (1914), 30 O.L.R. 523.
112/[1934] S.C.R. 133.

complete discharge of the responsibilities which under the BNA Act it was expected to assume touching such works.

vii   Federal-Provincial Agreements respecting Harbours

It has been seen that an exact determination of what is provincial and what is federal property in harbours may be a question of some nicety. To settle the problem in British Columbia, negotiations between the governments of that province and Canada were initiated in the early 1920s. These culminated in an agreement validated by virtually identical orders in council of Canada and British Columbia in 1924.[113] The agreement provided that the six harbours of Victoria, Esquimalt, Nanaimo, Alberni, Burrard Inlet, and New Westminster, as described in a schedule to the agreement, were and are the public harbours of British Columbia under section 108. It was further agreed that the ownership of all other ungranted foreshore and of all lands under water, except those within the Railway Belt, were vested in the province. However, grants or transfers between one government and the other were not to be affected; nor were any other transfers made to the Dominion under the BNA Act or otherwise. The province agreed that if other harbours were used as harbours before the passing of the orders in council, the province would consider transferring such parts thereof as might reasonably be required by the Dominion; it further agreed to set aside certain sites already occupied by the Dominion for marine administration and such further sites as may reasonably be required by the Dominion for the purpose. The Dominion agreed to furnish to the province full particulars of all grants, quit claims, leases, or other concessions granted by the Dominion in respect of foreshores and lands covered by water outside the limits of the six harbours or the Railway Belt to enable the province to consider and determine the terms and conditions upon which such concessions should be confirmed. The province, on its part, agreed to furnish similar information regarding concessions it had made of foreshore and water beds within the six harbours. Finally, paragraph 11 contains an important saving clause that provides that any foreshore or land under water which had theretofore been granted, quit-claimed, leased, or otherwise dealt with by the province within the six harbours would be confirmed by the Dominion, subject to such terms and conditions as the Dominion might prescribe; the paragraph contains a similar undertaking by the province in respect of foreshore or lands under water outside

113/P.C. 941 of 7 June 1924; B.C. order in council No. 507 of 6 May 1924. For an account of the agreement and terms of the orders in council, see *Attorney-General of Canada* v. *Higbie*, [1945] S.C.R. 385, *per* Rinfret C.J.

the six harbours and the Railway Belt that were granted or otherwise dealt with.

The effect of the agreement and orders in council has come up in several cases. In *Kapoor Sawmills Ltd.* v. *Deliko*,[114] Manson J. stated that the orders in council amounted to a conveyance of Burrard Inlet to the Dominion dating back to the original transfer. He pointed out, however, that the validity of the agreement, which was entered into without legislative sanction, was not argued before him. The matter came up before the Supreme Court of Canada in 1945 in *Attorney-General of Canada* v. *Higbie*,[115] where it was argued that the orders in council were invalid as lacking statutory sanction. All the judges were in agreement that the orders in council were valid as admissions of matters in dispute. Such admissions could be made by the Crown in the course of litigation and there was no reason why they should not be equally valid if made outside the course of litigation. But Rand J. indicated limits of such admissions in the following passage: "As between the two jurisdictions, such an acknowledgment concludes the question but as to private rights different considerations arise. Ordinarily third persons would not be concerned with either Crown right in ownership or legislative jurisdiction. But the Province could not bind its own prior grantee as to his own title by such an acknowledgment: and where accrued rights are claimed not derived from the Province, as by prescription, the third person likewise cannot be prejudiced by provincial action of that nature."[116] Rinfret C.J. and Taschereau J. were also of the opinion that, in addition to their effect as admissions, the orders in council were valid as conveyances, but Rand J. disagreed, holding that statutory authority was required. Kerwin and Hudson JJ. preferred to leave the question open. The point is discussed in detail in another part of this work.[117]

The last case on the matter, *Nanaimo Ice & Cold Storage Co.* v. *Blyth*,[118] deals with the saving clause in paragraph 11. The plaintiff claimed an indefeasible title to certain land under the British Columbia Registry Act, but the defence alleged, *inter alia,* that the land in question was part of the foreshore at Nanaimo and so belonged to the Dominion. O'Halloran J.A. pointed out that while the 1924 agreement made it clear that Nanaimo harbour passed to the Dominion, this was subject to paragraph 11 which provided that any foreshore or land under water which had theretofore been granted, quit-claimed, leased, or otherwise dealt with by the province would be confirmed by the Dominion, subject to such terms and conditions as the Dominion should prescribe. He held that such

114/(1940), 56 B.C.R. 433.   115/[1945] S.C.R. 385.   116/*Ibid.,* at 436.
117/See pp. 19–21.   118/[1946] 4 D.L.R. 524.

confirmation was not confined to provincial Crown grants but included grants made by issuing certificates of title and those made by statute. A provincial statute had approved a survey of the City of Nanaimo, including the land in question; consequently this was confirmed by the clause referred to. Robertson J. A. and Bird J. A. concurred, but on other grounds.

A similar agreement was entered into between Canada and Ontario on 26 September 1961.[119] Though there had been about sixty public harbours in use in Ontario in 1867, many of these were no longer suitable for development and management by the federal government.[120] Accordingly the agreement provides that only the twenty-seven described in a schedule should be public harbours of the Dominion;[121] the others belong to Ontario. It further provides that the Dominion owns all ungranted lands comprised within the description of its harbours, including lands covered by water and the foreshores, as well as all interests in lands, except mines and minerals (including gold and silver and base metals) which belong to Ontario. The agreement does not affect title to any lands transferred by Canada or Ontario before the date of the agreement, or any lands acquired by Canada otherwise than by virtue of item 2 of the third schedule to the BNA Act. Finally a number of grants and quit-claims made by Canada and Ontario and described in schedules to the agreement are confirmed. The agreement took effect on approval by the legislature of Ontario on 26 April 1963,[122] and by the parliament of Canada on 21 December 1963.[123]

The agreements with British Columbia and Ontario, and particularly the latter, afford business-like solutions to many of the problems concerning the extent of public harbours and the nature of the Dominion's interest in them. It is highly desirable that similar agreements be entered into with other provinces.

Certain other constitutional agreements respecting harbours may perhaps be mentioned. The British Columbia agreement, validated by the BNA Act, 1930, reserves the beds and foreshores of harbours theretofore established in the Railway Belt as well as certain wharves and wharf sites to the Dominion.[124] So too, paragraph (h) of term 33 of the terms

119/(1962–63), 11 & 12 Eliz. II, c.95(Ont.); (1963), 12 Eliz. II, c.39(Can.).
120/See *Debates of the Senate*, 1963, at 399–401.
121/The twenty-seven are the harbours of Amherstburg, Belleville, Brockville, Chatham, Collingwood, Fort William, Gananoque, Goderich, Kincardine, Kingston, Kingsville, Leamington, Oshawa, Owen Sound, Penetanguishene, Port Arthur, Port Burwell, Port Hope, Port Stanley, Prescott, Rondeau Bay, Sarnia, Sault Ste. Marie, Southampton, Toronto, Whitby, and Windsor.
122/(1962–63), 11 & 12 Eliz. II, c.95(Ont.).
123/(1963), 12 Eliz. II, c.39(Can.).
124/Para. 11; validated by the BNA Act, 1930, 21 Geo. V, c.26(Imp.).

of union with Newfoundland transfers "public harbours" to the Dominion.[125] This phrase would, no doubt, be interpreted in the same way as in the third schedule to the BNA Act, 1867.

RIVERS AND LAKE IMPROVEMENTS

Next to harbours, item 5, "Rivers and Lake Improvements," has received the closest judicial examination of any item in the third schedule. In several early cases it was argued that the item transferred to the Dominion not simply improvements on rivers and lakes, but lake improvements and the entire rivers; if improvements only had been intended (it was maintained), the item would have read "River and Lake Improvements." The contention was strengthened by the fact that the Dominion had legislative power over such matters as "Sea Coast and Inland Fisheries," "Navigation," and kindred heads. But the argument met with little success[126] and was finally rejected by the Privy Council in the *Fisheries* case.[127] The reasoning of Lord Herschell, which may throw light on the interpretation of other items, is as follows:

Upon the whole their Lordships, after careful consideration, have arrived at the conclusion that the Court below was right, and that the improvements only were transferred to the Dominion. There can be no doubt that the subjects comprised in the schedule are for the most part works or constructions which have resulted from the expenditure of public money, though there are exceptions. It is to be observed that rivers and lake improvements are coupled together as one item. If the intention had been to transfer the entire bed of the rivers and only artificial works on lakes, one would not have expected to find them thus coupled together. Lake improvements might in that case more naturally have been found as a separate item or been coupled with canals. Moreover, it is impossible not to be impressed by the inconvenience which would arise if the entire rivers were transferred, and only the improvements of lakes. How would it be possible in that case to define the limits of the Dominion and provincial rights respectively? Rivers flow into and out of lakes; it would often be difficult to determine where the river ended and the lake began.[128]

As was pointed out by Fisher J. (one of the Fathers of Confederation) in *Steadman* v. *Robertson*,[129] and Girouard J. in *In Re Provincial Fisheries*,[130] the Quebec Resolutions[131] by referring to "River and Lake

125/Validated by the BNA Act, 1949, 12 & 13 Geo. VI, c.22(Imp.).
126/See *Steadman* v. *Robertson* (1879), 18 N.B.R. 581 (in this case the Supreme Court of New Brunswick reversed its earlier finding in *Robertson* v. *Steadman* (1876), 16 N.B.R. 621); *R.* v. *Robertson* (1882), 6 S.C.R. 52, *per* Gwynne J., in the Exchequer Court; *In re Provincial Fisheries* (1895), 26 S.C.R. 444.
127/*Attorney-General of Canada* v. *Attorney-General of Ontario*, [1898] A.C. 700.
128/*Ibid.*, at 710–11.
129/(1879), 18 N.B.R. 581, at 598.
130/(1895), 26 S.C.R. 444, at 565.
131/Pope's *Confederation Documents* (Toronto, 1895), at 49.

Improvements" made it clear that only improvements were referred to, and the plural appeared in the later drafts of the BNA Act and the act itself by some inadvertence in copying.

The nature of the rights acquired by the Dominion in river and lake improvements transferred by section 108 were examined in *Attorney-General of Canada* v. *Higbie*[132] and has already been dealt with in connection with harbours works.

It is interesting to note that in the agreement with British Columbia on the Railway Belt and Peace River block, the beds of a number of rivers are reserved to the Dominion under the following portion of paragraph 11:

> **11** ... and there shall in addition be reserved and retained by Canada the foreshores and beds of the Fraser River and the Pitt River lying above the eastern boundaries of New Westminster Harbour and below lines to be ascertained and defined by agreement at the junction of Kanaka Creek with the Fraser River and at the point of the exit of the Pitt River from Pitt Lake.[133]

It should perhaps be noted that a similar transfer is effected by paragraph (d) of term 33 of the terms of union with Newfoundland which, in addition to public harbours, transfers 'wharves, breakwaters, and aids to navigation.'[134]

MILITARY PROPERTY

Item 9 of the third schedule transfers to the Dominion "Property transferred by the Imperial Government, and known as Ordnance Property." In the early days of Canada various tracts of land had been reserved and put under the control of Her Majesty's Ordnance or the commander of the forces for purposes connected with the defence of the province, or had been used or occupied for such purposes.[135] Early transactions in public lands were loosely conducted and a number of statutes were passed to regulate military reserves.[136] The most important was a statute of the province of Canada of 1843, the Ordnance Vesting Act,[137] which vested in the principal officers of Her Majesty's Ordnance all lands "set apart, used or occupied for purposes connected with the military defence of the

---

132/[1945] S.C.R. 385. See pp. 64–5.
133/Validated by the BNA Act, 1930, 21 Geo. V, c.26(Imp.).
134/Validated by the BNA Act, 1949, 12 & 13 Geo. VI, c.22(Imp.).
135/The following account is based on the judgments in *Commissioners for Queen Victoria Niagara Falls Park* v. *Howard* (1893), 23 O.R. 1, and (1896), 23 O.A.R. 355.
136/(1838), 2 Vict., c.21(L.C.); (1840), 4 Vict., c.18(L.C.); (1843), 7 Vict., c.11(Can.); (1855), 18 Vict., c.91(Can.); (1856), 19 Vict., c.45(Can.); (1859), 22 Vict., c.36(Can.); Burton J.A., in *Commissioners for Queen Victoria Niagara Falls Park* v. *Howard* (1896), 23 O.A.R. 355, at 373 refers to other statutes.
137/7 Vict., c.11(Can.).

Province, or placed under the charge and control of the officers of the Ordnance department, or of the Commander of the forces or other military officer ... or have been intended to be so set apart or transferred for any of the purposes aforesaid." Subsequently some of this ordnance property was retransferred to the province and it was provided by statute that certain parts of it should be used for the general public purposes of the province but other parts should be retained for military purposes. This, in broad terms, was the situation in the province of Canada when the BNA Act was passed. It is obvious that any problem on this item will require an examination of pre-Confederation grants and statutes.

The most important case dealing with the effect of item 9 is *Commissioners for Queen Victoria Niagara Falls Park* v. *Howard*.[138] The plaintiff claimed land under a patent from the Ontario government to which the defendant also claimed under a lease from the Dominion government. The land in question was a strip running along the bank of the Niagara River which had been reserved out of the original survey of the township of Stomford in 1787–88. The defendant claimed that the land had been reserved for military or ordnance purposes and had, under item 9, vested in the Dominion through whom he claimed. On the evidence before him, Boyd C. came to the conclusion that the strip was not reserved for purely military purposes but was held for public purposes in the largest sense, even though it was generally believed to be intended as a means of military communication. He then considered whether the property might have become ordnance property under the broad terms of the Ordnance Vesting Act, 1843, particularly the reference therein to lands intended to be set apart for military purposes. But he came to the conclusion that it was not enough that it was intended to set the land apart for military or ordnance purposes; the course of dealing with the land must have been conformable to such appropriation and must have continued to the date of the statute. Not having found any such course of dealing, he held that the land had not become ordnance property under the statute and consequently had not passed to the Dominion.

On appeal, Burton, Osler, and Maclennan JJ.A. agreed that the land was not originally ordnance property and the Act of 1843 had not made it so. Hagarty C.J.O. was also of the opinion that the property had not been transferred by item 9 but he arrived at the conclusion by another route. He agreed that the land had been originally considered not merely as a military work but as a road through an unsurveyed tract of country for the transit of military stores and the ordinary commerce of the country. But after the road was laid out, it was almost always looked upon and

138/(1893), 23 O.R. 1; aff'd (1896), 23 O.A.R. 355.

treated as in charge of the ordnance officers. For this reason it appeared likely to him that the land was caught by the broad language of the Ordnance Vesting Act, and had become ordnance property. Subsequently, however, this property was retransferred to the province. By a series of statutes passed between 1855 and 1859 some of this land was reserved for military purposes but other parts were released from ordnance control and merged with other public lands of the province of Canada and as such became part of the public lands of Ontario. The land in question fell in the latter group and so was not transferred to the Dominion under item 9. Burton J.A. seems to agree with this distinction, but he was of the opinion that, if the land had once been ordnance property, the transactions under which ordnance property was re-transferred to the province made it clear that this particular land would have continued to be ordnance property. As previously mentioned, however, he took the view that it had never been ordnance property.

As is true of other items in the third schedule, item 9 did not transfer to the Dominion any land that had been conveyed to private persons by the provinces before Confederation.[139] Nor, as the *Deadman's Island* case[140] shows, did it operate to transfer to the Dominion lands reserved for military purposes that remained under the administration of the Imperial government at Confederation. Such lands had to be expressly transferred by that government.

Item 9 is not the only provision specifically transferring military land. Item 7 lists military roads. And in the *Deadman's Island* case where it was argued that the island was transferred to the Dominion as military property, reliance was not placed on item 9 but on "Lands set apart for general Public Purposes" in item 10 to show that the island was transferred to the Dominion, and it is worthy of note that that phrase is preceded by the words "Armouries, Drill Sheds, Military Clothing, and Munitions of War."

Later constitutional provisions affecting military property should perhaps be mentioned. It is interesting to speculate whether a limitation is imposed on the Dominion's power over its property at Esquimalt by term 9 of the terms of union with British Columbia which provides:

9   The influence of the Dominion Government will be used to secure the continued maintenance of the naval station at Esquimalt.[141]

In that province, ordnance and admiralty lands transferred or to be transferred by the United Kingdom to Canada are expressly reserved from the

139/*Kennedy* v. *City of Toronto* (1886), 12 O.R. 211.
140/*Attorney-General of British Columbia* v. *Attorney-General of Canada*, [1906] A.C. 552.
141/See R.S.C., VI, 6263.

regrant to British Columbia of the Railway Belt and the Peace River block.[142] It is further provided that all ordnance and admiralty land in the province shall continue to be vested in Canada, but provision is made for the recognition by Canada of any alienation of such land previously made by the province.[143] It is also agreed to settle the boundaries of such lands by arbitration.[144] Finally, under term 33 of the terms of union with Newfoundland, the 'military and naval property, stores and equipment' of Newfoundland are transferred to Canada.[145]

OTHER ITEMS IN THE THIRD SCHEDULE

A few other items in the third schedule have been briefly discussed by the courts. Despite the holding respecting "Rivers and Lake Improvements,"[146] it was argued in *Macdonald* v. *R.* [147] that the transfer of a canal under item 1 operated to transfer the "navigations" of a river, making the Dominion liable for an accident thereon. The argument was, of course, rejected. Item 1 again came up for brief consideration in *Reference re Waters and Water-Powers*,[148] when the Supreme Court of Canada stated that "whatever subjects are comprehended under the phrase 'Water Power' in the 1st item of the third schedule, by section 108 passed to the Dominion, there was left to the provinces neither proprietary interest in, nor beneficial ownership of such subjects." And it added that the item did not, of course, comprise "water-powers ... 'created or made available by reason of extensions, enlargements or replacements made by the Dominion since Confederation,' or 'by works for the improvement of navigation constructed in whole or in part since Confederation.' "

The transfer of Sable Island to the Dominion under item 3 raises the interesting problem whether the transfer included the minerals and royalties. The considerations advanced in connection with the similar problem in relation to public harbours would indicate that any base metals may belong to the Dominion but not the precious metals or any other prerogative rights.[149] In determining what was transferred by the term "Sable Island" it is relevant to note that the transfer is linked with the transfer of lighthouses and piers and the Dominion legislative power over

---

142/Para. 6, British Columbia Railway Belt and Peace River block agreement, validated by the BNA Act, 1930, 21 Geo. V, c.26(Imp.).
143/*Ibid.*, para. 7.
144/*Ibid.*, para. 8.
145/Validated by the BNA Act, 1949, 12 & 13 Geo. VI, c.22(Imp.).
146/See pp. 68–9.
147/(1906), 10 Ex.C.R. 394.
148/[1929] S.C.R. 200, at 202; the quotation actually refers to section 106, but this is obviously a typographical error: see [1929] 2 D.L.R. 481, at 505.
149/See pp. 58–9.

the island is also coupled with "beacons, buoys and lighthouses."[150] There is thus indicated a limited purpose for the transfer which is fortified by section 7 of the BNA Act, 1867, which contemplates that the island shall remain within the limits of the province.

Item 4, transferring "Steamboats, Dredges, and Public Vessels" to the Dominion does not appear to have been discussed in the cases. The terms of union with Prince Edward Island, however, made some qualifications to the item.[151] A steam dredge boat then under construction was taken by the Dominion at a cost not exceeding twenty thousand dollars and a government steam ferryboat remained the property of the island. The terms of union with Newfoundland contain a clause similar to item 4.[152] Paragraph (g) of term 33 transfers public dredges and vessels, except those used for services that remain the responsibility of Newfoundland, and the nine Clarenville boats; paragraph (e) of the same term transfers the motor vessel *Malakoff* to the Dominion.

Item 6, transferring railways, railway stocks, mortgages, and other debts due by railway companies, was dealt with in *Western Counties Ry. Co.* v. *Windsor and Annapolis Ry. Co.*[153] which has already been discussed. In Prince Edward Island[154] and Newfoundland[155] the government railway systems were expressly taken over by the Dominion under the terms of union with those provinces.

By item 8, custom houses, post offices, and all other public buildings, except those appropriated by the government of Canada for the use of the provincial legislatures and governments, are transferred to the Dominion. The import of this item is limited by section 113 of the BNA Act which provides that the assets enumerated in the fourth schedule to the Act shall belong to the provinces of Ontario and Quebec conjointly. No case has arisen under the item, but its effect was dealt with in a report of the minister of Justice in 1893.[156] The report concerned a reserved New Brunswick bill purporting to declare that property described as 'government house property' was vested in the Crown in right of the province to the same extent as other provincial lands. The property in question had been transferred to the Dominion under item 8 of section 108, but by a Dominion order in council of 11 February, 1870 it had been appropriated to the use

150/See *Queddy River Driving Boom Co.* v. *R.* (1883), 10 S.C.R. 222, at 232; see also Lord Herschell's approach in *Attorney-General of Canada* v. *Attorney-General of Ontario*, [1898] A.C. 700, at 710–11; the statement is quoted at p. 68.
151/See R.S.C. 1952, VI, 6271, at 6274.
152/Validated by the BNA Act, 1949, 12 & 13 Geo. VI, c.22(Imp.).
153/(1882), 7 A.C. 178.
154/See R.S.C. 1952, VI, 6271, at 6274.
155/Validated by the BNA Act, 1949, 12 & 13 Geo. VI, c.22(Imp.).
156/W. E. Hodgins, *Dominion and Provincial Legislation, 1867–1896* (Ottawa, 1898), at 757–58.

of the government and legislature of the province. Sir John Thompson did not think the order constituted an appropriation of the property so as to change its character and convert it into ordinary provincial public property. This reasoning seems by no means free of doubt, as the minister himself admitted.

The terms of union with Prince Edward Island provide that the building then housing the law courts and registry office and land adjacent thereto are to be transferred to Canada on payment of sixty-nine thousand dollars.[157] Customs houses, post offices, and all public works and property used primarily for services taken over by Canada are also transferred under the terms of union with Newfoundland, and term 34 makes elaborate provisions for cases where public buildings are used partly for federal and partly for provincial purposes.[158]

Item 10 of the third schedule has already received attention in connection with military property.[159] The item was also dealt with in a rather oblique manner in the *Fisheries* case.[160] There it was argued on behalf of the Dominion that the large freshwater lakes, particularly the Great Lakes and waters of any description set apart for general public purposes, as well as the seacoast and the territorial waters, belonged to the Dominion as coming within this phrase. While the Privy Council[161] avoided the question by simply saying that whatever was vested in the provinces remained so vested unless expressly transferred by the BNA Act to the Dominion, the Supreme Court of Canada[162] was clear that all waters, except in public harbours, vested in the province. This would appear to involve a finding that these bodies of water do not fall within the description of "Lands set apart for general Public Purposes." Similarly in the *St. Catharine's Milling* case it was held that the phrase did not include Indian lands.[163] In connection with this item it is interesting to note the general reservation in the resources agreements with the Prairie provinces under which Canada retains any ungranted lands on which public money of Canada has been expended or which were in use or reserved by Canada for the purpose of the federal administration at the time of the agreements.[164]

157/See R.S.C. 1952, vol. VI, 6271, at 6274.
158/Validated by the BNA Act, 1949, 12 & 13 Geo. VI, c.22(Imp.).
159/See p. 71.
160/*Attorney-General of Canada* v. *Attorney-General of Ontario*, [1898] A.C. 700, affirming *In re Provincial Fisheries* (1896), 26 S.C.R. 444.
161/*Attorney-General of Canada* v. *Attorney-General of Ontario*, [1898] A.C. 700.
162/*In re Provincial Fisheries* (1895), 26 S.C.R. 444.
163/*St. Catherine's Milling and Lumber Co.* v. *R.* (1889), 14 A.C. 46, at 56.
164/Para. 18, Manitoba and Alberta agreements; para. 19, Saskatchewan agreement; validated by the BNA Act, 1930, 21 Geo. V, c.26(Imp.).

CHAPTER FIVE

Lands, Mines, Minerals, and Royalties

Section 109 of the British North America Act, 1867, provides that all lands, mines, minerals, and royalties belonging to the several provinces at the union shall belong to the provinces in which they are situate or arise. However, this grant is made subject to any trusts in respect thereof or to any interest therein other than that of the province. The section, of course, was originally applicable only to Ontario, Quebec, Nova Scotia, and New Brunswick, but it was extended to the provinces entering Confederation after 1867 by provisions in the instruments making them part of Canada. Consequently the section applies to British Columbia[1] and Prince Edward Island[2] as if they were expressly enumerated therein. In so far as Manitoba, Saskatchewan, and Alberta are concerned, specific provisions reserving natural resources to the Dominion seriously restricted the operation of the section, so that in Manitoba only the royalties,[3] and in Saskatchewan and Alberta only the royalties not incident to land,[4] were transferred to those provinces. But under the resources agreements between Canada and those provinces, validated by the BNA Act, 1930, the "Crown lands, mines, minerals (precious and base) and royalties derived therefrom" were specifically transferred to the provinces, subject to the same exceptions as in section 109.[5] Term 37 of the terms of union of Newfoundland with Canada puts that province in the same position.[6] The general effect of these sections, as we have seen, is to vest in the provinces all their natural resources and prerogative rights arising there, except such as have been expressly transferred to the Dominion and subject to excepted trusts and interests.[7] We must now examine what is meant by the expression "lands, mines, minerals, and royalties" in more detail.

LANDS, MINES, AND MINERALS

The word "lands" as used in the foregoing provisions means public lands, not all lands within the province. This is obvious from the corresponding

1/See p. 31.   2/See p. 33.   3/See pp. 29–31.
4/See pp. 34–5.   5/See pp. 35–8.   6/See p. 46.
7/See p. 25.

language of section 125 of the BNA Act, 1867 (exempting property belonging to Canada or the provinces from taxation), which could only apply to public property, and section 117 of that Act which specifically refers to public property.[8] The term comprises the beneficial use and proceeds of the lands,[9] including proceeds that had become due and payable before the transfer.[10] And, in exercising its beneficial interest in land, a province may do what any other proprietor may do, for example, attach conditions to its grants or licences, even if these touch upon matters ordinarily within the legislative jurisdiction of the federal parliament such as aliens and trade and commerce.[11] The term also includes the ordinary incidents of land. Thus it is clear that the word would be sufficient to include such mines and minerals as are ordinarily incident to land. This can be seen from the *Precious Metals* case[12] where it was stated that the conveyance of the "public lands" within the Railway Belt by British Columbia to Canada included the mines and minerals, so that the word "mines" and "minerals" in section 109 are redundant. It can also be seen from *Burrard Power Co. Ltd.* v. *R.*[13] where water commissioners, purporting to act under a British Columbia statute, granted certain water rights in the Railway Belt to the appellant company. The Canadian government, however, denied the validity of the grant, and its view was upheld by the Privy Council which asserted that the grant of the "public lands" in the Belt "passed the water rights incidental to those lands." Not only is the Crown entitled to rights on and under its land; it also possesses whatever rights belong to a landowner in the air space above by virtue of the common law maxim: *cujus est solum, ejus est usque ad caelum et ad inferos.*[14]

The term "lands," however, does not include prerogative rights connected with land. Thus in *Attorney-General of Ontario* v. *Mercer*[15] it was held that the term alone would be insufficient to transfer to the provinces

8/*Attorney-General of Ontario* v. *Mercer* (1882–83), 8 A.C. 767, at 775–76.
9/*St. Catherine's Milling and Lumber Co.* v. *R.* (1889), 14 A.C. 46, at 56.
10/*Attorney-General of Canada* v. *Attorney-General of Ontario*, [1897] A.C. 199, at 209. This is expressly provided for in section 109 of the BNA Act, 1867, and in term 37 of the terms of union with Newfoundland; this appears to be understood in para. 1 of the resources agreements.
11/See *Smylie* v. *R.* (1900), 27 O.A.R. 172; *Brooks-Bidlake and Whittall* v. *Attorney-General of British Columbia*, [1923] A.C. 450. These cases are discussed at pp. 164–5.
12/*Attorney-General of British Columbia* v. *Attorney-General of Canada* (1889), 14 A.C. 295.
13/[1911] A.C. 87.
14/A similar principle exists under the Civil Law: see the Quebec Civil Code, art. 414.
15/(1882–83), 8 A.C. 767.

the right to escheats, and in the *Precious Metals* case[16] it was held that the term "public lands" did not include precious metals, so that these did not pass to the Dominion with the lands in the Railway Belt. The right to gold and silver in land, like escheats, is not an incident to land but a prerogative right. However, these prerogative rights belong to the provinces as royalties,[17] and in the Prairie provinces precious minerals are expressly transferred.[18]

Finally, the word "lands" is not limited to lands in which the Crown has unlimited ownership, but includes all estates in land.[19] It, therefore, includes public lands reserved for Indians, though these are subject to a usufruct in favour of the Indians.[20]

FISHERIES AND NAVIGABLE WATERS

A major difficulty in the interpretation of the term "lands" has been whether it includes fisheries and the beds of navigable waters. There is no question that fisheries would *prima facie* appear to fall within the expression, for the owner of the bed of a stream has the exclusive right to fish in it as an incident to the ownership of the bed.[21] But, as has been shown, in several early cases it was argued that item 5 of the third schedule to the BNA Act, which transfers to the Dominion "Rivers and Lake Improvements," passed to the Dominion not simply improvements on rivers and lakes but the entire rivers as well. This, of course, would include the fisheries in the rivers. The argument was, however, laid to rest by the Privy Council in the *Fisheries* case.[22] Similarly, the argument that the large freshwater lakes, particularly the Great Lakes, as well as the seacoast and the territorial waters, belonged to the Dominion as "Lands set apart for general public purposes" within item 10 of the third schedule, was equally rejected.[23]

16/*Attorney-General of British Columbia* v. *Attorney-General of Canada* (1889), 14 A.C. 295; see also *Esquimalt and Nanaimo Ry.* v. *Bainbridge*, [1896] A.C. 561 and *Hudson's Bay Co.* v. *Attorney-General of Canada*, [1929] A.C. 285.
17/This is dealt with at pp. 79–83.
18/See the para. 1 of the resources agreements with Manitoba, Saskatchewan and Alberta, validated by the BNA Act, 1930, 21 Geo. V, c.26(Imp.).
19/*Attorney-General of Ontario* v. *Mercer* (1882–83), 8 A.C. 767.
20/See *St. Catherine's Milling and Lumber Co.* v. *R.* (1889), 14 A.C. 46; *Attorney-General of Canada* v. *Attorney-General of Ontario*, [1897] A.C. 199; *Ontario Mining Co.* v. *Seybold*, [1903] A.C. 73. Indian lands are discussed in chapter seven.
21/*R.* v. *Robertson* (1882), 6 S.C.R. 52; *Re Provincial Fisheries* (1895), 26 S.C.R. 444.
22/*Attorney-General of Canada* v. *Attorney-General of Ontario*, [1898] A.C. 700. For a discussion of the point, see pp. 68–9.
23/See *Re Provincial Fisheries* (1895), 26 S.C.R. 444.

But the most serious argument against provincial ownership of the fisheries was that the Dominion under its power to legislate respecting "Sea Coast and Inland Fisheries" had absolute control over the fisheries and could thereby exercise rights that were virtually proprietary. This problem is more germane to legislative power respecting fisheries and will be examined in detail in that connection. It is sufficient here to point out that the argument was found unacceptable by the Privy Council in the *Fisheries* case,[24] where Lord Herschell made the following statement:

It must also be borne in mind that there is a broad distinction between proprietary rights and legislative jurisdiction. The fact that such jurisdiction in respect of a particular subject-matter is conferred on the Dominion Legislature, for example, affords no evidence that any proprietary rights with respect to it were transferred to the Dominion. There is no presumption that because legislative jurisdiction was vested in the Dominion Parliament proprietary rights were transferred to it.

The similar argument that the Dominion owned the beds of navigable waters by virtue of its legislative power over navigation and shipping has also been held to be without foundation.[25]

The Privy Council has ruled that the provincial proprietary rights over fisheries are not limited to freshwater fisheries but extend to fisheries in tidal waters where the bed is vested in the province.[26] In tidal waters, however, provincial proprietary rights to ordinary fisheries are rather shadowy. For in the provinces governed by the common law the public has a paramount right to fish in tidal waters,[27] and in Quebec, by virtue of pre-Confederation legislation, the public has a right to fish in the deepsea fisheries and all fisheries that are natural adjuncts thereto, including coastal fisheries and those in tidal navigable waters;[28] the power to regulate these public rights is wholly within federal competence.[29] These public rights are, however, limited to ordinary fishing; they do not apply to fishing by kiddles, weirs, or other engines involving the use of the solum.

24/[1898] A.C. 700, at 709.
25/See *R.* v. *Moss* (1896), 26 S.C.R. 322; *Re Provincial Fisheries* (1896), 26 S.C.R. 444; *Fort George Lumber Co.* v. *Grand Trunk Pacific Ry.* (1915), 24 D.L.R. 527; *Montreal* v. *Montreal Harbour Commissioners*, [1926] A.C. 299.
26/*Attorney-General of British Columbia* v. *Attorney-General of Canada*, [1914] A.C. 153; *Attorney-General of Canada* v. *Attorney-General of Quebec*, [1921] 1 A.C. 413.
27/*Attorney-General of British Columbia* v. *Attorney-General of Canada*, [1914] A.C. 153.
28/(1865), 29 Vict., c.11(Can.); see *Attorney-General of Canada* v. *Attorney-General of Quebec*, [1921] 1 A.C. 413.
29/*Attorney-General of British Columbia* v. *Attorney-General of Canada*, [1914] A.C. 153; *Attorney-General of Canada* v. *Attorney-General of Quebec*, [1921] 1 A.C. 413.

Such fishing may be regulated by the Dominion, but the province, like any other landowner, has proprietary jurisdiction over the soil.[30]

ROYALTIES

In the context in which we are examining it, "royalties" may conceivably be used in two different senses. It may be construed restrictively to mean the dues based on production payable for the privilege of working a mine. Or it may be simply an English translation of *jura regalia, regalitates,* or *jura regia,* those casual revenues of the Crown derived from the Royal prerogative, such as, for example, the Queen's right to escheats, to the land between high- and low-water mark, to felon's goods, to treasure trove, and other rights owing their origin to the Queen's pre-eminence and dignity at common law. The question of which of these meanings should be attributed to the word first arose in the early case of *Attorney-General of Quebec* v. *Attorney-General of the Dominion (Church* v. *Blake)*[31] where there were conflicting claims by Canada and Quebec to the estate of one Edward Fraser, who died intestate leaving no heirs. The Quebec Court of Queen's Bench, Appeal side, decided in favour of the province for a variety of reasons, but we need concern ourselves only with those of Ramsay and Sanborn JJ. who held that escheats were among the minor prerogatives of the Crown, and so were royalties within the meaning of section 109 of the BNA Act. It should be noted that while the judges spoke solely of escheat, they were using the word to include *bona vacantia* as well, for the intestate's estate consisted of both real and personal property.

The matter arose again in connection with real estate in *Attorney-General of Ontario* v. *Mercer.*[32] Proudfoot V.C., who heard the case, and the Ontario Court of Appeal agreed with the reasoning in *Attorney-General of Quebec* v. *Attorney-General of the Dominion,* but in the Supreme Court of Canada the majority were of the view that royalties meant the dues for working mines existing in the Maritime provinces. On appeal to the Privy Council it was held that "royalties" must be given its primary sense of *jura regia,* and that the right to escheats was a royalty in this sense. It was further held that such royalties had been appropriated for the benefit of the provinces before the passing of the BNA Act, and consequently by section 109 of that Act they were assigned to the provinces.

30/*Ibid.* These matters are dealt with more extensively at pp. 155–7.
31/(1876), 2 Q.L.R. 236.
32/(1882–83), 8 A.C. 767; reversing (1881), 5 S.C.R. 538, which reversed 6 O.A.R. 576, which affirmed 26 Gr. 126.

Another type of royalty was discussed in *Attorney-General of British Columbia* v. *Attorney-General of Canada*:[33] the prerogative right of the Crown to precious metals, which is that, unless expressly granted "all mines of gold and silver within the realm, whether they be in the lands of the Queen or of subjects, belong to the Queen by prerogative, with liberty to dig and carry away the ores thereof, and with such other incidents thereto as are necessary to be used for the getting of the ore."[34] The facts of the case were that, when British Columbia entered Confederation, section 109 of the BNA Act was made applicable subject to the qualification that it should transfer to the Dominion the "public lands" in the British Columbia Railway Belt. Shortly after that land was transferred, gold was found and a dispute arose between the Dominion and the province concerning its ownership. The Privy Council held that the Crown's right to the gold was transferred to the province under the word "royalties" in section 109. The retransfer to the Dominion was of the lands only and whereas land includes as incidents the base mines and minerals therein, precious metals are not an appendage to land but a royalty and so were not re-transferred with the land.

In both the *Mercer*[35] and *Precious Metals*[36] cases their Lordships were careful to indicate that they were "not ... called upon to decide whether the word 'royalties' in section 109 of the British North America Act of 1867, extends to other Royal rights besides those connected with 'lands,' 'mines,' and 'minerals.' " But in *R.* v. *Attorney-General of British Columbia*[37] the question arose whether other royalties might not be included in the section, the royalty in question being *bona vacantia*, that is, personal property to which no one has a claim. It was argued that by virtue of the *ejusdem generis* rule the royalties in section 109 were confined to those connected with lands, mines, or minerals. The Privy Council, however, would not accept this argument, holding that *bona vacantia* fell within the section.[38] Their Lordships noted that the word "All" preceded the phrase "lands, mines, minerals, and royalties" and while they conceded that earlier judgments of the Board did refer to territorial revenues, they pointed out that this was in other contexts and that in the *Precious Metals*

33/(1889), 14 A.C. 295; followed in *Farwell* v. *R.* (1893–94), 22 S.C.R. 553.
34/*Attorney-General of British Columbia* v. *Attorney-General of Canada* (1889), 14 A.C. 295, at 302, citing from the *Mine's Case* (1567), 1 Plowd. 310, at 336; 75 E.R. 472, at 510.
35/(1882–83), 8 A.C. 769, at 779 where the statement quoted appeared.
36/(1889), 14 A.C. 295, at 305.
37/[1924] A.C. 213.
38/See also *Attorney-General of Alberta* v. *Attorney-General of Canada*, [1928] A.C. 475; *Attorney-General of Quebec* v. *Attorney-General of the Dominion* (*Church* v. *Blake*) (1876), 2 Q.L.R. 236.

case it had drawn a sharp distinction between the prerogative rights in precious metals and the rights to minerals arising from the ownership of land. They, therefore, held that the term "royalties" was used in its broadest sense, and was susceptible of including all prerogative revenues. But they nonetheless confined their judgment to *bona vacantia* and refused to give any opinion on whether "other jura regalia, such as flotsam and jetsam, deodands, swans and sturgeons, bona et catalla felonum and many others" were included in section 109, relying on the statement made in the *Mercer* case[39] that these prerogative rights were of a high political nature of far greater importance than their current pecuniary value.[40] At the same time there are remarks earlier in the judgment indicating that their Lordships would have been willing to include treasure trove among the royalties passing under section 109. Treasure trove is gold or silver in coin, plate, or bullion whose owner is unknown and which is concealed in a house, the earth, or other private place.[41]

The last case on provincial rights in royalties decided by the Privy Council was the *Fines* case: *Toronto* v. *R.*[42] Under a Dominion statute, certain fines were payable to the City of Toronto, but the province claimed them as a royalty under section 109 of the BNA Act. Their Lordships agreed that the sovereign has a prerogative to receive fines imposed on convicted persons and that this may with sufficient accuracy be described as a royalty, but they pointed out that the characteristics of royalties vary: some are absolute; others are qualified. In the case of fines, only those unappropriated by competent authority belong to the Crown. The competent authority in Canada is the Canadian parliament, for under section 91(27) of the BNA Act it is given exclusive authority to legislate respecting criminal law, and this power must include the manner of application of penalties; for if the power to create penalties were lodged in another authority it is easy to see how penal legislation might be seriously affected if not stultified. Since, therefore, the competent authority had enacted legislation appropriating the fines, the Crown in right of the province was not entitled to receive them even if this prerogative fell within section 109, a finding which their Lordships expressly refrained from making.

The wisdom of the Privy Council's policy of confining its judgments to the particular royalty in question can be seen from the only other cases on

39/*Attorney-General of Ontario* v. *Mercer* (1882–83), 8 A.C. 769, at 778.
40/See [1924] A.C. 213, at 221–22.
41/See *Attorney-General* v. *Moore*, [1893] 1 Ch. 676, at 683; the question whether the Queen owns treasure trove in right of the provinces or the Dominion may conceivably arise, for it may well be that pirate treasure has been buried in the Maritime provinces.
42/[1932] A.C. 98.

the meaning of the term as used in the BNA Act: *Perry* v. *Clergue*[43] and *In re International and Interprovincial Ferries*.[44] In *Perry* v. *Clergue* it was claimed that the defendant had interfered with the plaintiff's right, granted under a Dominion statute, to operate an exclusive ferry from Sault Ste Marie in Ontario to the town of the same name in Michigan. The defendant contended, *inter alia*, that the Dominion government never became entitled to grant the franchise because the right to do so was vested in the provincial authorities. Notwithstanding that legislative authority over "Ferries between a Province and any British or Foreign Country or between Two Provinces" is by section 91(13) of the BNA Act vested in parliament, Street J. upheld the contention of the defendant. He held that the right to grant and license ferries appears to have been a branch of the *jura regalia* or royalty appropriated for the benefit of the provinces before Confederation and consequently still retained by them under section 109 of the BNA Act.

As a result of this case, the Governor General in council immediately referred the question to the Supreme Court of Canada in *In re International and Interprovincial Ferries*. The court held that the parliament of Canada has jurisdiction to authorize the governor in council to establish and create ferries, and that the power given to that body to confer an exclusive ferry by licence or otherwise was valid. The reasons given by the court, however, are not remarkable for their clarity. Chief Justice Taschereau said that international and interprovincial undertakings, including ferries, were within federal power. The ferry in question and the right thereto did not exist before Confederation and consequently section 109 had no application and the right to these revenues fell to the Dominion under section 102. He distinguished the *Fisheries* case[45] on the ground that proprietary rights were in question there. He also noted that the provincial legislatures could not incorporate a company to run an interprovincial ferry. The reasons of Nesbitt J. (with whom Sedgewick and Girouard JJ. concurred) are somewhat more comprehensible. After setting out a number of pre-Confederation provincial statutes providing for the licensing and regulation of ferries and the fixing of tolls, he stated that it would appear that the Crown had abandoned certain prerogative rights such as the granting of charters, leaving them to the control of the legislatures, and that the exercise of such a right, at least in the colonies, was obsolete. He then pointed out that it was obvious from the whole scheme of Confederation that the BNA Act intended that all rights affecting navigation and ferries between the Dominion and foreign countries should be in parliament. Nothing, of course, was said of provincial ferries but it

43/(1903), 5. O.L.R. 357.   44/(1905), 36 S.C.R. 206.   45/[1898] A.C. 700.

has been held in other cases that the right to license and regulate these resides in the provinces, subject, however, to federal legislation relating to navigation and shipping under section 91(10) of the BNA Act.[46]

With respect, the reasoning of the Supreme Court appears unnecessarily tortuous. The simple fact is that the Imperial parliament, as it unquestionably had a right to do, gave legislative power to the Dominion parliament respecting international and interprovincial ferries by section 91(13) of the BNA Act. The regulation of ferries must, as the judges in the instant case point out, include the power to license them and determine their location. For, to paraphrase the language of the Privy Council in the *Fines* case,[47] if the power to license interprovincial and international ferries were to be dissociated from the power to make legislation respecting them, it is easy to see how such legislation might be seriously affected, if not stultified.

It is not proposed here to set forth the many other royalties that could conceivably give rise to problems;[48] enough has been said to indicate the approach the courts would take.

Finally, it should be remembered that minor royalties in Quebec are governed by French, not English law. Thus in *Ross* v. *Levy*[49] it was held that whatever the rights of the Queen to mines and minerals might be under English law, her rights in Quebec were no greater or less than those of the king of France.

TRUSTS AND NON-PROVINCIAL INTERESTS

Section 109 of the BNA Act, 1867, paragraph 1 of each of the resources agreements, and term 37 of the Newfoundland terms of union make the grant of the lands, mines, minerals, and royalties to the provinces subject to trusts existing in respect thereof and to any interest other than that of the province in the same. The word "trusts" may, of course, mean trusts or other equitable interests in the technical sense of a court of Chancery. This was the situation in *Warman* v. *Francis*.[50] There the province of New Brunswick had, shortly before Confederation, agreed to sell a portion of an Indian reserve under a statute authorizing such sale and the full purchase price had been paid but the letters patent were not issued until after

---

46/*Longueuil Navigation Co.* v. *City of Montreal* (1888), 15 S.C.R. 566, *per* Fournier J.; *Dinner* v. *Humberstone* (1896), 26 S.C.R. 264; *Validity and Applicability of the Industrial Relations and Disputes Investigation Act*, [1955] S.C.R. 529.
47/[1932] A.C. 98, at 104.
48/For a discussion of these, see Halsbury's *Laws of England* (3rd ed., London, 1954), VII, "Constitutional Law," at 453 *et seq.*
49/(1883), 6 L.N. 407. For the basis of this difference, see pp. 6–11.
50/(1960), 20 D.L.R. (2d) 627.

Confederation. It was held that title thereto passed in equity to the purchaser before Confederation and with it any Indian rights. The province, therefore, held the land subject to an equitable obligation to convey to the purchaser, and this amounted to a trust within the meaning of section 109.

But the word "trusts" is not limited to trusts in the technical sense. This can be seen from the following statement of the Privy Council in *Attorney-General of Canada* v. *Attorney-General of Ontario*[51] which defines the meaning of the concluding words of section 109. It reads:

> The expressions "subject to any trusts existing in respect thereof," and "subject to any interest other than that of the province," appear to their Lordships to be intended to refer to different classes of right. Their Lordships are not prepared to hold that the word "trust" was meant by the Legislature to be strictly limited to such proper trusts as a court of equity would undertake to administer; but, in their opinion, it must at least have been intended to signify the existence of a contractual or legal duty, incumbent upon the holder of the beneficial estate or its proceeds, to make payment, out of one or other of these, of the debt due to the creditor to whom that duty ought to be fulfilled. On the other hand, "an interest other than that of the province in the same" appears to them to denote some right or interest in a third party, independent of and capable of being vindicated in competition with the beneficial interest of the old province.

The cases dealing with this subject related to Indian lands and will be examined in that connection.[52] Here it may be briefly noted that in *St. Catharines' Milling and Lumber Co.* v. *R.*,[53] the Privy Council held that the usufructuary interest of the Indians in provincial lands reserved for them is an interest other than that of the province. On the other hand, a promise of an annuity to Indians in return for a surrender by them of their usufructuary interest is neither a trust nor an interest other than that of the province.[54] A more difficult question arises in relation to the privilege reserved by some tribes of Indians to hunt and fish on surrendered lands. Some statements of the Privy Council appear to indicate that this privilege may be a trust or interest in the land,[55] but Greene, J. of the Ontario High Court later held the contrary in *R.* v. *Commanda*.[56]

51/[1897] A.C. 199, at 210–11.
52/See chapter seven.
53/(1889), 14 A.C. 46.
54/*Attorney-General of Canada* v. *Attorney-General of Ontario*, [1897] A.C. 199; *Dominion of Canada* v. *Province of Ontario*, [1910] A.C. 637.
55/*St. Catherine's Milling and Lumber Co.* v. *R.* (1889), 14 A.C. 46, at 60; *Ontario Mining Co.* v. *Seybold*, [1903] A.C. 73, at 79.
56/[1939] 3 D.L.R. 635.

CHAPTER SIX

Offshore Submarine Resources

Until recent years the possibility of federal-provincial controversy over what Lord Hale was wont to describe as "the great waste of the sea" would have seemed unthinkable. But when modern technology made it possible to extract oil and other resources from the bed of the sea and other bodies of water, it was inevitable that conflicting claims to ownership and control of the resources of the subsoil of the adjoining seas should be made by the federal and provincial governments. The recent decision of the Supreme Court of Canada in the reference *Re: Offshore Mineral Rights of British Columbia*[1] has settled the question so far as the territorial sea and continental shelf of British Columbia is concerned, but the situation regarding at least some of the other coastal provinces will require further clarification.

The subject raises complex problems both of constitutional and international law. But though the solution of particular problems would require a close examination of the principles and application of international law, only such reference will be made to these as is necessary to an exposition of the general constitutional position.

Under international law a coastal state's claim to submarine resources may be based on its jurisdiction over either inland waters, territorial waters, or the continental shelf. Each of these raises separate, though related, problems.

INLAND WATERS

Inland waters consist of "a State's ports and harbours, bays and gulfs, land-locked seas, straits and rivers."[2] Such waters are so intimately connected with the territory of the state that, under international law, they are considered as much the territory of a state as if they were dry land,[3] and consequently the state "possesses the right to carry out the exploitation

1/[1967] S.C.R. 792. As this book was going to press the federal government made an offer to the provinces for the division of the resources and jurisdiction offshore.
2/C. J. Colombos, *The International Law of the Sea* (5th ed., London, 1962), at 158; see also L. Oppenheim, *International Law* (8th ed. by Lauterpacht, London, 1955), vol. I, "Peace," at 460–63.
3/Colombos, *ibid.*, at 78–9; Oppenheim, *ibid.*, at 460–63.

of both the surface and its subsoil by tunnelling or mining for coal and other minerals."[4] The Geneva Convention on the Territorial Sea and the Contiguous Zone clearly recognizes that the sovereignty of a state extends to its inland waters.[5]

The common law position in England is that inland waters (or waters *intra fauces terrae* as they are often called) form part of the adjoining county.[6] The situation in the colonies depends to some extent on which of two competing theories one accepts. The more convincing theory is that the English rule that inland waters form part of the adjoining county, like other parts of the common law, applies to the colonies. This is supported by the fact that whenever it was convenient to do so, the boundaries of the provinces were defined by reference to inland waters. Thus the western boundary of Nova Scotia, when it included New Brunswick, was drawn across the entrance to the Bay of Fundy;[7] later the provinces were defined by a line drawn in the middle of that bay.[8] And part of the boundary

4/Colombos, *ibid.*, at 79; see also Oppenheim, *ibid.*, at 460–63.

5/Geneva Convention on the Territorial Sea and the Contiguous Zone, art. 5: UN Doc. A/Conf. 13/L. 52; reproduced in (1958), 52 *Amer. J. Int. Law* 834.

6/See *R.* v. *Cunningham* (1859), Bell's C.C. 72; followed in *Direct United States Cable Co.* v. *Anglo-American Telegraph Co.* (1876–77), 2 A.C. 394; *The Fagernes*, [1927] P. 311; *Re Dominion Coal Co. and County of Cape Breton* (1963), 40 D.L.R. (2d) 593; see also the authorities collected by Sir Cecil Hurst in "The Territoriality of Bays" (1922–23), 3 *Br. Year Book Int. Law* 42. At common law a bay lies *intra fauces terra* if a man can reasonably discern from shore to shore, a rule that is none too clear: see *Direct United States Cable Co.* v. *Anglo-American Telegraph Co.*, *supra*.

7/See the boundaries as drawn in the original grant of that province to Sir William Alexander, dated 10 Sept. 1621 in J. M. Moore, *History and Digest of the International Arbitrations to which the United States has been a Party* (Washington, 1898), vol. I, at 33, 50.

8/For example, the boundaries of Nova Scotia as described in the Royal Commission to Lord Elgin of 1 Sept. 1846 read as follows: "Our said Province of Nova Scotia in America, the said Province being bounded on the westward by a line drawn from Cape Sable across the entrance to the centre of the Bay of Fundy; on the northward by a line drawn along the centre of the said Bay to the mouth of the Musquat River by the said river to its source, and from thence by a due East line across the Isthmus into the Bay of Verte; on the Eastward by the said Bay of Verte and the Gulf of St. Lawrence to the Cape or Promontory called Cape Breton in the Island of that name, including the said Island, and also including all Islands within six Leagues of the Coast, and on the Southward by the Atlantic Ocean from the said Cape to Cape Sable aforesaid, including the Island of that name, and all other Islands within forty leagues of the Coast, with all the rights, members and appurtenances whatsoever thereunto belonging." This description was supplied by officials of the Department of the Attorney-General of Nova Scotia; see also J. B. Moore, *History and Digest of the International Arbitrations to which the United States has been a Party* (Washington, 1898), vol. I, at 33–4, 50–1. For the boundaries of New Brunswick, see Can. Sess. Pap. 1883, no. 70, at 47; for a more accurate reproduction, see *Collections of the New Brunswick Historical Society* (Saint John, 1905), No. 6, at 394–95.

between Quebec and New Brunswick is drawn in the middle of the Baie des Chaleurs.[9]

As a rule, however, inland waters were not expressly mentioned in the letters patent, royal commissions, or other instruments establishing the provinces, though they may well have been comprised in general phrases appearing in some of these. Thus in the early commissions to the governors of Nova Scotia[10] and New Brunswick,[11] these provinces are defined as including not only the area therein described but all islands within a certain number of leagues from the coast and "all the rights, members and appurtenances thereunto belonging"; the commission to Governor Patterson establishing Prince Edward Island (then called the Island of Saint John) as a separate colony, describes it as "our island of Saint John, and Territories adjacent thereto in America, and which now are or which heretofore have been dependent thereupon. ..."[12]

Certainly numerous pre-Confederation statutes appear to have been enacted on the assumption that the inland waters adjacent to a province fell within the province. Thus, beginning as early as 1799, New Brunswick passed several statutes treating Miramichi Bay as within the county of Northumberland,[13] and in 1835 it passed a statute exercising jurisdiction over Passamaquoddy Bay;[14] indeed in the first revised statutes of the province, in 1854, the Interpretation Act provides that any county bounded by any sea, bay, gulf, or river shall extend therein to the boundary of the province.[15] There were numerous other instances of exercises of jurisdiction by the Maritime provinces during the nineteenth century;[16] indeed those provinces exercised general jurisdiction over adjacent inland waters.[17] Such jurisdiction may be justified under the general phrases in the constitutional instruments previously referred to, but Newfoundland also exercised jurisdiction over all its inland waters,[18] and Lower Canada

9/(1851), 44 & 45 Vict., c.63(Imp.). 10/*Supra* note 8.
11/Can. Sess. Pap. no. 70, at 47; see also *Collections of the New Brunswick Historical Society* (Saint John, 1905), no. 6, pp. 394–95.
12/Can. Sess. Pap. 1883, no. 70, at 2.
13/(1799), 39 Geo. III, c.5; (1810), 50 Geo. III, c.5; (1823), 4 Geo. IV, c.23; (1829), 9 & 10 Geo. IV., c.3; (1834), 4 Wm. IV, c.31(N.B.).
14/(1835), 5 Wm. IV, c.41(N.B.).
15/R.S.N.B. 1854, c.161, s.10.
16/See the many statutes reproduced in *Proceedings in the North Atlantic Fisheries Arbitration, 1910* (Washington, 1912), vol. 5, appendix to the Case of Great Britain, part III.
17/(1836), 6 Wm. IV, c.8(N.S.); (1843), 6 Vict., c.14(P.E.I.); (1853), 16 Vict., c.69(N.B.).
18/(1844), 17 Vict., c.2; (1847), 20 Vict., c.1; (1862), 25 Vict., c.2; C.S.N. 1872, c.102; (1874), 37 Vict., c.2(Nfld.).

exercised jurisdiction over the Baie des Chaleurs long before the British parliament defined the province as extending into the bay.[19] These various exercises of jurisdiction were proprietary, for they applied not only to residents of the provinces, but to foreigners as well. The provinces were not alone in taking this view of their legislative powers; it accorded with that of the Imperial authorities, for it should be remembered that these authorities closely supervised colonial legislation, and some of these statutes were expressly approved by the Queen in council.[20] Moreover the British parliament in some statutes acted on the basis that inland waters were within the jurisdiction of a colony.[21]

These historical instances have thus far been treated as manifestations of the colonial application of the English common law rule that inland waters form part of the adjoining county. But they are also consistent with another theory which receives some support from the general approach of the Supreme Court of Canada in *Re: Offshore Mineral Rights of British Columbia*:[22] that the colonies were entitled to only such jurisdiction over inland waters as had been delegated to them by the British Crown.[23] Such jurisdiction might be conveyed, for example, by expressly including certain waters within the boundaries of a province as in the case of the Baie des Chaleurs and the Bay of Fundy or by recognizing the rights of a province over certain waters by statute, as in the case of Conception Bay.[24] In fact, it would appear sufficient if the colony exercised legislative jurisdiction without express delegation.[25] Even under this more restrictive theory, however, the Maritime provinces and Newfoundland, in particular, have, as is apparent from the foregoing historical account, very extensive rights.

19/(1807), 47 Geo. III, c.12; (1824), 4 Geo. IV, c.1(L.Can.) dealing with the Baie des Chaleurs before it was expressly within the boundaries of that province.
20/The hovering acts of Nova Scotia (1836), 6 Wm. IV, c.8(N.S.), Prince Edward Island (1843), 6 Vict., c.14(P.E.I.), and New Brunswick (1853), 16 Vict., c.69(N.B.) were so approved: see *Proceedings in the North Atlantic Fisheries Arbitration, 1910* (Washington, 1912), vol. 5, appendix to the Case of Great Britain, at 962, 963, 1055.
21/For example, the British statute implementing the treaty of Washington (1872), 35 & 36 Vict., c.45(Imp.), recognized Newfoundland's jurisdiction over its bays: *Direct U.S. Cable Co.* v. *Anglo-American Telegraph Co.* (1876–77), 2 A.C. 394, at 421–22.
22/[1967] S.C.R. 792.
23/In *Direct U.S. Cable Co.* v. *Anglo-American Telegraph Co.* (1876–77), 2 A.C. 394, both theories are relied on. In *Re Dominion Coal Co. and County of Cape Breton* (1963), 40 D.L.R. (2d) 593, Macdonald J. seems to rely on this second theory, though the other judges rely on the first.
24/See *Direct U.S. Cable Co.* v. *Anglo-American Telegraph Co.* (1876–77), 2 A.C. 394.
25/*Re Dominion Coal Co. and County of Cape Breton* (1963), 40 D.L.R. (2d) 593. per Macdonald J.; see also *R.* v. *The "John J. Fallon"* (1916), 16 Ex.C.R. 332.

Whatever the exact limits of the inland waters of the provinces may have been at union, it is clear that, by virtue of sections 109 and 117 of the British North America Act, any inland waters then belonging to the provinces continued to do so unless previously conveyed to individuals or expressly surrendered to the Dominion, for example under section 108. As the Privy Council put it in the *Fisheries*[26] case, whatever proprietary rights were possessed by the provinces at the date of union remained vested in them unless expressly transferred to the Dominion. The same conclusion is inherent in the many cases delimiting the ownership of the Dominion in harbours[27] and defining its right to regulate the fisheries requiring use of the subsoil.[28] But the clearest statement of the law is by Duff J. in *Capital City Canning Co.* v. *Anglo-British Packing Co.*[29] Speaking of the ownership of a site believed to be in inland waters, he said: "It was not disputed, and I assume for the purpose of this application, that this site is *intra fauces terrae*. The bed of the sea in such places is part of the territorial possessions of the Crown; and – except in the case of public harbours, within the disposition of the Provincial Legislature ..." The opinion of Duff J. here, it should be observed, presupposes the first of the foregoing theories respecting colonial ownership of inland waters.

The case for provincial ownership of inland waters expressly within the boundaries of a province is, of course, even stronger. For by section 6 of the BNA Act Ontario and Quebec are to have the limits of the former provinces of Upper and Lower Canada, respectively, and by section 7 Nova Scotia and New Brunswick are to continue to have the same limits as before. The terms of union with Newfoundland also expressly continue the pre-existing boundaries of Newfoundland and the same is inherent in the terms of union with British Columbia and Prince Edward Island. On this ground the Supreme Court of Canada in *Mowat* v. *McPhee*[30] held that the southern half of the Baie des Chaleurs formed part of Restigouche County in New Brunswick, and the Supreme Court of New Brunswick in *R.* v. *Burt*[31] held that a point in the northern half of the Bay of Fundy, within a mile and a half of the coast, was part of New Brunswick. Whatever questions may arise as to the status of the latter bay in international law,[32] therefore, for internal purposes the declaration of the boundaries by

26/*Attorney-General of Canada* v. *Attorney-General of Ontario*, [1898] A.C. 700.
27/See pp. 49–64.
28/See pp. 78, 157.
29/(1905), 11 B.C.R. 333, at 339; see also *Re Dominion Coal Co. and County of Cape Breton* (1963), 40 D.L.R. (2d) 593.
30/(1880), 5 S.C.R. 66.
31/(1932), 5 M.P.R. 112; see also *Re: Offshore Mineral Rights of British Columbia*, [1967] S.C.R. 792.
32/For a discussion of the status of the bay, see G. V. La Forest, "Canadian Inland

the early commissions have the same force as a statute.[33] An equally strong case can be made for provincial ownership of bays, such as Conception Bay, which before Confederation were recognized by British legislation as belonging to a province.[34]

Without going into detail it may be mentioned that the inland waters of the provinces at union were quite extensive. They included all bays and straits, or parts thereof, capable of being enclosed by lines of six marine miles or less from shore to shore.[35] But these were not all. Historic claims could be made to the Baie des Chaleurs, Conception, Fundy, and Miramichy bays as well as all other bays in the Maritime provinces and Newfoundland.[36] There are also vast expanses of inland waters in British Columbia. In fact a case can be made that all Canadian bays are territorial, for Great Britain, several of the provinces, and later Canada have exercised uninterrupted legislative jurisdiction over them since 1819.[37]

As already seen, the better view is that all the bays adjacent to the various provinces at Confederation belong to the provinces, and at any rate this is so of all such bays over which jurisdiction had been delegated by Great Britain to the colonies. But there are a number of bays and other inland waters that would seem clearly to belong to the Dominion. One of these is Hudson Bay. That bay, despite its large area, has from early times been claimed by Great Britain and Canada as an inland bay[38] but, while Ontario, Quebec, and Manitoba, after Confederation, were extended northerly until they were partially bounded by the bay and adjacent waters,

Waters of the Atlantic Provinces and the Bay of Fundy Incident" (1963), 1 *Can. Yearbook Int. Law* 149.

33/*Re Cape Breton* (1846), 5 Moo. P.C. 259; 13 E.R. 489; see also *Campbell* v. *Hall* (1774), 1 Cowp. 204; 98 E.R. 1045; *Taylor* v. *Attorney-General* (1837), 8 Sim. 413; 59 E.R. 164; *St. Catherine's Milling and Lumber Co.* v. *R.* (1887), 13 S.C.R. 577; *R.* v. *McMaster*, [1926] Ex.C.R. 68; *Re Dominion Coal Co. and County of Cape Breton* (1963), 40 D.L.R. (2d) 593; *R.* v. *George* (1964), 45 D.L.R. (2d) 709; *R.* v. *White and Bob* (1965), 50 D.L.R. (2d) 613, *per* Norris J.A.

34/*Direct U.S. Cable Co.* v. *Anglo-American Telegraph Co.* (1876–77), 2 A.C. 394; *Re: Offshore Mineral Rights of British Columbia*, [1967] S.C.R. 792.

35/See Oppenheim, *International Law* (8th ed. by Lauterpacht, London, 1955) at 505 *et seq.*, and 510 *et seq.*

36/For a discussion of these claims, see La Forest, "Inland Waters of the Atlantic Provinces and the Bay of Fundy Incident" (1963), 1 *Can. Yearbook Int. Law* 149; in addition to the acts in that article, see (1862), 25 Vict., c.2; C.S.N. 1872, c.102; (1874), 37 Vict., c.2(Nfld.).

37/See *ibid.*

38/See V. K. Johnston, "Canada's Title to Hudson Bay and Hudson Strait" (1934), 15 *Br. Year Book Int. Law* 1; see also the Hon. Davie Fulton in *Proceedings in the Senate Standing Committee on Natural Resources* on 9 Jan. 1958, at 50–1; cf., T. W. Balch, "Is Hudson Bay a Closed or Open Sea?" (1912), 6 *Amer. J. Int. Law* 409; Mitchell P. Strohl, *The International Law of Bays* (The Hague, 1963), c.6, at 232 *et seq.*

these provinces are clearly defined as following along the shore.[39] This would seem to exclude all provincial interest beyond high-water mark. In *Esquimalt and Nanaimo Ry. Co.* v. *Treat*[40] British Columbia had by statute transferred a belt of land (the Railway Belt) to Canada as part of the arrangements for the entry of the province into the union. The western limit of this belt was defined as bounded by the coast line of Vancouver Island, and the Privy Council held that Dominion ownership ended at high-water mark and excluded the foreshore.

Waters that have become inland waters of Canada since Confederation would also appear to belong to the Dominion. Among these may be mentioned bays between six and twenty-four marine miles in width, unless these were already inland waters at Confederation by historic title; since the Geneva Convention waters enclosed by headlands distant up to twenty-four miles are inland waters.[41] Again, Canada, in the Territorial Sea and Fishing Zones Act, has provided for measuring the baseline of territorial waters according to the straight baselines system.[42] This system involves drawing straight lines from various points along the coast instead of following the sinuosities of the coast. Such a system is permissible under international law where the coast is deeply indented or there is a fringe of islands along the coast.[43] Since waters within the baseline of territorial waters are inland waters,[44] it follows that Canada may, by adopting a system of straight baselines, extend its inland as well as its territorial waters. In addition, beginning in 1949 Canada has on several occasions expressed its intention of contending that the whole of the Gulf of St. Lawrence is an inland sea.[45] Since these waters accrue, or would accrue, to Canada from its political activities as a sovereign state and the prerogative power over external relations belongs to the Dominion, it follows from the reasoning of the Supreme Court of Canada in *Re: Offshore Mineral Rights of British Columbia*[46] (to be examined with more particularity in relation to territorial waters) that this additional territory belongs to the Dominion. Moreover in *Re Dominion Coal Co. and County of Cape*

39/(1912), 2 Geo. V, cc.32, 40, 45(Can.).
40/[1919] 3 W.W.R. 356.
41/Geneva Convention on the Territorial Sea and the Contiguous Zone, art. 7(5): U.N. Doc. A/Conf. 13/L. 52; reproduced in (1958), 52 *Amer. J. Int. Law* 834.
42/(1964), 13 Eliz. II, c.22, s.5(Can.).
43/Geneva Convention on the Territorial Sea and the Contiguous Zone, art. 4: U.N. Doc. A/Conf. 13/L. 52; reproduced in (1958), 52 Amer. Jo. Int. Law 834.
44/*Ibid.*, art. 1; Territorial Sea and Fishing Zones Act (1964), 13 Eliz. II, c.22, s.3(2).
45/*Debates of the House of Commons*, 1949, I, at 368; *Debates of the House of Commons*, 1957–58, II, at 1168–9.
46/[1967] S.C.R. 792.

Breton[47] Macdonald J. stated that to consider waters added to Canadian territory as belonging to the province would amount to a redefinition of the boundaries of the province. These in his view are fixed by the BNA Act and can only be altered by the action of both the federal and provincial legislatures. The provinces might, of course, argue that all inland waters, whenever they become such, are a mere appendage to the adjoining province, but in the light of the previous considerations it is doubtful, to say the least, that the argument has any chance of success.

TERRITORIAL WATERS

Stretching from low-water mark and the outer edge of inland waters is a belt of water called the territorial waters, the territorial sea, or the marginal sea. While there is no definite rule under international law respecting the breadth of the belt, a claim to three marine miles is clearly valid,[48] and Canada abides by that limit, though it has now provided for a fishing zone of twelve miles.[49] The sovereignty of a coastal state extends to its territorial sea,[50] and accordingly in a federal state like Canada the problem of which level of government may exercise proprietary and legislative jurisdiction over it inevitably arises.

This was the problem put to the Supreme Court of Canada in relation to the territorial waters of British Columbia in the recent reference *Re: Offshore Mineral Rights of British Columbia*.[51] There the court was asked the following questions respecting "the lands, including the minerals and other natural resources, of the sea bed and subsoil" of the territorial sea off the coast and islands of British Columbia: (a) Are the said lands the property of Canada or British Columbia? (b) Has Canada the right to explore and exploit the said lands? (c) Has Canada or British Columbia legislative jurisdiction in relation to the said lands? To each of these questions the court replied: "Canada."

47/(1963), 40 D.L.R. (2d) 593.
48/See J. L. Brierly. *The Law of Nations* (5th ed., Oxford, 1955), at 177–78; Oppenheim, *International Law* (8th ed. by Lauterpacht, London, 1955), vol. I; "Peace," at 488–92.
49/Territorial Sea and Fishing Zones Act (1964), 13 Eliz. II, c.22, ss.3, 4; for a discussion of Canada's inland and territorial waters, see Jacques-Yvan Morin, "Les eaux territoriales du Canada au regard du Droit international" (1963), I *Can. Yearbook Int. Law* 82.
50/Geneva Convention on the Territorial Sea and the Contiguous Zone, art. 1: U.N. Doc. A/Conf. 13/L. 52; reproduced in (1958), 52 *Amer. J. Int. Law* 834.
51/[1967] S.C.R. 792; for discussions, see Head, "The Legal Clamour over Canadian Offshore Minerals" (1967), 5 *Alta. Law Rev.* 312; Jacques Brossard in *Le Devoir*, 22 November 1967, at 5, cols. 1–4; Head, "The Canadian Offshore Mineral Reference" (1968), 18 *U. of T. L.J.* 131; Hubbard, note in (1967), 2 *Ottawa Law Rev.* 213.

The province's case rested largely on the application of sections 109 and 117 of the BNA Act. The general effect of these sections, as interpreted by the Privy Council, was that whatever proprietary rights were vested in the provinces at union remained so vested unless transferred to the Dominion by express provision, such as section 108 of the Act.[52] But this, in the view of the court, left untouched the problem it had to face – whether the territorial sea was within the province at Confederation.

There were two conflicting lines of authority between which the court had to choose in deciding this question: one indicating that the territorial sea was part and parcel of the realm, another that the realm ended at low-water mark. The first is much the older of the two; it first found expression in the works of such early writers as Coke and Lord Hale.[53] It is true, as the court and the Privy Council before pointed out,[54] that these writers were speaking of a claim to a much larger expanse of water, England's narrow seas, which may now be regarded as obsolete; but the same attitude found expression in numerous cases during the nineteenth century after the three-mile limit was established but before Confederation.[55] For example, in *Attorney-General* v. *Chambers*[56] in 1854 Lord Cranworth stated: "The Crown is clearly ... according to all the authorities entitled to the 'littus maris' [i.e., the shore] as well as the soil of the sea adjoining the coasts of England." The ownership of the three-mile zone by the Crown was also recognized in the House of Lords by Lord Wensleydale and Lord Cranworth in the Scottish case of *Gammell* v. *Lord Advocate*[57] in 1859, and by Lord Wensleydale and Lord Chelmsford in *Gann* v. *Free Fishers of Whitstable*[58] in 1865. A similar view was expressed in 1868 in *Duchess of Sutherland* v. *Watson*.[59]

In addition to these judicial authorities, there were before 1867 clear exercises of property rights by the British parliament over the three-mile

52/*Attorney-General of Canada* v. *Attorney-General of Ontario*, [1898] A.C. 700.
53/See Co. Litt., s.439; Hale, *De Jure Maris*, c.6, at 31. The early authorities are collected in *R.* v. *Keyn* (1876–77), 2 Ex. 63, especially *per* Lindley L.J. and Brett J.A.; Sir Cecil Hurst, "Whose is the Bed of the Sea?" (1923–24), 4 *Br. Year Book Int. Law* 34; D. P. O'Connell, "Problems of Australian Coastal Jurisdiction" (1958), 34 *Br. Year Book Int. Law* 199, at 204, n1.
54/*Attorney-General of British Columbia* v. *Attorney-General of Canada*, [1914] A.C. 153.
55/In addition to the cases in the text, see *Blundell* v. *Catterall* (1821), 5 B. & Ald. 268; 106 E.R. 1190; *Benest* v. *Pipon* (1829), 1 Knapp 60; 12 E.R. 243; *Officers of State* v. *Smith* (1846), 8 Sess. Cas. 711; *aff'd*: *Smith* v. *Stair* (1849), 6 Bell's A.C. 487; *The Leda* (1856), Swab. 40; 166 E.R. 1007; *R.* v. *Hanmer* (1858), 6 W.R. 804.
56/(1854), 4 De G.M. & G. 206, at 213; 43 E.R. 486, at 489.
57/(1859), 3 Macq. 419.
58/(1865), 11 H.L.C. 192, at 218; 11 E.R. 1305, at 1316; see also, *per* Erle C.J. in the court below: (1861), 11 C.B. (N.S.) 387, at 413; 142 E.R. 847, at 857.
59/(1868), 6 Sess. Cas. 199, at 213.

zone. The most important example is the Cornwall Submarine Mines Act of 1858 which, on the basis of an award in a controversy between the Crown and the Duchy of Cornwall concerning the ownership of mines below low-water mark, enacted and declared that the mines and minerals below low-water mark belonged to the Queen in right of her Crown.[60] A number of local acts contained similar exercises of sovereignty.[61]

Up to this point, then, the authorities all seemed to point to one conclusion: that the Crown owned the resources of the territorial sea in the same way as it owns other property, the seashore, for example. But this consistent line of authority came to an abrupt end with the decision of *R. v. Keyn*[62] in 1876. The question there was whether the Central Criminal Court, as successor of the High Admiral's Court, had jurisdiction to try for manslaughter the master of a foreign ship that had negligently struck an English ship within three miles of the English coast. By the narrow majority of seven to six, the court decided that it lacked jurisdiction. The majority had no doubt that parliament could exercise jurisdiction over the three-mile belt, but until it did so the courts had no jurisdiction; the realm of the common law ended at low-water mark. Statutes such as the Cornwall Submarine Mines Act were examples of such parliamentary action. One of the majority, Lush J., in a passage quoted by the Supreme Court, put it thus:

I think that usage and the common consent of nations, which constitute international law, have appropriated these waters to the adjacent State to deal with them as the State may deem expedient for its own interests. They are, therefore, in the language of diplomacy and of international law, termed by a convenient metaphor the territorial waters of Great Britain, and the same or equivalent phrases are used in some of our statutes denoting that this belt of sea is under the exclusive dominion of the State. But the dominion is the dominion of Parliament, not the dominion of the common law. That extends no further than the limits of the realm. In the reign of Richard II. the realm consisted of the land within the body of the counties. All beyond low-water mark was part of the high seas. At that period the three-mile radius had not been thought of. International law, which, upon this subject at least, has grown up since that period, cannot enlarge the area of our municipal law, nor could treaties with all the nations of the world have that effect. That can only be done by Act of Parliament. As no such Act has been passed, it follows that what was out of the realm then is out of the realm now, and what was part of the high seas then is part of the high seas now; and upon the high seas the Admiralty juris-

---

60/(1858), 21 & 22 Vict., c.109(Imp.).
61/See, for example, the Norfolk Estuary Act (1846), 9 & 10 Vict., c.388(Imp.) and Lincolnshire Estuary Act (1851), 14 & 15 Vict., c.136(Imp.), cited by Hurst, "Whose is the Bed of the Sea?" (1923–24), 4 *Br. Yearbook Int. Law* 34, at 37, n2.
62/(1876–77), 2 Ex. 63; see also *General Iron Screw Co.* v. *Schurmann* (1860), 1 J. & H. 180; 70 E.R. 712.

diction was confined to British ships. Therefore, although, as between nation and nation, these waters are British territory, as being under the exclusive dominion of Great Britain, in judicial language they are out of the realm, and any exercise of criminal jurisdiction over a foreign ship in these waters must in my judgment be authorized by an Act of Parliament.[63]

R. v. *Keyn* could, of course, be looked upon as authority for the narrow point before the court, namely the extent of jurisdiction of the Central Criminal Court. But, in the following year the case was followed in *Harris* v. *Franconia*[64] and *Blackpool Pier Co.* v. *Fylde Union*.[65] The latter case is especially important because it was heard by three of the minority judges in *R.* v. *Keyn*, Coleridge C.J., Grave J., and Denman J., who accepted that the *ratio decidendi* of *R.* v. *Keyn* was that the realm ends at low-water mark.

In the same year, following severe strictures of the *Keyn* case,[66] the British parliament enacted the Territorial Waters Jurisdiction Act, 1878,[67] which provided that all offences committed within one marine league of Her Majesty's dominions were within the jurisdiction of the admiral, and took the unusual step of declaring in the preamble that the Queen's jurisdiction has always extended over the open seas adjacent to the United Kingdom and other parts of Her Majesty's dominions.

Following this the pre-*Keyn* tradition began to revive. From 1891 to 1916 four cases were decided containing statements asserting Crown ownership in the territorial sea, including a Scottish case in the House of Lords and one in the Privy Council.[68] Moreover, in *Carr* v. *Fracis Times*[69] in the House of Lords, Lord Halsbury appears to have tried to explain the *Keyn* case as turning on the narrow point that the court could only be given jurisdiction over the territorial sea by statute.

The most important of the cases during this period was *Secretary of State for India* v. *Chellikani Rama Rao*[70] before the Privy Council. There it was held that islands arising in the seas within three miles of India belonged to the Crown. The Board's judgment was clearly based on the proposition that the territorial sea was the property of the Crown in the same

---

63/*Ibid.*, at 238–39.
64/(1877), 2 C.P.D. 173.
65/(1877), 36 L.T. 251; 46 L.J.M.C. 189.
66/For an account, see *The Lotus Case* (1927), P.C.I.J., Ser. A., No. 10, at 74–5, *per* Judge John Bassett Moore (*diss.*).
67/41 & 42 Vict., c.73(Imp.).
68/*Lord Advocate* v. *Clyde* (1891), 19 Rettie 174; *Lord Advocate* v. *Wemyss*, [1900] A.C. 48; *Lord Fitzhardinge* v. *Purcell*, [1908] 2 Ch. 139; *Secretary of State for India* v. *Chellikani Rama Rao* (1916), 32 T.L.R. 652; 85 L.J.P.C. 222.
69/[1902] A.C. 176, at 181.
70/(1916), 32 T.L.R. 652; 85 L.J.P.C. 222.

manner as the foreshore and other Crown lands. Lord Shaw quoted with approval, from the Scottish case of *Lord Advocate* v. *Clyde Navigation*,[71] the following statement of Lord Kyllachy:

With respect to the nature of the Crown's right in what is acknowledged to be part of the territory of the kingdom – viz., the strip or area of sea within cannon-shot or three miles of the shore. Is the Crown's right in that strip of sea, proprietary, like the Crown's right in the foreshore, and in the land? Or is it only a protectorate for certain purposes and particularly navigation, and fishing? I am of opinion that the former is the correct view, and that there is no distinction in legal character between the Crown's right in the foreshore, in tidal and navigable rivers, and in the bed of the sea within three miles of the shore. In each case it is of course a right largely qualified by public uses. In each case it is, therefore, to a large extent *extra commercium*; but none the less is it in my opinion a proprietary right – a right, which may be the subject of trespass and which may be vindicated like other rights of property.

The Board also relied on the following statement by Lord Watson in *Lord Advocate* v. *Wemyss*,[72] another Scottish case in the House of Lords: "I see no reason to doubt that by the law of Scotland, the solum underlying the waters of the ocean, whether within the narrow seas, or from the coast outward to the three mile limit, and also the minerals beneath it are vested in the Crown." Of *R.* v. *Keyn*[73] the Board simply said that "It should not be forgotten that the case had reference on its merits solely to the point as to the limits of Admiralty jurisdiction; nothing else fell to be decided there. It was marked by an extreme conflict of judicial opinion ..."

A few years before this case, however, the Board, in *Attorney-General of British Columbia* v. *Attorney-General of Canada*,[74] had refused to enter into the question of proprietary ownership of the three-mile zone on the ground that it was not desirable that a municipal court should pronounce itself upon the question, since it was a question of international law which could not be satisfactorily disposed of until it had been settled by a conference of the various nations. The same approach was again taken by the Board in *Attorney-General of Canada* v. *Attorney-General of Quebec*[75] in 1921, five years after the *Chellikani Rama Rao* case.

This was the state of the English authorities when the reference *Re: Offshore Mineral Rights of British Columbia* was heard. In Canada, there was also some conflict of authority, and these may briefly be reviewed in chronological order. The early trend was all in favour of provincial ownership. Thus in two Newfoundland cases, *Direct United States Cable Co.* v. *Anglo-American Telegraph*[76] in 1875 and *The Queen* v. *Delepine*[77] in

71/(1891), 19 Rettie 174, at 177.   72/[1900] A.C. 48, at 66.
73/(1876–77), 2 Ex. 63.   74/[1914] A.C. 153.
75/[1921] 1 A.C. 413.   76/(1876), 6 Nfld. L.R. 28, at 33.
77/(1889), 7 Nfld. L.R. 378, at 385; see also *Rhodes* v. *Fairweather* (1888), 7 Nfld. L.R. 321.

1889 the view is expressed that that colony extended into the three-mile belt. Again, in *Re Provincial Fisheries*,[78] in 1895, one could surmise that the Supreme Court of Canada thought the territorial belt belonged to the province. In that case, the court was asked whether the Dominion or the provinces owned the beds of every conceivable type of water in the provinces, including "waters directly and immediately connected with the seacoast and *waters not so connected*" and "waters separating ... two or more provinces ... or ... separating the Dominion from a foreign nation." The court replied that the bed of all waters, without distinction, belonged to the provinces. Counsel had argued on the basis that the question referred to territorial waters,[79] and one judge, Girouard J., expressly dealt with these.[80] On appeal, however, the Privy Council limited its answer to saying that whatever belonged to the provinces before union continued to do so unless expressly transferred to the Dominion.[81] Again in *Re Quebec Fisheries*,[82] three of the four majority judges in the Quebec Court of King's Bench, Appeal Side, expressed the view that the territorial sea belonged to that province. As already mentioned, however, the Privy Council refused to enter into the question when the case came before it on appeal. Then in 1932 in *R.* v. *Burt*,[83] the Supreme Court of New Brunswick, following the *Chellikani Rama Rao* case, held that the three-mile limit adjacent to New Brunswick fell within the province, and it repeated the same view in 1934 in *Filion* v. *New Brunswick Paper Co.*[84]

In 1956, however, the Supreme Court of Prince Edward Island in *Gavin* v. *R.*[85] followed *R.* v. *Keyn*. The final Canadian case before the Reference was *Re Dominion Coal Co. and County of Cape Breton*[86] before the Supreme Court of Nova Scotia, en banc, in 1963. The question there was whether the county of Cape Breton had power to levy municipal taxes against under-sea coal workings of the company. The court held that some of these workings were under inland waters and so taxable as being within the county, but certain parts were situated under Spanish Bay which it held (Currie J. dissenting), was not an inland water and so was outside the county. This was the *ratio* of the case, but Macdonald and Currie JJ. engaged in a discussion of the ownership of the territorial sea. Macdonald J. favoured the *Keyn* decision, and was of the view that the Territorial Waters Jurisdiction Act, 1878, was directed to redefining criminal jurisdiction respecting offences in territorial waters, and did not affect the juridical character of these waters as being outside the realm, or confer property rights in them. He doubted, indeed, whether property rights

78/(1895), 26 S.C.R. 444. 79/*Ibid.*, at 458–59, 510.   80/*Ibid.*, at 569 *et seq.*
81/*Attorney-General of Canada* v. *Attorney-General of Ontario*, [1898] A.C. 700.
82/(1917), 35 D.L.R. 1.   83/(1932), 5 M.P.R. 112.
84/(1934–35), 8 M.P.R. 88, at 95.   85/(1956), 3 D.L.R. (2d) 547.
86/(1963), 40 D.L.R. (2d) 593.

could exist in territorial waters, especially in a federal system, citing in support the American tidelands cases.[87] Currie J., on the other hand, favoured the line of authority culminating with the *Chellikani Rama Rao* case. In his view the preamble to the Territorial Waters Jurisdiction Act, 1878, indicated that parliament regarded the majority opinion in *R. v. Keyn* as being in error.

This then was the judicial background when the question of the ownership of the submarine resources in the territorial sea off British Columbia was raised in the Supreme Court of Canada. The court decided that the *Keyn* case correctly stated the law. In their view "that case decided that the territory of England and the sovereignty of the Queen stopped at low-water mark (except where under special circumstances and in special Acts, Parliament had thought fit to extend it)." The Territorial Waters Jurisdiction Act, 1878, "did not enlarge the realm of England, nor did it purport to deal with the juridical character of British territorial waters and the sea-bed beneath them"; it merely enlarged the jurisdiction of the admiral to include offences committed within one marine league of the coast of Her Majesty's dominions. There was no historical record evidencing a different rule for British Columbia, so that that colony ended at low-water mark at the date of union, and nothing had been done since union to change the situation. Accordingly the territorial sea and its underlying resources did not belong to British Columbia.

The court dismissed the contrary view in the nineteenth-century British cases as *dicta*, and accepted the explanation of Cockburn C.J. in the *Keyn* case that the Cornwall Submarine Mines Act, 1858, dealt solely with a particular dispute, and could not be read as a general assertion of the right of the Crown over the territorial sea. The *Chellikani Rama Rao* case could not be so easily disposed of because the *dicta* quoted with approval by Lord Shaw were "undoubtedly based on the proposition that the islands were Crown lands because located in the territorial sea." But the Supreme Court saw an alternative explanation in a statement from Oppenheim to the effect that where islands are created by alluvium in the territorial sea they are considered accretions to the neighbouring land.[88] Finally, a number of Canadian cases were distinguished as dealing with inland, not territorial, waters.

This was sufficient to dispose of British Columbia's case. But it was not enough to establish a case for the federal government, for there is nothing in the BNA Act transferring the submarine resources of the terri-

87/See *United States* v. *California* (1947), 332 U.S. 19; *United States* v. *Louisiana* (1950), 339 U.S. 699; *United States* v. *Texas* (1950), 339 U.S. 707.
88/Oppenheim, *International Law* (8th ed. by Lauterpacht), vol. I, at 565.

torial sea to it. The court, however, saw such a transfer in the acquisition by Canada of authority over external affairs formerly vested in the British authorities. Before 1871, when British Columbia became part of Canada, the British Crown asserted jurisdiction over the territorial sea in respect of British Columbia and continued to do so in respect of Canada after that date. Before 1919 Canada had only limited rights to legislate in respect of the territorial waters, and in its legislation these were referred to as "British waters"; not until 1928 did Canadian legislation refer to the "territorial waters of Canada."[89] By a process beginning with its separate signature of the Treaty of Versailles in 1919 and culminating with the Statute of Westminster, 1931, Canada acquired the status of a sovereign state. It is the state now recognized by international law as having rights in the territorial sea off British Columbia, and it has signed and implemented treaties with several foreign countries.[90] The effect of Canada's claim under the Territorial Sea and Fishing Zones Act, 1964,[91] to a three-mile territorial belt, coupled with the Geneva Convention on the Territorial Sea and the Contiguous Zone[92] (which accords sovereignty to a state over its territorial sea) is that Canada is recognized in international law as having sovereignty over a territorial sea three nautical miles wide; it is part of the territory of Canada. Canada as a sovereign state, not British Columbia, has the right to explore and exploit the subsoil of this territory, and has exclusive legislative jurisdiction over it either under section 91(1A) or under the peace, order, and good government clause of the BNA Act. It falls within the latter clause because, the territory being outside the province, it is a matter affecting Canada generally and goes beyond local or provincial concern or interest.

The reference appears to assume throughout that the legislature having jurisdiction over external affairs is the only body able to acquire new areas of jurisdiction made available under international law. However, there is recent authority in England supporting the view that legislative intervention may be unnecessary. In R. v. Kent Justices, Ex Parte Lye[93] a divisional court held that the Crown in the exercise of its prerogative

89/Cf., The Customs Act (1867), 31 Vict., c.6, s.1 and An Act Respecting Fishing by Foreign Vessels (1868), 31 Vict., c.61, s.1 with An Act to Amend the Customs Act (1928), 18 & 19 Geo. V, c.16, s.1(Can.).
90/The confusion between Canada as a sovereign state and Canada as the federal government is criticized by Jacques Brossard in Le Devoir, 22 November 1967, at 5, cols. 1–4; Head, "The Canadian Offshore Minerals Reference" (1968), 18 U. of T. L.J. 131.
91/13 Eliz. II, c. 22(Can.).
92/UN Doc. A/Conf. 13/L. 52; reproduced in (1958), 52 Amer. J. Int. Law 834.
93/[1967] 2 W.L.R. 765; approved: Post Office v. Estuary Radio Ltd., [1967] 1 W.L.R. 1396.

might lay down limits of territorial waters, and this right was not generally abrogated by the fact that the Queen had assented to the Territorial Waters Jurisdiction Act, 1878, which set limits for the purposes of that Act. In Canada such prerogative rights would be exercised on the advice of the federal government. Since Canada has set limits for territorial waters under a general act, the point is not currently relevant in relation to territorial waters, but it may be of some importance in relation to the continental shelf.

The reference *Re: Offshore Mineral Rights of British Columbia*, of course, judicially settles the competing claims of the Dominion and British Columbia towards the territorial waters adjacent to that province. But what of the other provinces? The court concedes that a different result could follow if a province established an historical claim before Confederation. It stated at one point: "We are not disputing the proposition that while British Columbia was a Crown Colony the British Crown might have conferred upon the Governor or Legislature of the colony rights to which the British Crown was entitled under international law but the historical record of the colony does not disclose any such action."[94]

The problem does not arise in relation to the land-locked provinces of Alberta and Saskatchewan; the only salt-water boundaries of Manitoba and Ontario are on Hudson Bay and related waters, but those provinces expressly extend only to the shores of those waters.[95] This is true also of the boundaries of Quebec on those waters.

The problem does arise, however, in relation to Quebec's boundary on the Gulf of St. Lawrence. There are some pre-Confederation exercises of jurisdiction by Lower Canada beyond its land territories. The acts relating to the Baie des Chaleurs have already been mentioned, though it may have been looked on as an inland water.[96] But this cannot be said of legislation discussed in the *Quebec Fisheries* case[97] extending the right to the king's subjects to fish in the Gulf of St. Lawrence. When that case was before the Quebec Court of King's Bench, Appeal Side, it will be remembered that three of the majority judges thought the territorial sea belonged to the province,[98] but the Privy Council refused to express any opinion on the point.

But the strongest historical case is that of the Maritime provinces and Newfoundland. Two of these provinces – Nova Scotia and New Brunswick

94/[1967] S.C.R. 792, at 808.
95/See pp. 90–1.
96/(1807), 47 Geo. III, c.12; (1824), 4 Geo. IV, c.1 (L.C.)
97/*Attorney-General of Canada* v. *Attorney-General of Quebec*, [1921] 1 A.C. 413.
98/*Re Quebec Fisheries* (1917), 35 D.L.R. 1.

– are described as including "all rights, members and appurtenances whatsoever thereunto belonging."[99] In this context the phrase may well refer to territorial waters, for these are sometimes described as an appurtenance of a coastal state.[100] Prince Edward Island is described as including "the territories adjacent thereto."[101]

But more important are the numerous exercises of jurisdiction in the three-mile belt, and sometimes beyond, by these provinces before Confederation. As early as 1770, Nova Scotia enacted a statute prohibiting the throwing into the sea within three leagues of the provincial coasts of any heads, bones, or other offal, and establishing a penalty.[102] In addition to particular examples, Nova Scotia in 1836, Prince Edward Island in 1843, and New Brunswick in 1853, began exercising general jurisdiction over their territorial waters under a series of statutes often called the "hovering acts."[103] These acts empowered customs and excise officers to board any ship within any port or bay in the province as well as those hovering within three marine miles of the coasts, ports, or bays, and to examine and forfeit them to the Crown if found fishing within these waters. That these statutes met with the views of the British Crown is evident from the fact that they were confirmed by British orders in council.[104] Indeed, if they had conflicted with British policy, they would undoubtedly have been disallowed. One further example from Nova Scotia should be mentioned. Leases of mining rights under the sea off Cape Breton had already begun before Confederation[105] and continued afterwards.[106]

Similarly, beginning in 1893 Newfoundland enacted hovering legislation like that of the Maritime provinces,[107] and also exercised customs jurisdiction over the three-mile belt.[108] At a later period it enacted several statutes that may even apply beyond the three-mile belt. The Crown Lands

99/See p. 87.
100/See, for example, *The Ship "North"* v. *R.* (1906), 37 S.C.R. 385, at 401; *The Grisbadarna Arbitration* (1916), Scott Hague Reports 121, at 127; *Anglo-Norwegian Fisheries Case* (1951), I.C.J. Rep. 112, at 128.
101/See p. 87.
102/(1770), 10 Geo. III, c.10(N.S.).
103/(1836), 6 Wm. IV, c.8(N.S.); (1843), 6 Vict., c.14(P.E.I.); (1853), 16 Vict., c.69(N.B.); for later general legislation, see R.S.N.B. 1854, c.101; see also G. V. La Forest, "Canadian Inland Waters of the Atlantic Provinces and the Bay of Fundy Incident" (1963), 1 *Can. Yearbook Int. Law* 149.
104/See *Proceedings in the North Atlantic Fisheries Arbitration, 1910* (Washington, 1912), vol. 5, appendix to the Case of Great Britain, at 962, 963, 1055.
105/See Lease from Nova Scotia to William Sword dated 1 June 1867, in the *Case*, at 425–26, to *Re: Offshore Mineral Rights of British Columbia*.
106/See Mines Act, R.S.N.S. 1954, c. 179, ss. 1(ah), 47(1), 105–11.
107/(1893), 56 Vict., c.6; (1905), 5 Edw. VII, c.4; (1906), 6 Edw. VII, c.1(Nfld.).
108/(1898), 61 Vict., c.13(Nfld.).

Act of 1930, which was re-enacted in 1952, deals with mining locations "covered by the sea or public tidal waters,"[109] and the Oyster Fisheries Act exercises jurisdiction over the "banks" of the province.[110]

In the judicial field, too, there was considerable authority favouring the view that these provinces had at Confederation a proprietary interest in the three-mile belt. Hoyles C.J. of the Supreme Court of Newfoundland in *Anglo-American Telegraph Co.* v. *Direct United States Cable Co.*[111] had this to say in 1875:

I hold that the territorial jurisdiction of the sovereign extends to three miles outside of a line drawn from headland to headland of the bay ...; that the local government, being the Queen's government, representing and exercising within the limits of the Governor's commission, which contains nothing restrictive upon this point, her authority and jurisdiction is, in this respect, the same with the Imperial government ... and that, subject to the royal instructions and the Queen's power of dissent, the Acts of the local legislature have full effect and operation to the full extent of that territorial jurisdiction.

The court again repeated the view in *Rhodes* v. *Fairweather*[112] in 1888 and *The Queen* v. *Delepine*[113] in 1889.

The same approach was taken in New Brunswick. In *R.* v. *Burt*[114] in 1932 the Appeal Division of the Supreme Court of New Brunswick had to consider whether the accused was rightly convicted of having intoxicating liquor within the province, the offence having occurred on board ship in the Bay of Fundy within three miles of the coast. Chief Justice Baxter, giving the judgment of the court, stated that the area was in New Brunswick on the ground either that the Bay of Fundy was an inland bay or that it was within the three-mile zone. He continued: "On the grounds ... both of property and jurisdiction there can be no doubt that the Province of New Brunswick includes the territory in which the offence was committed."[115] Though the Supreme Court of Canada in *Re: Offshore Mineral Rights of British Columbia* refers to the case as one dealing with inland waters, the fact is that it was based on both grounds, and indeed Chief Justice Baxter appears to have had more confidence in the holding that the area in question was within New Brunswick because it was within three miles of the coast. In any event, a few years later, again giving the

109/(1930), c.15, s.168(Nfld.); re-enacted: R.S.N. 1952, c.175, s.67. An earlier version of the Act is dealt with in *McNeily* v. *Blandford* (1904–11), 9 Nfld. L.R. 571.
110/C.S.N. 1916, c.165; see now R.S.N. 1952, c. 204.
111/(1875), 6 Nfld. L.R. 28, at 33.
112/(1888), 7 Nfld. L.R. 321.
113/(1889), 7 Nfld. L.R. 378.
114/(1932), 5 M.P.R. 112.
115/*Ibid.*, at 118–19.

unanimous judgment of the Appeal Division, he repeated the view in *Filion* v. *New Brunswick International Paper Co.*[116]

However, as we have seen, the Supreme Court of Prince Edward Island, in *Gavin* v. *The Queen*,[117] in 1956, followed *R.* v. *Keyn.*[118] And the same is true of Macdonald J., *obiter*, in *Re Dominion Coal Co. Ltd. and County of Cape Breton*[119] in 1963. However, in the latter case, Currie J., also *obiter*, referred to Nova Scotia's pre-Confederation "hovering Act," and the extraction of coal offshore from the early days of the colony, and concluded: "Prior to Confederation, Nova Scotia exercised jurisdiction over an area of territorial waters three miles in width measured from its coasts, bays and rivers. See particularly the 'hovering' Act, 1836, 6 Wm. iv, c. 8, approved by the King in Council, thus recognizing that the control and administration of these waters reposed in the Province of Nova Scotia ... By virtue of s. 109, *B.N.A. Act*, all property rights held by Nova Scotia before Confederation were retained."[120]

It should perhaps be mentioned that even if it were held that the Atlantic provinces owned the resources of the subsoil of the territorial sea, their right of exploiting them would have to be exercised subject to federal power to legislate respecting defence, navigation, and other matters falling within section 91.[121] The federal government could also settle the line of demarcation with foreign countries, for such treaties touching as they do on sovereignty are self-implementing.[122]

CONTINENTAL SHELF

It is a universally recognized rule of international law that the open seas are not within the sovereignty of any one state,[123] and until recent years it was tempting to assume that the bed of the sea was also a *res nullius* or a *res communis*.[124] But there has for long been some recognized rights of

---

116/(1934), 8 M.P.R. 89, at 118–19; see also *City of Saint John* v. *Belyea* (1919), 47 N.B.R. 155, which, though based on a broader view, now untenable since *Re: Offshore Mineral Rights of British Columbia*, [1967] S.C.R. 792, also appears to favour the view that the territorial waters adjacent to New Brunswick are part of the province.

117/(1956), 3 D.L.R. (2d) 547. 118/1876), 2 Ex.D. 63.

119/(1963), 40 D.L.R. (2d) 593. 120/*Ibid.*, at 620.

121/For an example of how this might operate, see *Underwater Gas Developers Ltd.* v. *Ontario Labour Relations Board* (1960), 21 D.L.R. (2d) 345.

122/*Francis* v. *R.*, [1956] S.C.R. 618, *per* Rand and Cartwright JJ.

123/See J. L. Brierly, *The Law of Nations* (5th ed., Oxford, 1955), at 236–42.

124/See *ibid.*, at 183; Sir Cecil Hurst, "Whose is the Bed of the Sea?" (1923–24), 4 *Br. Year Book Int. Law* 34; E. Borchard, "Resources of the Continental Shelf" (1946), 40 *Amer. J. Int. Law* 52.

coastal states to exploit certain resources under the open sea. For example, coal mining has been conducted under the open seas beyond the three-mile limit off Cumberland in Great Britain.[125] Again, sedentary fisheries, such as oysters and chanks which live close to the sea bed, are claimed by numerous coastal states, notably Great Britain and its colonies, even when they are found beyond territorial waters. This right is usually justified either on the ground that the fisheries are appurtenances of the coastal state or on the ground of prescription, but it would in any case seem to be limited to the coastal state.[126] Again, no one has ever questioned the right of Great Britain and France to construct a tunnel under the English Channel.[127]

Only in recent years has more extensive exploitation of the resources of the bed of the sea become practicable and the question of the ownership of these resources acquired importance. This has resulted in the development of the doctrine of the continental shelf.[128] The term "continental shelf" is in its origin a geological not a legal term. On most coasts of the continents the sea bed does not at once descend precipitously but slopes downward gradually for a considerable distance, and then more abruptly plunges to the great depths of the sea. It is commonly[129] though erroneously,[130] believed that this plunge often occurs when the sea reaches a depth of 100 fathoms (600 feet) or 200 metres. Actually this is an oversimplification. Sometimes the sea bed drops in a series of falls; often shortly after a space of deep sea there is higher ground forming a shelf; some coasts have no shelf, the bed dropping almost immediately to the ocean floor. As the term is understood legally, the continental shelf

125/J. L. Brierly, *The Law of Nations* (5th ed., Oxford, 1955), at 181.
126/See Sir Cecil Hurst, "Whose is the Bed of the Sea?" (1923–24), 4 *Br. Year Book Int. Law* 34; E. Borchard, "Resources of the Continental Shelf" (1946), 40 *Amer. J. Int. Law* 52; L. Oppenheim, *International Law* (8th ed. by H. Lauterpacht, London, 1955), vol. I, "Peace," at 628–31.
127/See C. J. Colombos, *The International Law of the Sea* (5th ed., London, 1962), at 75–7.
128/See M. W. Mouton, *The Continental Shelf* (The Hague, 1952); among the many articles, see E. Borchard, "Resources of the Continental Shelf" (1946), 40 *Amer. J. Int. Law* 52; F. A. Vallat, "The Continental Shelf" (1946), 23 *Br. Year Book Int. Law* 333; H. Lauterpacht, "Sovereignty over Submarine Areas" (1950), 27 *Br. Year Book Int. Law* 376; R. Young, "The Legal Statue of the Submarine Areas beneath the High Seas" (1951), 45 *Amer. J. Int. Law* 225; D. P. O'Connell, "Sedentary Fisheries and the Australian Continental Shelf" (1955), 49 *Amer. J. Int. Law* 185. For short accounts, see J. L. Brierly, *The Law of Nations* (5th ed., Oxford, 1955), at 180–85; L. Oppenheim, *International Law* (8th ed. by H. Lauterpacht, London, 1955), vol. I, "Peace," at 629–35.
129/See, for example, J. L. Brierly, *The Law of Nations* (5th ed., Oxford, 1955), at 181.
130/See H. Lauterpacht, "Sovereignty over Submarine Areas" (1950), 27 *Br. Year Book Int. Law* 376; R. Young, "The Legal Status of the Submarine Areas beneath the High Seas" (1951), 45 *Amer. J. Int. Law* 225.

includes not only the shelves of continents but those adjoining islands and places where, strictly speaking, there is no continental shelf at all, such as the Caspian Sea. It is now possible to extract oil from the continental shelf as so understood, by installations in the open seas. The importance of the matter to Canada is obvious; for example, the continental shelf off the northeastern shores of Canada extends for a distance of over 200 miles from Newfoundland.[131] Canada has granted licences to search for oil off several provinces.[132]

By the early 1950s it was becoming generally accepted in international law that a coastal state has the right to explore and exploit the resources of the continental shelf.[133] Whatever doubt existed[134] has now been removed by the Geneva Convention on the Continental Shelf of 1958 which permits a coastal state to explore and exploit the submarine area off its coasts beyond the territorial sea to a depth of 200 metres or beyond that where the depths of the water admits of the exploitation of the natural resources.[135]

When the conflicting claims of the federal government and British Columbia were raised in *Re: Offshore Mineral Rights of British Columbia*[136] the provinces could point to the fact that a number of claims to resources beyond the three-mile zone had been recognized under international law and under English law.[137] Again, early common law writers had maintained that the "great waste of the sea" belonged to the Crown.[138] Moreover, Great Britain and its colonies, including some of the provinces before union, had frequently exercised both legislative and proprietary jurisdiction beyond or without restriction to the three-mile limit before

131/*Debates of the House of Commons*, 1957, II, at 1770, *per* The Hon. James Sinclair, then Minister of Fisheries; see the maps in J. G. Castel, *International Law Chiefly as Interpreted and Applied in Canada* (Toronto, 1965), at 362–65.
132/See Castel, *ibid.*
133/See E. Borchard, "Resources of the Continental Shelf" (1946), 40 *Amer. J. Int. Law* 52; H. Lauterpacht, "Sovereignty over Submarine Areas" (1950), 27 *Br. Year Book Int. Law* 376; J. L. Brierly, *The Law of Nations* (5th ed., Oxford, 1955), at 183–84; Oppenheim, *International Law* (8th ed. by H. Lauterpacht, London, 1955), vol. I, "Peace," at 629–35.
134/In *The Abu Dhabi Arbitration* (1952), 1 *Int. & Comp. L.Q.* 247, Lord Asquith did not think it had yet become an established rule of international law.
135/UN Doc. A/Conf. 13/L. 55; reprinted in (1958), 52 *Amer. J. Int. Law* 858. Though Canada has yet to ratify this treaty, there is no question that it expresses customary international law that applies to Canada: see a letter by the Under-Secretary of State for External Affairs in (1965), 3 *Can. Yearbook Int. Law* 325–26; *Re: Offshore Mineral Rights of British Columbia*, [1967] S.C.R. 792.
136/*Ibid.*
137/See p. 104.
138/See Co. Litt., vol. 2, s.439; Hale, *De Jure Maris*, c.4, at 10–11, c.6 at 31. The early authorities are collected in *R. v. Keyn* (1876–77), 2 Ex. 63, especially *per* Lindley L.J. and Brett J.A., and in Sir Cecil Hurst, "Whose is the Bed of the Sea?" (1923–24), 4 *Br. Year Book Int. Law* 34.

Confederation.[139] It was, therefore, possible to conclude that all exploit-able resources of the sea adjacent to the coast belonged to a coastal state and were vested in the Crown. The right to explore the continental shelf on this basis could be looked upon as a mere development of the Crown's right to explore and exploit "the great waste of the sea." Such a Crown right, it could be argued, was a royalty (i.e., a right arising to the Crown by prerogative)[140] retained by the provinces under section 109 of the BNA Act, or "property" under section 117 which retained all undisposed public property in the provinces.

The foundation for the argument was completely removed when the Supreme Court held that the province of British Columbia ended at low-water mark. The court's reasoning in support of property and legislative jurisdiction over the continental shelf lying in Canada and not the province was succinctly expressed in the following passage:

> As with the territorial sea, so with the continental shelf. There are two reasons why British Columbia lacks the right to explore and exploit and lacks legislative jurisdiction:
> (1) The continental shelf is outside the boundaries of British Columbia, and
> (2) Canada is the sovereign state which will be recognized by international law as having the rights stated in the Convention of 1958, and it is Canada, not the Province of British Columbia, that will have to answer the claims of other members of the international community for breach of the obligations and responsibilities imposed by the Convention.
> There is no historical, legal or constitutional basis upon which the Province of British Columbia could claim the right to explore and exploit or claim legislative jurisdiction over the resources of the continental shelf.[141]

In the face of this judgment it would seem difficult for any province to mount a successful historical argument in favour of ownership of the resources of the continental shelf. There is, however, some material upon which such an argument might be framed. Quebec could point to the statutes of Lower Canada exercising jurisdiction in relation to fisheries up to six leagues at sea in the Baie des Chaleurs region, and giving a public right to fish in the Gulf of St. Lawrence.[142]

Nova Scotia and New Brunswick might rely on the early commis-

---

139/See pp. 93–4, 101–2.
140/See pp. 79–83.
141/*Re: Offshore Mineral Rights of British Columbia*, [1967] S.C.R. 792, at 821.
142/See pp. 87–88, 100.
143/See p. 87.
144/See the articles cited *supra* note 133. The United States proclamation of 1946 (10 Fed. Reg. 12303) provides a convenient example: see *Re: Offshore Mineral Rights of British Columbia*, [1967] S.C.R. 792 where it is cited. See also *The Anna* (1805), 8 C.Rob. 373; 165 E.R. 809 where mud islands beyond the three-mile limit were treated as "appendant" to the coast.

sions establishing the provinces which purport to include "all the Rights, Members and Appurtenances" to the described areas.[143] For the doctrine of the continental shelf was to no little extent developed through the concept of appurtenance.[144] Moreover, the early Nova Scotia act of 1770, previously mentioned, treated the sea within three leagues as being within the jurisdiction of the colony,[145] and counties in New Brunswick have since 1854 been defined as extending into any adjoining "Sea, Bay, Gulf or River, to the boundary of the Province ... in the same manner as if it were land."[146]

The strongest case is perhaps that of Newfoundland. Despite the view expressed by Lord Asquith in the *Abu Dhabi Arbitration*[147] in 1952, that the doctrine of the continental shelf was not yet accepted under international law, there was considerable state practice supporting such a doctrine before Newfoundland's entry into Confederation in 1949. Beginning with the annexation of part of the Gulf of Paria by Great Britain in 1942,[148] and President Truman's proclamation of 1945 claiming the continental shelf off the coasts of the United States as "appertaining" to that country and "subject to its jurisdiction and control,"[149] no less than thirty states had issued proclamations claiming similar jurisdiction, and none had been objected to by other states except where claims had been made to the superjacent waters. From this, some noted authorities had concluded that the doctrine was established long before its adoption into the Geneva Convention on the Continental Shelf.[150]

Moreover, Newfoundland had on several occasions, in language that could easily be construed as extending its rights beyond the three-mile limit, exercised jurisdiction over the sea bed. The Oyster Fishery Act before union applied to the "banks" of the province,[151] and the Crown Lands Act has long dealt with mining locations "covered by the sea or public tidal waters."[152] However, the Newfoundland Supreme Court has on more than one occasion asserted that its jurisdiction did not extend beyond the three-mile limit,[153] and these statutes would probably be restrictively interpreted.

145/(1770). 10 Geo. III, c.10(N.S.).
146/R.S.N.B. 1854, c.161.
147/(1952), 1 *Int. & Comp. L.Q.* 247.
148/The Submarine Areas of the Gulf of Paria (Annexation) Order, 1942; (1942), B.T.S. no. 10.
149/(1945), 10 Fed. Reg. 12303.
150/See the article cited *supra* note 133.
151/C.S.N., 1916, c.165; see now R.S.N. 1952, c.204.
152/(1930), c.15, s.168(Nfld.); re-enacted by R.S.N. 1952, c.175, s.67. An earlier version is dealt with in *McNeily* v. *Blandford* (1904–11), 9 Nfld. L.R. 571.
153/*Rhodes* v. *Fairweather* (1888), 7 Nfld. L.R. 321; *The Queen* v. *Delepine* (1889), 7 Nfld. L.R. 378.

CHAPTER SEVEN

Property in Indian Lands

At common law, the Crown is the owner of all ungranted lands in a settled colony.[1] The same was true of French law when Canada was settled;[2] in 1763 when France ceded to Great Britain all her rights of sovereignty, property, and possession over Canada, full title to the territory ceded became vested in the English sovereign.[3] Consequently all ungranted land in Canada belongs to the Queen. But the numerous Indian tribes that roamed the vast territory of what is now Canada considered themselves the owners of the land. In the early colonies attempts were made to take the land without regard for the Indians' interests, but this led to frequent frontier wars involving great sacrifices of life and property and expenditures of money which proved burdensome to the colonies. The impolicy of this mode of dealing, coupled possibly with motives of humane consideration for the aborigines, led the British to adopt a more liberal method of dealing with the Indians, which included the recognition of the Indian title. Whenever land occupied by the Indians was required it was obtained by a surrender from the Indians in return for a consideration, often a payment in money which frequently took the form of an annuity. This policy resulted in peace obtaining between the white man and the Indian.[4]

Variations in the manner of implementing this policy naturally occurred in the different provinces and further changes have come about through agreements between the Dominion and the provinces. Still, the bulk of the lands reserved for Indians were governed, or influenced by the royal proclamation of 7 October 1763, following the conquest of Canada,[5] and it seems best to begin with the law under the proclamation, and then to examine the variations that exist in various parts of Canada.

1/*Mercer* v. *Attorney-General of Ontario* (1883), 5 S.C.R. 538; *St. Catherine's Milling and Lumber Co.* v. *R.* (1887), 13 S.C.R. 577; *Doe d. Burk* v. *Cormier* (1891), 30 N.B.R. 142.
2/See *St. Catherine's Milling and Lumber Co.* v. *R.* (1887), 13 S.C.R. 577, *per* Taschereau J., at 644.
3/See *ibid.*, at 645; see also in the same case Boyd C. in 10 O.R. 196 and the Privy Council in (1889), 14 A.C. 46, at 53.
4/See the judgments of Strong and Taschereau JJ., in *St. Catherine's Milling and Lumber Co.* v. *R.* (1887), 13 S.C.R. 577; see also *Church* v. *Fenton* (1878), 28 U.C.C.P. 384; *R.v. White and Bob* (1965), 50 D.L.R. (2d) 613, *per* Norris J.A.
5/See R.S.C. 1952, VI, at 6127.

France,[6] like other European powers,[7] also followed a policy of recognizing the Indian title and on the capitulation of Canada attempts were made to protect the Indians. In the Articles of Capitulation, signed at Montreal in 1760, the fortieth article provides:

40 – The savages or Indian Allies of His Most Christian Majesty shall be maintained in the lands they inhabit, if they choose to reside there; they shall not be molested on any pretence whatsover, for having carried arms and served His Most Christian Majesty ...[8]

This was followed by the Treaty of Paris, 1763, by which what then comprised Canada was ceded by France to Great Britain. One of the earliest acts of government by the British regarding the territory ceded was the royal proclamation of 7 October 1763. This proclamation had the force of statute, for the king has power to legislate for a newly conquered country by virtue of his prerogative.[9] After establishing four colonies in the ceded territories – Quebec, West Florida, East Florida, and Grenada – and providing for their government, the proclamation deals with Indian lands in the following passages:

And whereas it is just and reasonable, and essential to our Interest, and the security of our Colonies, that the several Nations or Tribes of Indians with whom We are connected, and who live under our Protection, should not be molested or disturbed in the Possession of such Parts of Our Dominions and Territories as, not having been ceded to or purchased by Us, are reserved to them or any of them, as their Hunting Grounds – We do therefore, with the Advice of our Privy Council, declare it to be our Royal Will and Pleasure, that no Governor or Commander in Chief in any of our Colonies of Quebec, East Florida, or West Florida, do presume, upon any Pretence whatever, to grant Warrants of Survey, or pass any Patents for Lands beyond the Bounds of their respective Governments, as described in their Commissions; as also that no Governor or Commander in Chief in any of our other Colonies or Plantations in America do presume for the present, and until our further Pleasure be Known, to grant Warrants of Survey, or pass Patents for any Lands beyond the Heads or Sources of any of the Rivers which fall into the Atlantic Ocean from the West and North West, or upon any

6/See *St. Catherine's Milling and Lumber Co.* v. *R.* (1887), 13 S.C.R. 577, *per* Taschereau J.; *Lazare* v. *St. Lawrence Seaway Authority*, [1957] Que. S.C. 5.
7/See *St. Catherine's Milling and Lumber Co.* v. *R.* (1887), 13 S.C.R. 577, and the American cases cited therein.
8/Cited in *St. Catherine's Milling and Lumber Co.* v. *R.* (1887), 13 S.C.R. 577, at 585.
9/*Campbell* v. *Hall* (1774), 1 Cowp. 204; 98 E.R. 1045; *St. Catherine's Milling and Lumber Co.* v. *R.* (1887), 13 S.C.R. 577; *R.* v. *McMaster*, [1926] Ex.C.R. 68; *Attorney-General of Canada* v. *George* (1964), 45 D.L.R. 709; *R.* v. *White and Bob* (1965), 50 D.L.R. (2d) 613, *per* Norris J.A.

Lands whatever, which, not having been ceded to or purchased by Us as aforesaid, are reserved to the said Indians, or any of them.

And We do further declare it to be Our Royal Will and Pleasure, for the present as aforesaid, to reserve under our Sovereignty, Protection, and Dominion, for the use of the said Indians, all the Lands and Territories not included within the Limits of Our Said Three New Governments, or within the Limits of the Territory granted to the Hudson's Bay Company, as also all the Lands and Territories lying to the Westward of the Sources of the Rivers which fall into the Sea from the West and North West as aforesaid;

And We do hereby strictly forbid, on Pain of our Displeasure, all our loving Subjects from making any Purchases or Settlements whatever, or taking Possession of any of the Lands above reserved, without our especial leave and Licence for that Purpose first obtained.

And, We do further strictly enjoin and require all Persons whatever who have either wilfully or inadvertently seated themselves upon any Lands within the Countries above described, or upon any other Lands which, not having been ceded to or purchased by Us, are still reserved to the said Indians as aforesaid, forthwith to remove themselves from such Settlements.

And Whereas Great Frauds and Abuses have been committed in purchasing Lands of the Indians, to the Great Prejudice of our Interests, and to the Great Dissatisfaction of the said Indians; In order, therefore, to prevent such Irregularities for the future, and to the End that the Indians may be convinced of our Justice and determined Resolution to remove all reasonable Cause of Discontent, We do, with the Advice of our Privy Council strictly enjoin and require, that no private Person do presume to make any Purchase from the said Indians of any Lands reserved to the said Indians, within those parts of our Colonies where, We have thought proper to allow Settlement; but that, if at any Time any of the said Indians should be inclined to dispose of the said Lands, the same shall be Purchased only for Us, in our Name, at some public Meeting or Assembly of the said Indians, to be held for that Purpose by the Governor or Commander in Chief of our Colony respectively within which they shall lie; and in case they shall lie within the limits of any Proprietary Government, they shall be purchased only for the Use and in the name of such Proprietaries, conformable to such Directions and Instructions as We or they shall think proper to give for that Purpose ...[10]

In summary the proclamation makes the following provisions regarding the lands it reserves for Indians: the Indians are not to be molested or disturbed in their possession of such lands; the various colonial governors are not to give grants of such lands; private individuals are not to purchase lands from the Indians; if any persons have settled on such lands, they are to leave them; and if the Indians wish to dispose of such lands, they may only be purchased in the king's name after a meeting of the Indians for

10/See R.S.C. 1952. VI, at 6130–31.

that purpose has been held by the governor of the colony where the land is located (or in a proprietary government, in the name of the proprietaries in accordance with directions of the king or the proprietary).

The provisions of the proclamation respecting Indian lands applied to vast tracts of territory. The proclamation expressly provides that there shall be reserved for the use of Indians all the territories not included within the limits of the colonies of Quebec and East and West Florida or within the lands granted to the Hudson's Bay Company; and all the territories lying to the westward of the sources of the rivers that fall into the Atlantic Ocean from the west and northwest. As Strong J. pointed out in the *St. Catherine's* case[11] "all the territories" there referred to must be limited to "the countries and islands" ceded by the Treaty of Paris. It is true that the Privy Council in the same case[12] broadly stated that the proclamation applied in favour of all Indians then living under the sovereignty and protection of the British Crown but this is demonstrably too wide because the proclamation expressly exempts the land within the three colonies mentioned, as well as the territory of the Hudson's Bay Company.[13] The line of demarcation between the lands reserved by the proclamation and Hudson's Bay Company land is impossible to define with precision because the Hudson's Bay Company land is vaguely described as including the vast territories the waters of which empty into Hudson Bay.[14] Broadly, however, it may be said that the lands reserved under the proclamation include large portions of the area now comprising Ontario, Quebec, the Prairie provinces, and probably British Columbia; it has even been held that the Maritimes fell within the area reserved by the proclamation, but this seems doubtful. The situation in each province and the territories will be examined later.

NATURE OF INDIAN TITLE
UNDER THE PROCLAMATION OF 1763

Some of the land reserved by the proclamation had been surrendered by the Indians before Confederation but the bulk remained subject to the proclamation. In the British North America Act, 1867, the only provision dealing expressly with Indian lands is section 91(24) which gives

11/*St. Catherine's Milling and Lumber Co.* v. *R.* (1887), 13 S.C.R. 577, at 628.
12/(1889), 14 A.C. 46, at 54.
13/This is underlined by the Supreme Court of Canada in the recent case of *Sigeareak E1-53* v. *R.*, [1966] S.C.R. 645.
14/See E. H. Oliver, *The Canadian North-West* (Ottawa, 1914), vol. I, 135, at 143–44.

the Dominion legislative power over "Indians, and Lands reserved for the Indians." The sections distributing property do not specifically refer to these lands.

The nature of the Indian title and the respective rights of the Dominion and the provinces to Indian lands reserved by the proclamation can best be discussed by reference to the leading case of *St. Catherine's Milling and Lumber Co.* v. *R*.[15] There by a formal treaty (the North-West Angle Treaty, No. 3) of 3 October 1873, between commissioners appointed by the government of Canada on behalf of the Queen and the chiefs of the Salteaux tribe of the Ojibway Indians, the Indians surrendered to the government of Canada, for certain considerations, their right over 50,000 square miles of the land described in the proclamation, not less than 32,000 miles of which were situated in Ontario. Acting on the assumption that this land now vested in the Crown in right of the Dominion, the Dominion government issued to the St. Catherine's Milling and Lumber Company a timber permit to a specified area of the surrendered land. The company having availed itself of the permit, the Attorney-General of Ontario began an action against it on the ground that the beneficial owner-ship of the land was vested in the province of Ontario. Boyd V.C. gave judgment for the province[16] and his judgment was affirmed by the Ontario Court of Appeal[17] and a majority of the Supreme Court of Canada.[18] Appeal was then taken to the Privy Council. The Dominion argued that under the proclamation the Indians held the land in fee simple, for the proclamation recited that the land had never been surrendered to the Crown, and consequently on its surrender by the treaty of 1873 it had passed to the Dominion. This contention was rejected; it was held that the land belonged to the Crown, subject to whatever right it had granted the Indians. The Privy Council thus described the nature of the Indian title under the proclamation:

It was suggested in the course of the argument for the Dominion, that inasmuch as the proclamation recites that the territories thereby reserved for Indians had never "been ceded to or purchased by" the Crown, the entire property of the land remained with them. That inference is, however, at variance with the terms of the instrument, which shew that the tenure of the Indians was a personal and usufructuary right, dependent upon the good will of the Sover-eign. The lands reserved are expressly stated to be "parts of Our dominions and territories;" and it is declared to be the will and pleasure of the sovereign that, "for the present," they shall be reserved for the use of the Indians, as their hunting grounds, under his protection and dominion. There was a great deal of learned discussion at the Bar with respect to the precise quality of the Indian right, but their Lordships do not consider it necessary to express any

15/(1889), 14 A.C. 46.   16/(1885), 10 O.R. 196.
17/(1886), 13 O.A.R. 148.   18/(1887), 13 S.C.R. 577.

opinion upon the point. It appears to them to be sufficient for the purposes of this case that there has been all along vested in the Crown a substantial and paramount estate, underlying the Indian title, which became a plenum dominium whenever that title was surrendered or otherwise extinguished.[19]

Though the Privy Council refused to go into the exact nature of the Indian title, it does seem to imply that the interest is related to Indian habits and mode of life.[20] Their usufructuary interest would not seem to give Indians the right, for example, to conduct large-scale mining operations on the land. However, the matter is by no means clear, and some Dominion-provincial agreements provide that the Indians are to benefit from royalties from mines on reserves.[21] The title does not authorize the Indians to sell, lease, or otherwise dispose of their interest except to the Crown,[22] or to bring action for interferences with it.[23] An Indian on a reserve has no equitable title to the land on which he resides; all he has is a personal usufructuary title based on the goodwill of the Crown,[24] though the Indian Act now gives him considerable power of disposition to other Indians.[25] In fact, the rights of the Indians respecting lands reserved for them are now largely regulated by that act; the limits of federal power in this respect are examined in chapter eight.

Having decided that the Crown has a paramount title underlying the Indian title, the next problem facing the Privy Council in the *St. Catherine's* case was whether the Dominion or the provinces had the beneficial interest in the Crown's title. Their Lordships pointed out that the beneficial interest in Crown lands in the province of Canada, including lands reserved for Indians, had been transferred to the province by the Union Act in 1840.[26] This continued to be the situation at the passing of the BNA Act, so it was necessary to examine the sections of that act distributing property between the Dominion and the provinces. Turning to those sections, the Privy Council held that no title had passed to the Dominion

19/(1889), 14 A.C. 46, at 54–5.
20/See also *Lazare* v. *St. Lawrence Seaway Authority*, [1957] Que. S.C. 5; *R.* v. *Discon and Baker* (1968), 67 D.L.R. (2d) 619.
21/See p. 133.
22/See *Easterbrook* v. *R.*, [1931] S.C.R. 210; see now Indian Act, R.S.C. 1952, c.149, s.88(1).
23/Cf., *D'Ailleboust* v. *Bellefleur* (1918), 25 R.L.N.S. 50 and *Pap-Wee-In* v. *Beaudry*, [1933] 1 W.W.R. 138.
24/*Point* v. *Diblee Construction Co.*, [1934] 2 D.L.R. 785; on the latter point see also *St. Catherine's Milling and Lumber Co.* v. *R.* (1889), 14 A.C. 46, at 54–5 (see passage quoted *supra*); *Attorney-General of Canada* v. *Toth* (1959), 17 D.L.R. (2d) 273.
25/R.S.C. 1952, c.149; see esp. ss.24 and 45.
26/3 & 4 Vict., c.43. It was not until 1860, however, that the Imperial authorities surrendered complete control over Indians to the Canadian authorities; see (1860), 23 Vict., c.151(Can.).

under section 108 because that section only conveys to the Dominion the property enumerated in the third schedule to the Act and Indian lands did not appear there; nor were they included in the phrase "lands set apart for general public purposes" in that schedule. Section 102 (which assigns to the Dominion the duties and revenues formerly appropriated to the provinces) must, their Lordships pointed out, be read subject to section 109 which assigns all lands belonging to the provinces at Confederation to the provinces and section 117 which retains for the provinces all such property not otherwise transferred. There was thus no ground for holding the Indian lands to be federal property under these sections.

The Dominion also relied on section 91(24) of the BNA Act, arguing that its power to legislate respecting "Indians, and Lands reserved for the Indians" carried with it by necessary implication any patrimonial interest the Crown might have had in the reserved land. But the Privy Council also rejected this argument. The right to legislate respecting Indians and lands reserved for Indians undoubtedly carried with it the power to accept surrenders of the Indian title, but this surrender did not take away from Ontario any interest in any lands assigned to it under the BNA Act. That being so, their Lordships held the province entitled to the Indian lands under sections 109 and 117. Section 109, however, adds that the title assigned thereunder is subject to "any Trusts existing in respect thereof, and to any Interest other than that of the provinces in the same." The Indian title was an interest in the land other than that of the province and the provincial title was, therefore, subject to it.

One more point should be made. In the course of the case, the provinces had argued that "Lands reserved for the Indians" in section 91(24) referred only to lands specially reserved for Indians in treaties or in statutes and not to the extensive tracts of land reserved by the proclamation. The Board also rejected this argument, holding the expression applicable to both types of reserved lands. Since a later case[27] has held that the legislative power includes the power of administration and control, it follows that the administration and control of the lands reserved for Indians under the proclamation or otherwise is in the federal government, even though the land belongs to the provinces.

In summary, then, the underlying title to lands reserved for the Indians under the proclamation is vested in the Crown for the benefit of the provinces. The provincial title is subject, however, to the usufructuary title of the Indians thereto. This Indian title is under the control and administration of the Crown in right of the Dominion by virtue of its legislative power over "Indians, and Lands reserved for the Indians," and in exercis-

27/*Attorney-General of Canada* v. *Attorney-General of Ontario*, [1897] A.C. 199.

ing this right of control, the Dominion may accept a surrender, which under the 1763 proclamation was the only way the Indians could surrender their title.[28] But once the Indians surrender their title the province has the complete beneficial interest in the land and the federal government ceases to have the control and administration thereof. In most of the provinces, however, the Dominion government, by virtue of Dominion-provincial agreements, now has the beneficial title in surrendered Indian lands or the power to sell or otherwise dispose of it and use the proceeds for the benefit of the Indians. These agreements will be dealt with later.[29]

COMPENSATION FOR SURRENDER

A vast part of the lands reserved by the proclamation have now been surrendered by the Indians under a network of treaties.[30] The Indians do not surrender their lands without consideration. In return they receive compensation, usually by way of annuities, the establishment of more compact reserves, and hunting and fishing privileges over the ceded territory.

We must now examine who is responsible for fulfilling the promises made to the Indians in return for the surrender. The question first came up in connection with a pre-Confederation treaty in *Attorney-General of Canada* v. *Attorney-General of Ontario*.[31] There a tribe of Indians had, in 1850, entered into two treaties with the governor of Canada on behalf of the Queen and the government of the province of Canada whereby the Indians ceded to the province certain lands theretofore occupied by them as reserves. In consideration therefor, a sum was immediately paid to the Indians and a promise was given to pay them a perpetual annuity of £ 400 under one treaty and £ 600 under the other. In addition, both treaties provided that if at a future time the territories ceded should produce an income permitting the provincial government to do so without loss, the annuities would be increased up to a certain limit. As their Lordships pointed out, the effect of the treaties was that while the lands ceded continued to vest in the Crown, the beneficial interest in them, together with the right of disposal and appropriation of the proceeds, passed to the provincial government. The land, being situate in what became

28/The federal parliament has modified the method of surrender, and could abolish the Indian title, see pp. 157–8.
29/See pp. 126–33.
30/See *Indian Treaties and Surrenders* (Ottawa), vols. I, II (1905), and III (1912).
31/[1897] A.C. 199.

Ontario, became, by virtue of section 109 of the BNA Act, part of the public domain of that province. In 1873, the Indians claimed increased annuities as from the date of the treaties on the ground that from the beginning the proceeds from the land had been large enough to enable the stipulated increases to be paid without loss. The problem then was to determine the respective liability of the Dominion and the province to pay the increased annuity. The Dominion contended that Ontario was liable on the ground that the treaty rights to an increase of annuity were either a trust burdening the surrendered lands and their proceeds or an interest other than that of the province in the same within the meaning of section 109 of the BNA Act. Ontario, on the other hand, asserted that the annuity was a mere debt of the province of Canada and was consequently payable in the first instance by the Dominion under section 111 of the BNA Act (which provides that "Canada shall be liable for the Debts and Liabilities of each Province existing at the Union") subject to reimbursement from both Ontario and Quebec under section 112 of the Act, which provides that these provinces are conjointly liable to Canada for debts of the province of Canada in excess of $62,500,000. The Privy Council accepted the contention of the province. All the Indians received was a promise to pay the annuities as and when they became due. The annuities were not a "trust" within section 109 because that word was intended to signify a contractual or legal duty upon the province to make payment out of the land or its proceeds, whereas it was never intended that the annuity should be derived from those sources. Nor was the annuity "an interest other than that of the province in the same," for this referred to a right or interest independent of that of the old province and capable of being vindicated in competition with it, and the Indian interest was not such an independent interest. Since the annuity was a mere debt of the old province, the Dominion was primarily liable under section 111 of the BNA Act, subject to being reimbursed by Ontario and Quebec under section 112. It follows that Quebec had to share equally with Ontario the payment of the annuities though the revenues from the land accrued to Ontario. This result was confirmed by the Supreme Court of Canada in *Province of Quebec* v. *Dominion of Canada*.[32]

These cases were concerned with pre-Confederation treaties. As regards treaties made by the Dominion there was for a time authority for the view that the provinces were responsible for paying the compensation promised for a surrender. For Lord Watson had stated in *St. Catherine's Milling*[33] case that: "Seeing that the benefit of the surrender accrues to her, Ontario

32/(1898), 30 S.C.R. 151.
33/*St. Catherine's Milling and Lumber Co.* v. *R.* (1889), 14 A.C. 46, at 60.

must, of course, relieve the Crown, and the Dominion, of all obligations involving the payment of money which were undertaken by Her Majesty, and which are said to have been in part fulfilled by the Dominion Government." The statement was not necessary to the decision and the point was again raised in *Dominion of Canada* v. *Province of Ontario*[34] where the Dominion sought to be recouped from Ontario for so much of the payments and other burdens assumed by the Dominion under a treaty providing for the surrender of lands by Indians as might properly be attributed to the part of such lands situated in Ontario. The Privy Council held that the Dominion could not recover. In negotiating the treaty the Dominion was in no way acting on behalf of the province, but was acting with a view to promoting great national interests within its jurisdiction without the consent of the province, believing that the lands did not belong to the province. The Board accepted the view of Duff and Idington JJ.[35] that Lord Watson may have referred to the principles of fair play that should be followed between governments but that, if that was not what he meant, the passage should be regarded as *obiter*.

Except as provided in Dominion-provincial agreements (to be examined later),[36] there is now no question that lump-sum payments and annuities promised in consideration of a surrender of Indian lands are the responsibility of the federal government. But sometimes the consideration for a surrender relates to the ceded land. Such a situation arose in *Ontario Mining Co.* v. *Seybold*.[37] In the treaty already discussed in the *St. Catherine's* case, the Dominion had agreed to set aside certain portions of the lands surrendered as reserves for the Indians. In intended compliance with the agreement the federal authorities purported to appropriate portions of the land as reserves, including Reserve 38B on which the Rat Portage Band of the Salteaux Indians resided. On 8 October 1886 the band surrendered a portion of Reserve 38B to the Crown in trust to sell the land, invest the proceeds, and pay the interest from the investments to the Indians and their descendants forever. The Dominion conveyed a portion of the land that had formed part of Reserve 38B to the predecessors in title of the Ontario Mining Company by letters patent in 1889. The company now claimed to be entitled to the land as against the respondent who claimed an interest in the same land under provincial letters patent of 1899. The whole point then was whether the Dominion or the province had the right to convey the land. Boyd C., who heard the case,[38] disposed of it on the ground that even assuming that the Dominion could validly establish Reserve 38B, the subsequent surrender in 1886 had the effect

34/[1910] A.C. 637.   35/(1908–9), 42 S.C.R. 1.
36/See p. 128.   37/[1903] A.C. 73.   38/(1899), 31 O.R. 386.

of leaving the sole proprietary ownership in the province, and accordingly the defendant's title prevailed. His judgment was adopted by the Supreme Court of Canada.[39] The Privy Council found it unnecessary to discuss this aspect of the case but stated that they did not dissent from this opinion. The judgment of the Board is based on the view that the first surrender gave the province the full beneficial interest in the land, and so the disposition of the land by the Crown could only be effected on the advice of the provincial ministers. Even assuming "... that the Government of the province, taking advantage of the surrender of 1873, came at least under an honourable engagement to fulfil the terms on the faith of which the surrender was made, and, therefore, to concur with the Dominion Government in appropriating certain undefined portions of the surrendered lands as Indian reserves ... the choice and location of the lands to be so appropriated could only be effectively made by the joint action of the two Governments."[40]

It might be noted in passing that Ontario complied with its "honourable engagement." On 16 April 1894, the province and the Dominion entered into a statutory agreement[41] whereby Ontario agreed to make a full enquiry respecting the reserves with a view to acquiescing in their location unless some good reason presented itself, and that if it was dissatisfied with the reserves selected, a joint commission was to be appointed to settle the question. Following full enquiry, Ontario in 1915 passed an act[42] acquiescing in the location of all but one of the reserves, but excepting certain rights to water power.[43] The federal government now has agreements with most of the provinces under which these problems may be avoided in the future.[44]

While the promises to the Indians in the cases thus far discussed related to the land surrendered, the Indian's usufructuary right to the land had been surrendered. Some treaty provisions, however, might well be interpreted as a reservation of a part of the usufructuary right, rather than as a mere promise not attached to the land. Thus in the treaty examined in the *St. Catherine's* case,[45] there is the following provision: "... the Indians are to have right to pursue their avocations of hunting and fishing throughout the surrendered territory, with the exception of those portions of it

39/(1901), 31 S.C.R. 125.   40/[1903] A.C. 73, at 82–3.
41/(1891), 54 & 55 Vict., c.5(Can.); (1891), 54 Vict., c.3(Ont.).
42/5 Geo. V, c.12(Ont.).
43/For an account of the matter, see *Ontario and Minnesota Power Co.* v. *R.*, [1925] A.C. 196; the water powers excepted are similar to those in the agreement discussed at pp. 128–30.
44/See pp. 126–33.   45/(1889), 14 A.C. 46, at 51–2.

which may, from time to time, be required or taken up for settlement, mining, lumbering, or other purposes." Many other treaties of cession have similar provisions. While "other purposes" in such treaties has been interpreted broadly so as to except game reserves from the operation of the provision,[46] such a provision, if it is binding on the province, may curtail the freedom of action of the provincial legislature in connection, for example, with its game and fishing regulations. In the *St. Catherine's* case,[47] the only references to this clause indicate that the Dominion has legislative power to regulate the Indians' privilege and that questions might arise respecting the right to determine to what extent, and at what periods, the territory over which the Indians exercise these rights is to be taken up for settlement. These statements appear to recognize the hunting and fishing rights as against the province and this seems to be the view taken of the case in *Ontario Mining Co.* v. *Seybold*,[48] where it is said:

> It was decided by this Board in the *St. Catherine's Milling Co.'s Case* that prior to that surrender the province of Ontario had a proprietary interest in the land, under the provisions of s. 109 of the BNA Act, 1867, subject to the burden of the Indian usufructuary title, and upon the extinguishment of that title by the surrender the province acquired the full beneficial interest in the *subject only to such qualified privilege of hunting and fishing as was reserved to the Indians in the treaty.*

From this it can certainly be argued that the right to hunt and fish is an unsurrendered portion of the usufructuary right of the Indians in lands reserved for them, and consequently that it is a trust or an interest other than that of the provinces in such lands. It would follow that, subject to the exceptions in the treaty, the right would come within the exclusive jurisdiction of the federal authorities as relating to Indians and lands reserved for Indians. But this was not the view taken in *R.* v. *Commanda*.[49] There the appellant, an Ojibway Indian, was convicted of having in his possession parts of two moose and a deer, contrary to the Ontario Game and Fisheries Act. The appellant contended that the legislation was *ultra vires* in so far as it included Ojibway Indians hunting in territory surrendered under the Robinson Treaty of 1850, which contained a provision granting those Indians a privilege of hunting and fishing similar to that mentioned in the *St. Catherine's* case. That privilege, he alleged, was a trust or interest other than that of the province within the meaning of section 109 of the BNA

46/*R.* v. *Smith*, [1935] 3 D.L.R. 703; *R.* v. *Hill* (1951), 101 C.C.C. 343; but cf., *R.* v. *Strongquill*, [1953] 2 D.L.R. 264.
47/(1889), 14 A.C. 46, at 60.
48/[1903] A.C. 73, at 79 (italics mine).
49/[1939] 3 D.L.R. 635.

Act. Greene J., who heard the appeal, rejected the contention. He equated the hunting and fishing rights to the annuities discussed in *Attorney-General of Canada* v. *Attorney-General of Ontario*;[50] they are not property rights, he held, but mere promises. He distinguished the observations in the *St. Catherine's* case on the ground that the treaty in that case was a post-Confederation treaty, whereas the treaty under consideration was entered into before Confederation. With respect, this would appear to make no difference. If a portion of the Indians' usufructuary title that remains after a post-Confederation surrender of the major part can subsist as a trust or interest other than that of the province under section 109, it is difficult to understand why a similar portion remaining after a pre-Confederation surrender could not subsist and be preserved under section 109.

Though there are *dicta* in the recent case of *R.* v. *Sikyea*[51] supporting Greene J.'s approach to hunting rights, the approach seems out of line with the equitable treatment heretofore accorded Indian rights by the courts. In the previous cases there was no question that the promise of an annuity would be kept. As the court said in *Attorney-General of Canada* v. *Attorney-General of Ontario*, it did not matter to the Indians where the money was coming from. It does, of course, matter to them where they hunt and fish; the privilege is thus attached to land and would appear to constitute a trust or interest other than that of the province in the land. But if the view in *R.* v. *Commanda* is to prevail, there seems no reason why it should not extend to post-Confederation treaties; the remarks in the *St. Catherine's* case and in *Ontario Mining Co.* v. *Seybold* were *obiter* and by no means clear. However, there are other doctrines under which these Indian hunting rights are protected from provincial legislation; these are discussed in chapter nine.

JUDICIAL ATTITUDE TOWARDS LANDS
NOT RESERVED BY THE PROCLAMATION

Thus far we have been concerned with property in lands reserved for Indians under the proclamation of 1763. As already seen, however, these comprise only a portion of the lands reserved for Indians. Thus the proclamation does not in terms apply to the territory then comprising Quebec (which now forms a substantial portion of Quebec and Ontario) and the Hudson's Bay Company territory (which now forms a substantial portion of the western provinces and the territories). Nor does it reserve land in the

50/[1897] A.C. 199.
51/(1964), 43 D.L.R. (2d) 150, at 154; *Sikyea* v. *R.*, [1964] S.C.R. 642.

Maritimes or Newfoundland, and whether it applied to some parts of British Columbia and the territories is a matter of controversy.

In the areas not reserved by the proclamation, reserves were established under many different types of authorities and instruments. Thus, reserves had been established in New France even before the conquest; others were set up by British colonial governors by deeds, treaties, and other instruments made under prerogative power; still others can be traced to pre-Confederation statutes.[52] A recent judgment even asserts that an Indian aboriginal right existed apart from grant, the 1763 proclamation merely confirming the right,[53] but this is not in accord with other cases.[54] There must somehow have been a grant to give the Indians rights to land; they do not acquire interests in land simply because they occupy it over a long period. Thus, in *R.* v. *Bonhomme*[55] Indians from a nearby reserve had at various times occupied property beneficially owned by the province of Quebec. It was held that such possession could not remove the fee from the Crown, and there could be no prescription because "les uns possedent par les autres." Only lands specifically set apart and reserved for Indians could be lands reserved for Indians.

As can be seen, the situation is extremely complex and much of the history is obscure. But while variations in different parts of Canada must be kept in mind, there is considerable uniformity in the law throughout the country. This has come about partly by statute and partly by a strong tendency on the part of the courts to construe Indian rights to land in a uniform manner. The attitude of the courts is not surprising, for the granting of reserves followed the general British policy previously outlined, and the courts have taken this into consideration in deciding cases. This can be seen from *Attorney-General of Quebec* v. *Attorney-General of Canada*.[56] There the question was whether, on surrender by the Indians in 1882 of lands appropriated for their use pursuant to Canadian statutes of 1850 and 1851, title vested in the Dominion or the province. If the

---

52/For the many different types of instruments relating to Indian reserves, see *Indian Treaties and Surrenders* (Ottawa), vols. I, II (1905), and III (1912). See also the cases referred to in this chapter. There were, of course, special reserves established by individuals where title is not in the Crown. The Indian Act applies equally to these reserves; see R.S.C. 1952, c.149, s.36.

53/*R.* v. *White and Bob* (1965), 50 D.L.R. (2d) 613, *per* Norris J.A.

54/*R.* v. *Bonhomme* (1917), 16 Ex.C.R. 437; *aff'd* (1918), 59 S.C.R. 679; *In the Matter of the Boundary Between the Dominion of Canada and the Colony of Newfoundland in the Labrador Peninsula*, [1927] 2 D.L.R. 701; *R.* v. *White and Bob* (1965), 50 D.L.R. (2d) 613, *per* Sheppard and Lord JJ.A. (diss.).

55/*Ibid.*

56/[1921] 1 A.C. 401.

Indians had the full beneficial title, there could be no doubt that it would on surrender vest in the Dominion; if, as in the *St. Catherine's* case[57] the province had the beneficial title subject to a usufructuary title in the Indians, the province would have complete beneficial title on the surrender of the Indian title. This required an examination of the statutes under which the reserves were created. The statutes provided for the appropriation of Crown lands and their vesting in a commissioner in trust for the Indians in occupation of them. The commissioner was deemed to be in occupation and possession of lands so appropriated, to be entitled to recover the rents and profits and to defend any rights appertaining to the proprietor or possessor of such land. He was also given full power to concede, lease, or charge such land as any lawful proprietor might do, but he was made subject to instructions of the governor and was bound to report to him and give an account of moneys received. As can be seen, the language of the statute was susceptible of having the meaning attributed to it by the Dominion, that is, as giving the Indians the full beneficial ownership; indeed, this was the view taken by Duff, Anglin, and Idington JJ. in the Supreme Court of Canada in the case of *Attorney-General of Canada* v. *Giroux*.[58] But the Privy Council (in a judgment given, interestingly enough, by Duff J.) did not accept this view. Looking at the recitals and language of the Act and "the policy of successive administrations in the matter of Indian affairs," their Lordships came to the conclusion that the interest of the Indians in the land was "a usufructuary right only and a personal right in the sense that it is in its nature inalienable except by surrender to the Crown." They refused to interpret the power of the commissioner to "concede" the land as including the power of sale.

In the light of this case it would appear to require very strong language indeed to permit a court to interpret Indian rights to land as anything more than a usufructuary right. Some instruments, however, do use very strong terms. For example, after the American Revolutionary War the Mohawk Indians who had supported the British were, by a deed of Governor Haldimand, permitted to settle in an area described therein. This alone would not seem to give anything more than a usufructuary title but on 14 January 1793 a further deed was made by Governor Simcoe under which the King did "Give and Grant to the Chiefs, Warriors, Women and People of the Said Six Nations and their Heirs forever" the land described "To Have and to Hold ... to and for the sole use and Behoof of them and their Heirs forever" and confirmed to them "the full and entire possession,

57/[1889] A.C. 46.
58/(1916), 53 S.C.R. 172; see also *Gouin* v. *Star Chrome Mining Co.* (1917), 24 R.L.N.S. 271.

use, benefit and advantage of the said ... territory." The deed, however, prohibited the Indians from disposing of the land, and following the decision in the case we have just examined, the Indians' interest would appear to be a usufructuary and personal interest.[59]

The tendency to interpret Indian rights in the same manner as in the *St. Catherine's* case[60] can also be seen in the courts' dealings with Indian titles in the former Hudson's Bay Company territory. That territory, it will be remembered, is expressly excluded from the lands reserved by the 1763 proclamation. What rights to the land were possessed by the Indians during the period when the Hudson's Bay Company had jurisdiction over the land is not clear,[61] but in the instruments by which this territory was surrendered to Canada there are several provisions dealing with the matter. Thus the order in council of 23 June 1870, admitting Rupert's Land and the North-Western Territory into the union, provides:[62]

14 Any claims of Indians to compensation for lands required for purposes of settlement shall be disposed of by the Canadian Government in communication with the Imperial Government and the Company shall be relieved of all responsibility in respect of them.

This order in council has appended to it as schedule A an address from the Senate and House of Commons which contains the following clause:[63]

And furthermore that, upon the transference of the territories in question to the Canadian Government the claims of the Indian tribes to compensation for lands required for purposes of settlement will be considered and settled in conformity with the equitable principles which have uniformly governed the British Crown in its dealings with the aborigines.

And schedule B contains the following resolution:[64]

That upon the transference of the territories in question to the Canadian Government it will be the duty of the Government to make adequate provision for the protection of the Indian tribes whose interest and well being are involved in the transfer.

From these provisions, the Appellate Division of the Alberta Supreme Court in *R.* v. *Wesley*[65] reasoned that

... the Indian inhabitants of these Western plains were deemed to have or at least treated by the Crown as having rights, titles and privileges of the same

59/The above documents appeared in *Logan* v. *Styres* (1960), 20 D.L.R. (2d) 416.
60/[1889] A.C. 46.
61/It should be noted that the proclamation makes reference to proprietary colonies.
62/See R.S.C. 1952, VI, 6237, at 6241.
63/*Ibid.*, at 6243.
64/*Ibid.*, at 6248.
65/[1932] 4 D.L.R. 774, at 787.

kind and character as those enjoyed by those Indians whose rights were considered in the *St. Catherine's Milling* case because it is a matter of common knowledge that the Dominion has made treaties with all of the Indian tribes of the North West within the fertile belt in each of which they have given recognition to and provided for the surrender and extinguishment of the Indian title.

This case was followed by Sissons J. of the Territorial Court of the Northwest Territories, who held that the lands of the Eskimos (who are Indians within the meaning of the 1763 proclamation and the BNA Act)[66] are covered by the 1763 proclamation, and, in so far as they are situate within lands formerly owned by the Hudson's Bay Company, they have a similar right pursuant to the documents just mentioned. Consequently they have a right to hunt, trap, and fish at all times on all unoccupied lands in the Arctic.[67] The Northwest Territories Court of Appeal, however, held that it was doubtful, to say the least, whether the Indians of at least the western part of the Northwest Territories could claim any rights under the proclamation. However, it added that this was not important because the government of Canada has treated all Indians across Canada, including those living on Hudson's Bay Company lands, as having an interest in the lands requiring a treaty to effect a surrender.[68] The latter judgment was later affirmed by the Supreme Court of Canada.[69] Yet one must not carry the reasoning of the Northwest Territories Court of Appeal too far. The recognition during the first part of the century by the government of Canada of the Indian title in the Prairie provinces and the territories may certainly be looked upon as giving the Indians a usufructuary right because the lands in the Prairie provinces were vested in the Dominion until 1930 and this is still the case in the territories. But mere recognition of the Indian title by the government of Canada in other parts of Canada can hardly give a title to the Indians, as *Ontario Mining Co.* v. *Seybold*[70] shows. In any event, however, the courts have recognized that the rights of Indians in the territories are governed by rights similar to those accorded by the proclamation.

A similar attitude has been adopted in New Brunswick,[71] and there are

---

66/*Reference as to whether "Indians" includes Eskimos*, [1939] S.C.R. 104.
67/*R.* v. *Kogogolak* (1959), 28 W.W. R. 376; *R.* v. *Sikyea* (1962), 40 W.W.R. 494; *R.* v. *Koonungnak* (1963), 45 W.W.R. 282; *R.* v. *White and Bob* (1965), 50 D.L.R. (2d) 613, *per* Norris J.A.
68/*R.* v. *Sikyea* (1964), 43 D.L.R. (2d) 150; se also *R.* v. *White and Bob, ibid., per* Sheppard and Lord JJ.A. (diss.).
69/*Sikyea* v. *The Queen*, [1964] S.C.R. 642.
70/[1903] A.C. 73.
71/*Doe d. Burk* v. *Cormier* (1891), 30 N.B.R. 142; *Warman* v. *Francis* (1906), 20 D.L.R. (2d) 627.

judicial pronouncements that a similar situation prevailed in British Columbia,[72] though some judges have expressed a contrary opinion.[73]

VARIATIONS AMONG THE PROVINCES

We may now turn to a more detailed examination of the situation in each province. Newfoundland has no Indian reserves, but in the *Labrador Boundary* case[74] it was argued that the proclamation of 1763 applied to the Indians who were settled between the Atlantic seaboard of Labrador and the watershed. However, the Privy Council rejected the contention, pointing out that the reservation is confined to "the said Indians," that is, Indians described in the preceding paragraph of the proclamation as nations or tribes of Indians with whom the king was connected and who lived under his protection. From the report of the Lords of Trade of 8 June 1763, on which the proclamation was based, their Lordships determined that the Indians so described consisted of the tribes of the Six Nations settled round the Great Lakes or beyond the sources of the rivers which fell into the St. Lawrence from the north. This would exclude Indians residing beyond the sources of the rivers which flow into the Gulf of St. Lawrence or into the Atlantic; further, the lands occupied by these Indians would not fall within the description of "lands and territories lying to the westward of the sources of the rivers which fall into the sea from the west and north-west."

The reserves for Indians in the Maritimes would appear to have been of a similar character to those covered by the proclamation of 1763. This certainly is true of New Brunswick. There has never been any doubt that Indian lands in that province, like all ungranted lands, remained vested in the Crown.[75] This view was confirmed by an act of 1844[76] which permitted the governor to sell portions of the reserves and use the proceeds for the benefit of Indians. The act was continued by the Revised Statutes of 1854[77] and was in force at Confederation. In *Doe d. Burk* v. *Cormier*,[78] Allen C.J. expressed the view that the reserves in New Brunswick were not affected by the proclamation, though he agreed that they were of the

72/See *per* Boyd C. in *St. Catherine's Milling and Lumber Co.* v. *R.* (1886), 10 O. R. 196; *R.* v. *White and Bob* (1965), 50 D.L.R. (2d) 613, *per* Norris J.A.; see also H. B. Hawthorn, C. S. Belshaw, and S. M. Jamieson, *The Indians of British Columbia* (London, 1958), c.5.
73/*R.* v. *White and Bob, ibid., per* Sheppard and Lord JJ.A. (diss.).
74/*In the Matter of the Boundary Between the Dominion of Canada and the Colony of Newfoundland in the Labrador Peninsula*, [1927] 2 D.L.R. 401.
75/*Doe d. Burk* v. *Cormier* (1891), 30 N.B.R. 142; *Warman* v. *Francis* (1960), 20 D.L.R. (2d) 627.
76/7 Vict., c.47(N.B.).   77/R.S.N.B. 1854, c.85.   78/(1891), 30 N.B.R. 142.

same character, but Anglin J. in *Warman* v. *Francis*[79] was of the opinion that the proclamation applied to New Brunswick reserves if and when made. It seems clear from the words of the proclamation that it did not reserve lands in New Brunswick, but one need not speculate on the matter; both cases are clear that the protection accorded to reserves established there is similar to that accorded under the proclamation.

It is interesting to note that in 1762 the Governor of Nova Scotia (then including New Brunswick and Prince Edward Island) issued a proclamation, in accordance with royal instructions, affording a protection to lands reserved for Indians similar to that later inserted in the proclamation of 1763.[80] This would indicate that reserves in Nova Scotia and Prince Edward Island are in the same position. And as Boyd C. pointed out in the *St. Catherine's* case,[81] the legislatures of both provinces appear to have acted on that basis.[82] In these three provinces there never seems to have been any general grant like the proclamation of 1763,[83] though grants of specific reserves were made from time to time.[84] When land was reserved for the Indians it continued to belong to the Crown for the benefit of the province, subject to a usufructuary right in favour of the Indians. The underlying title remained in the province after Confederation.[85]

In recent years, however, an important modification has been made in two of the provinces. New Brunswick, in 1958,[86] and Nova Scotia, in 1959,[87] entered into identical agreements with the federal government under which the provinces transferred to Canada all their rights and interests in reserved lands, except minerals, a term that is broadly defined to include, *inter alia*, oil and natural gas, and lands lying under highways.

79/(1960), 20 D.L.R. 627.
80/See *ibid.*
81/*R.* v. *St. Catherine's Milling and Lumber Co.* (1888), 10 O.R. 196, at 221 *et seq.*
82/See R.S.N.S. 1851, c.28, esp. s.5, and c.58, s.3; R.S.P.E.I. 1856, c.10.
83/Note that in a treaty signed at Boston on 15 December 1725 and ratified at Fort Annapolis, Nova Scotia, on 13 May 1728 and in the Articles of Submission signed at Boston, 15 August 1749, the Indians acknowledged the dominion of His Majesty over all the territories now comprising the Maritime provinces; see in this connection *R.* v. *Syliboy*, [1928] 1 D.L.R. 307; see the Boston treaty in *Indian Treaties and Surrenders* (Ottawa), 1905), vol. II, at 198–204. The treaty is referred to in *R.* v. *Syliboy* and in *R.* v. *Simon* (1958), 43 M.P.R. 101.
84/See *R.* v. *St. Catherine's Milling and Lumber Co.* (1888), 10 O.R. 196. See also *Indian Treaties and Surrenders* (Ottawa), vols. I, II (1905), and III (1912). The establishment of the New Brunswick reserves is briefly discussed in W. S. MacNutt, *New Brunswick, A History: 1784–1867* (Toronto, 1963), at 300–1.
85/*Doe d. Burk* v. *Cormier* (1891), 30 N.B.R. 142; *Warman* v. *Francis* (1960), 20 D.L.R. (2d) 627.
86/7 & 8 Eliz. II, c.47(Can.); 7 Eliz. II, c.4(N.B.).
87/7 & 8 Eliz. II, c.50(Can.); 8 Eliz. II, c.3(N.S.).

Consequently, on a surrender by the Indians, the whole beneficial interest vests in Canada. However, the provinces may, under the agreement, elect to purchase the land at a price to be agreed upon, and if agreement is not reached in thirty days, at a price to be settled by arbitration. There is also a provision under which Canada is to revest the land in the province if the band residing on it becomes extinct, but this expression does not include enfranchisement. Paragraph 2 of the agreement also confirms previous grants made by the federal government of lands surrendered by the Indians, except in so far as such grants purport to transfer minerals. Finally, the mining regulations under the Indian Act are to apply to prospecting, mining, and other dealings in minerals on reserves and all minerals referred to in paragraph 2 of the agreements, and any payment made under such regulations is to be paid to the receiver general of Canada for the benefit of the Indian band from whose reserves such monies are derived.

In Ontario and Quebec the Indian lands are of several types. The colony of Quebec as defined in the proclamation of 1763 did not come within the lands reserved by the proclamation. In the area formerly part of that colony, some of the reserves originated before the conquest; others arose under pre-Confederation statutes; still others were created by grants made pursuant to the governor's executive power.[88] Part of the lands reserved by the proclamation were added to the colony by the Quebec Act of 1774.[89] When, by the operation of the Constitutional Act of 1791[90] Quebec was divided into Upper and Lower Canada, part of the original colony and the land so reserved fell within Upper Canada and part within Lower Canada; and since by the operation of section 6 of the BNA Act, 1867, Upper and Lower Canada became Ontario and Quebec, respectively, it follows that the Indian lands in those provinces at Confederation consisted of some falling under the proclamation and others owing their origin to other instruments. Further tracts of land reserved by the proclamation were added to those provinces by the Ontario Boundaries Extension Act, 1912,[91] and the Quebec Boundaries Extension Act, 1912.[92] These acts, which extended Ontario and Quebec to the shores of Hudson Bay also contained lands formerly belonging to the Hudson's Bay Company. As we have seen, the lands formerly held by that company are in a similar position to those reserved by the proclamation but in any

88/For different types of instruments relating to Indian reserves, see *Indian Treaties and Surrenders* (Ottawa), vols. I, II (1905), and III (1912); see also the cases referred to in this chapter; a pre-conquest reserve modified by later statute is discussed in *Mowat v. Casgrain* (1897), 6 Que. Q.B. 12.
89/14 Geo. III, c.83(Imp.).   90/31 Geo. III, c.31(Imp.).
91/2 Geo. V, c.40(Can.).   92/2 Geo. V, c.45(Can.).

case the boundary extension acts have provisions under which the Indian title in the lands transferred to the provinces thereby is recognized and continued under the management of the federal government.[93] These acts go on to provide that while the surrender of reserves may be obtained by the provinces, they can only do so with the approval of the governor in council. However, unlike the situation that would have existed under the proclamation, the province concerned must bear the charges and expenditures in connection with such surrenders. As can be seen, these provisions avoid some of the problems relating to the surrender of reserves and the compensation payable to the Indians. Much of the Indian lands in Ontario and Quebec have now been surrendered in exchange for smaller reserves, compensation, and often a right to hunt and fish on the ceded territories.[94]

Any discussion of the situation in Ontario must be in the light of a Dominion-provincial agreement of 24 March 1924, validated by statutes of both jurisdictions.[95] The agreement deals not only with property in Indian reserves but also with their administration; and although the latter is more germane to legislative power, for clarity the whole agreement will be examined here. It first provides (in paragraph 1) that the reserves in the province are to be administered by the Dominion for the benefit of the Indian bands to which they have been allotted, and authorizes the Dominion government, upon surrender by any such band for the purpose, to sell, lease, or otherwise dispose of such reserves, the proceeds thereof to be applied for the benefit of such band, but if the band becomes extinct or its reserve is declared by the superintendent general of Indian affairs to be no longer required for the band, the reserve shall thereafter be administered by the province; any balance of the proceeds from any disposition made pursuant to the agreement which is no longer required for the band shall be paid to the province with accrued unexpended simple interest thereon. Paragraph 2 then provides that dispositions made under paragraph 1 may include or may be limited to minerals (including precious minerals) but are subject to the provisions of the Ontario Bed of Navigable Waters Act. Paragraphs 3 to 6 provide for prospecting and mining claims on the reserves. Persons authorized under Ontario law to prospect for minerals are to be permitted to enter, prospect, and stake claims on reserves in accordance with that law, on obtaining permission from the Indian agent and complying with the conditions laid down by him, and no other person is to be permitted to prospect thereon. However, the

93/2 Geo. V, c.40, s.2(a) to (c) (Can.); 2 Geo. V, c.45, s.2(c) to (e) (Can.).
94/See *Indian Treaties and Surrenders* (Ottawa), vols. I, II (1905), and III (1912). See also the cases referred to in this chapter.
95/(1924), 14 & 15 Geo. V, c.48(Can.); (1924), 14 Geo. V, c.15(Ont.).

staking of a mining claim on a reserve is to give only such rights as are provided for in the Indian Act or other law dealing with the disposition of Indian lands. Paragraph 6 provides that any consideration, whether by way of purchase money, rent, royalty, or otherwise in respect of any disposition of a mining claim, or of any reserve where, to the knowledge of the Department of Indian Affairs, the consideration was affected by the existence or supposed existence of minerals in the land, shall be divided into two parts, one half to be paid to the province, the other to be dealt with by the Dominion as provided in paragraph 1 of the agreement. Paragraph 7 provides that paragraph 6 shall not apply to Indian reserves established under a treaty of 1873 therein described, and that nothing in the agreement is to detract from the rights of the Dominion to lands granted for the use of Indians by letters patent under the Great Seal of Upper Canada, the province of Canada, or Ontario, or in any minerals vested for such use by the operation on such letters patent of any statute of Ontario. Paragraph 8 prohibits the Dominion from disposing of water power in reserves which, in their natural condition, have a greater capacity than 500 horsepower, except with the consent of the government of Ontario and in accordance with such agreement as may be made for the division of any consideration given therefor. Paragraph 9 validates earlier dispositions of reserves by the Dominion, subject to the Ontario Bed of Navigable Waters Act and to the appropriation of the proceeds therefrom as provided in paragraph 1, but any consideration received by Ontario from earlier dispositions of reserves is to continue to remain under the exclusive control of the province. Finally, paragraph 11 provides that nothing in the agreement, except the provisions respecting the Bed of Navigable Waters Act shall affect the interpretation of any letters patent, conveyance, or contract made under the direction of either government.

The Prairie provinces – Manitoba, Saskatchewan, and Alberta – were carved out of land reserved under the proclamation and territories formerly held by the Hudson's Bay Company.[96] The latter territories have been held to be subject to Indian rights similar to those provided for under the proclamation.[97] But the law respecting Indian lands in those provinces is now governed by provisions of the resources agreements of 1930.[98] Each of these agreements provides that Indian reserves, including those selected and surveyed but not yet confirmed, shall continue to be vested in the Crown and administered by the government of Canada for

96/See pp. 27–8, 29, 34.
97/*R.* v. *Wesley*, [1932] 4 D.L.R. 774; *R.* v. *Kogogolak* (1959), 28 W.W.R. 376; *R.* v. *Sikyea* (1962), 40 W.W.R. 494; *R.* v. *Koonungnak* (1963), 45 W.W.R. 282.
98/Paras. 11 to 13, Manitoba agreement; paras. 10 to 12, Saskatchewan and Alberta agreements; validated by the BNA Act, 1930, 21 Geo. V, c.26(Imp.).

the purposes of Canada. In addition, the provinces, upon request of the superintendent general of Indian affairs, are to set aside, out of unoccupied Crown lands transferred to them by the agreements, such further areas as the superintendent, in agreement with the provincial minister of mines and natural resources, may select as necessary to Canada to fulfil its obligations under the treaties with the Indians, and such areas shall thereafter be administered by Canada as if they had not been transferred to the province under the agreements. However, paragraphs 1 to 6 and 8 of the agreement between the Dominion and Ontario of 24 March 1924 (except so far as they relate to the Bed of Navigable Waters Act) are to apply to reserves so set aside by the provinces; these provisions also apply to the reserves selected and surveyed before the making of the resources agreements except that such lands or the proceeds of the disposition thereof shall not become administrable by or be paid to the province. Finally, the resources agreements give the Indians the right to trap and fish at all seasons on unoccupied Crown lands; this right is more germane to legislative power over Indian lands and will be examined in that connection.[99]

The Yukon and Northwest Territories consist partially of Hudson's Bay Company lands.[100] The remainder is considered by some judges to fall within the proclamation,[101] but higher authority has it that some or all of it was probably *terra incognita* when the proclamation was issued.[102] But the practical result is the same. Those who hold these lands not to be covered by the proclamation have held that the territories are subject to rights like those which exist under the proclamation because the government of Canada has treated all Indians, including those living on Hudson's Bay Company lands, as having an interest in the land requiring a treaty to effect its surrender.[103] But the Dominion parliament has complete legislative jurisdiction over these areas and could make whatever alterations it wished to these rights, whatever their origin may be. Consequently a careful examination of the Indian Act and any other statute applying to the territories would have to be made to determine the extent to which such rights have been altered. It is also arguable that the Dominion government may, by virtue of its right of administration flowing from parliament's legislative power over lands reserved for Indians, make whatever alterations to these rights it may desire by executive act, so long as it does nothing inconsistent with the Indian Act or other statute. The proclama-

99/See pp. 180–2.
100/*R.* v. *Kogogolak* (1959), 28 W.W.R. 376; *R.* v. *Sikyea* (1962), 40 W.W.R. 494; *R.* v. *Koonungnak* (1963), 45 W.W.R. 282.
101/*Ibid.*
102/*R.* v. *Sikyea* (1964), 43 D.L.R. (2d) 150; *aff'd*: *Sikyea* v. *R.*, [1964] S.C.R. 642.
103/*Ibid.*

tion only gives a usufructuary right to the Indians "for the present until our [that is, the Queen in council's] further pleasure be Known."[104] These matters will be discussed in chapter eight.

Indian lands in British Columbia have an exceedingly complicated history.[105] For the purposes of a general exposition of their legal nature it is unnecessary to go into this history in any detail, but it is interesting to note that in the pre-Confederation period the governors of Vancouver Island and later of British Columbia acted on the principle that all lands in those colonies belonged to the Crown. There was some recognition of the Indian title and a number of treaties were entered into under which Indians surrendered lands for a consideration, but there was no general policy of having a surrender from the Indians of all tracts of lands appropriated by the white man or of paying compensation to the Indians as was the case in Ontario and the Prairie provinces. Nor was there any general policy regarding reserves; a few had been set aside in areas of settlement but they were much smaller than those of old Canada. The nature of the original Indian title on Vancouver Island was recently discussed by the British Columbia Court of Appeal in *R. v. White and Bob*.[106] Norris J.A. there held that aboriginal rights existed in favour of the Indians from time immemorial and was confirmed by the proclamation of 1763. The other two majority judges expressed no opinion on the point, though they pointed out that the policy of the Crown and of the Hudson's Bay Company was to purchase the land from the Indians, and they recognized the hunting rights reserved by the Indians under such a purchase by the Hudson's Bay Company as being valid notwithstanding provincial legislation; provincial legislation in violation of such rights would be void as contravening section 91(24) of the BNA Act. The dissenting judges, Sheppard and Lord JJ.A., were of the opinion, however, that the 1763 proclamation had no application to Vancouver Island since it was then unknown to the Crown. The same view was recently taken by Schultz Co. Ct. J. who also held that aboriginal rights have no legal validity unless recognized by treaty or statute.[107]

For present purposes we need not consider these divergent views because the existing nature of the Indian title to reserved lands in British Columbia has been settled by a series of Dominion-provincial agreements.

104/See *St. Catherine's Milling and Lumber Co.* v. *R.* (1889), 14 A.C. 46; *R.* v. *Sikyea, ibid.; aff'd: Sikyea* v. *R., ibid.*
105/See H. B. Hawthorn, C. S. Belshaw, and S. M. Jamieson, *The Indians of British Columbia* (London, 1958), c.5 on which the following account is based. See also, *per* Boyd C., in *St. Catherine's Milling and Lumber Co.* v. *R.* (1888), 10 O.R. 196.
106/(1965), 50 D.L.R. (2d) 613; affirmed without reference to the point: (1966), 52 O.L.R. (2d) 481.
107/*R.* v. *Discon and Baker* (1968), 67 D.L.R. (2d) 619; Clement shared this view, see his *Canadian Constitution* (3rd ed., London, 1916), at 634.

The first of these was comprised in term 13 of the terms of union of the province with Canada, which reads as follows:

13 The charge of the Indians, and the trusteeship and management of the lands reserved for their use and benefit, shall be assumed by the Dominion Government, and a policy as liberal as that hitherto pursued by the British Columbia Government shall be continued by the Dominion Government after the Union.

To carry out such policy, tracts of land of such extent as it has hitherto been the practice of the British Columbia Government to appropriate for that purpose, shall from time to time be conveyed by the Local Government to the Dominion Government in trust for the use and benefit of the Indians on application of the Dominion Government; and in case of disagreement between the two Governments respecting the quantity of such tracts of land to be so granted, the matter shall be referred for the decision of the Secretary of State for the Colonies.[108]

After Confederation discontent arose among the Indians of British Columbia and a continuing dispute went on between the Dominion and the province regarding the size of reserves; the Dominion sought to have reserves of areas similar to those in eastern Canada; the province was convinced that a system of extensive reserves was unsuitable to the west-coast Indians. The dispute continued for many years; numerous agreements were entered into and several royal commissions were appointed, but it was not finally settled until the 1930s. From our point of view, the important question is whether the reversionary interest in the reserves is owned by the province or the Dominion. In an early agreement with British Columbia the Dominion had agreed that any "extra land required by any reserve shall be allotted from Crown lands, and any land taken off a reserve shall revert to the province."[109] From this, Boyd C., in the *St. Catherine's* case,[110] concluded that, from a legal standpoint, the reserves in British Columbia were in the same position as those in other parts of Canada. Certainly the agreement made it clear that the reversionary right to Indian lands was in the province. But this was altered by the McKenna-McBride Agreement of 24 September 1912, under which the province abandoned its reversionary interest to the Dominion subject to the condition that

... in the event of any Indian tribe or band in British Columbia at some future time becoming extinct, then any land within the territorial boundaries of the Province which have been conveyed to the Dominion as aforesaid for such tribe or band, and not sold or disposed of as hereinbefore mentioned, or any unexpended funds being the proceeds

108/See R.S.C. 1952, VI, at 6264.
109/See *R. v. St. Catherine's Milling and Lumber Co.* (1888), 10 O.R. 196, at 234.
110/*Ibid.*

of any Indian reserve in the Province of British Columbia, shall be conveyed or repaid to the Province.[111]

The McKenna-McBride arrangement did not originally apply to the lands in the Railway Belt and the Peace River block, but it was made applicable to them by Dominion-provincial agreement of 22 March 1929.[112] Under this agreement it was provided that Indian reserves should be excepted from the reconveyance of the Railway Belt and Peace River block, by the Dominion to the province, and that such reserves should be held in trust and administered by the Dominion under the terms and conditions of the McKenna-McBride Agreement. Consequently Indian reserves were not affected by the transfer of the Railway Belt and Peace River block to the province in 1930, the agreement being expressly continued by paragraph 13 of the agreement providing for the transfer.[113]

Finally, in 1943, a further agreement was entered into regarding mining on the reserves in the province.[114] The agreement recites that, though the reserves had been conveyed to the Dominion in trust for the Indians, precious minerals are not incidents of land and so continued to belong to the province; since both precious and base minerals are closely associated, the development of minerals in the reserves was impractical. To remedy the situation the agreement provides that the administration, control, and disposal of all minerals and mineral claims, precious and base, in all Indian reserves in the province shall be subject to the laws of the province. Several provisos are made. Existing leases under section 50(2) of the Indian Act, as it then existed, are not affected; the permission of the Indian agent to enter or prospect on reserves is given only to persons approved by the gold commissioner and is then subject to such terms and conditions as may be specified by the Indian agent; and base minerals and mineral rights come under the agreement only upon being surrendered pursuant to the Indian Act. In the definition of minerals there are important exclusions, notably coal, petroleum, and natural gas, and any stone mined for building purposes. All the revenues resulting from the minerals or mineral claims, whether by way of purchase money, royalty, licence fees, or otherwise are to be collected by the Department of Mines of British Columbia. Half of such moneys belong to the province, the rest is to be paid yearly to the Dominion to be dealt with as provided in paragraph 7 of the McKenna-McBride agreement of 1912.

111/*Report of Royal Commission on Indian Affairs for the Province of British Columbia* (Ottawa, 1916), 10, at 11. The province interprets "extinct" as including enfranchisement.
112/Confirmed by P.C. 208 of 3 Feb. 1930 (Can.).
113/Validated by the BNA Act, 1930, 21 Geo. V, c.26(Imp.).
114/Confirmed by (1943), 7 Geo. V, c.19(Can.).

CHAPTER EIGHT

Federal Legislative and Executive Power

LEGISLATIVE POWER RESPECTING
FEDERAL PROPERTY

Section 91 (1A) of the British North America Act, 1867 (formerly section 91(1) but re-numbered by the BNA Act (No. 2), 1949)[1] expressly provides that the federal parliament has exclusive power to make laws respecting "The Public Debt and Property," though the power might well have existed by virtue of the prerogative.[2] The section, of course, refers to the public debt and property of the Dominion only, not to that of the provinces.[3] To fall within the section, property need not be owned by the Crown directly; legislative jurisdiction under section 91(1A) extends to lands and goods held by federal Crown corporations.[4] The section also gives legislative authority to the Dominion over new areas of territory and new jurisdictional rights, such as offshore mineral rights, that may be available to Canada under international law.[5] Nor does it matter how the Dominion acquired the property, whether under a constitutional provision (such as section 108 of the BNA Act), purchase, confiscation, or expropriation.[6] In a word, the term "property" in section 91(1A) is used in its broadest sense and includes every kind of asset and partial interest.[7] But,

1/13 Geo. VI, c.81(Imp.); note that in Newfoundland, legislative authority over property transferred to the Dominion under the terms of union is expressly given to the Dominion parliament: see term 36, validated by the BNA Act, 1949, 12 & 13 Geo. VI, c.22(Imp.).
2/See F. R. Scott, "The Constitutional Background of the Taxation Agreements" (1955), 2 *McGill L.J.*, at 6; F. R. Scott, "Our Changing Constitution" (1961), 55 *Proc. Royal Soc. Can.*, 3rd ser., at 83.
3/*Deeks McBride Ltd.* v. *Vancouver Associated Contractors Ltd.*, [1954] 4 D.L.R. 844.
4/See, inter alia, *R.* v. *Powers*, [1923] Ex.C.R. 131; *R.* v. *Red Line Ltd.* (1930), 54 C.C.C. 271; *Reid* v. *Canadian Farm Loan Board*, [1937] 4 D.L.R. 248; *Validity and Applicability of the Industrial Relations and Disputes Investigation Act*, [1955] S.C.R. 529, at 554, per Rand J.; *Lazare* v. *St. Lawrence Seaway Authority*, [1957] Que. S.C. 5; *City of Ottawa* v. *Shore & Horwitz Construction Co. Ltd.* (1960), 22 D.L.R. (2d) 247.
5/*Re: Offshore Mineral Rights of British Columbia*, [1967] S.C.R. 792.
6/*Deeks McBride Ltd.* v. *Vancouver Associated Contractors Ltd.*, [1954] 4 D.L.R. 844.
7/*Reference re Employment and Social Insurance Act*, [1936] S.C.R. 427, per

on a complete transfer of property to anyone else, it ceases to be public property and is no longer subject to the jurisdiction of parliament as such.[8] This applies even though there may still be some obligations remaining upon the grantee in connection with the grant, as where the grantee is still liable to pay the costs of survey and a small sum of money for incidental expenses.[9]

It follows from this broad definition of property that the Dominion's legislative power under this head is quite extensive. In exercising the power it may pass laws that would normally fall within provincial competence. Thus, in *R. v. Red Line Ltd.*,[10] it was held that the Federal District Commission might validly regulate the use of its roadways and consequently grant the exclusive privilege to any person to run sightseeing buses thereon. Moreover, if the federal government has an interest in property it may legislate respecting that property in such a way as to displace ordinary provincial law. For it should be observed that the Dominion may legislate respecting its property notwithstanding anything in the BNA Act.[11] Thus sections 33 and 34 of the Soldier Settlement Act which provide that, in the absence of the Board's consent, livestock sold to a settler by the Board should be exempt from provincial laws requiring registration of documents, and that such livestock could not be alienated or encumbered to the prejudice of the Board's rights, have been held *intra vires*.[12] Again in *Spooner Oils Ltd. v. Turner Valley Gas Conservation Bd.*,[13] the Supreme Court of Canada made clear that rights given to a lessee of Dominion public lands either by Dominion regulations or under the lease could not be interfered with by provincial legislation. In *Maunsell v. Lethbridge Northern Irrigation District*,[14] however, Stuart J. doubted whether

Duff C.J. and Davis J. (diss.), at 431; see also *R. v. Bell Telephone Co.* (1935), 59 Que. K.B. 205, at 212; for ownership of partial interests, see *inter alia*, *R. v. Powers*, [1923] Ex.C.R. 131; *Spooner Oils Ltd. v. Turner Valley Gas Conservation Bd.*, [1933] S.C.R. 629.

8/See *Attorney-General of British Columbia v. Attorney-General of Canada* (1889), 14 A.C. 295; *McGregor v. Esquimalt and Nanaimo Ry.*, [1907] A.C. 462; *Burrard Power Co. v. R.*, [1911] A.C. 87; *Spooner Oils Ltd. v. Turner Valley Gas Conservation Bd.*, [1933] S.C.R. 629; *Mercury Oils Ltd. v. Vulcan-Brown Petroleums Ltd.*, [1943] S.C.R. 427.

9/See *Calgary and Edmonton Ry. v. Attorney-General of Alberta* (1911), 45 S.C.R. 170; *Mercury Oils Ltd. v. Vulcan-Brown Petroleums Ltd.*, [1943] S.C.R. 37.

10/(1930), 54 C.C.C. 271; *Validity and Applicability of the Industrial Relations and Disputes Investigation Act*, [1955] S.C.R. 529, at 554, *per* Rand J.; *R. v. Hughes* (1958), 122 C.C.C. 198; see also *R. v. Glibbery* (1963), 36 D.L.R. (2d) 548.

11/Section 91 so provides; see *Reference re Employment and Social Service Insurance Act*, [1936] S.C.R. 427.

12/*R. v. Powers*, [1923] Ex.C.R. 131.

13/[1933] S.C.R. 629.

14/[1925] 4 D.L.R. 70.

the mere ownership of property in the streams in Alberta was sufficient to clothe the Dominion with legislative power as against the civil rights of other parties to whom the Crown in right of the Dominion grants an interest in the waters in the land. If this means that the Dominion cannot, under the guise of legislating respecting its public property, make laws that in pith and substance fall within provincial competence, the statement appears to be well founded; but if it means that the Dominion cannot legislate respecting the rights of grantees of partial interests in Dominion lands in such a way as to affect the rights of other persons relating to such interests, then, as the foregoing cases show, it is clearly wrong.

THE FEDERAL "SPENDING POWER"

By far the most important problem relating to section 91(1A) is the extent of the authority it gives the federal parliament to expend money, or, as it is often called, the federal "spending power." For it is evident that if section 91(1A) is broadly construed, it constitutes, along with the extensive powers of taxation under section 91(3), a powerful instrument for implementing policies not otherwise falling within the purview of section 91. To give some notion of the dimensions of the problem, some of the expenditures of Parliament relating to matters not otherwise governed by section 91 must be mentioned. In addition to the subsidies guaranteed under various constitutional instruments,[15] the federal parliament pays the provinces vast subsidies under authority of federal statutes.[16] Again, it makes extensive grants to individuals, organizations, and public authorities as well as to the provinces, not only for schemes falling under other

15/The first constitutional provision was section 118 of the BNA Act, 1867, 30 & 31, c.31(Imp.), followed by terms in the terms of union with British Columbia (see R.S.C. 1952, VI, 6259, at 6262 (term 3)) and with Prince Edward Island (R.S.C. 1952, 6271, at 6273–7) and the Alberta Act (1905), 4 & 5 Edw. VII, c.3, ss.18–20 (Can.) and the Saskatchewan Act (1905), 4 & 5 Edw. VII, c.42, ss.18–20(Can.). These provisions were made obsolete by the BNA Act, 1907, 7 Edw. VII, c.11(Imp.) and section 118 of the BNA Act, 1867, was repealed by the Statute Law Revision Act, 14 Geo. VI, c.6(Imp.). See also the agreements with Manitoba (paras. 20–22), Saskatchewan (paras. 21–23), Alberta (paras. 20–22), and British Columbia (para. 24) validated by the BNA Act, 1930, 21 Geo. V, c.26(Imp.) and terms 26, 28, and 29 of the terms of union with Newfoundland, validated by the BNA Act, 1949, 12 & 13 Geo. VI, c.22(Imp.).
16/Among these may be mentioned the Provincial Subsidies Act, R.S.C. 1952, c.221; The Maritime Provinces Additional Subsidies Act, 1942 (1942–43), 6 Geo. VI, c.14(Can.). See also Federal Provincial Fiscal Arrangements Act (1960–61), 9 & 10 Eliz. II, c.58; amended (1962–63), 11 & 12 Eliz. II, c.14(Can.); (1965), 14 Eliz. II, c.18, s.30(Can.); (1966–67), 14, 15 & 16 Eliz. II, c.89. See J. A. Maxwell, "A Flexible Portion of the British North America Act," (1933), 11 *Can. Bar Rev*, at 148.

federal heads of power, but for many ordinarily governed by provincial law.[17] By attaching conditions to such grants, it can powerfully influence the scope and direction of such schemes. The federal spending power is today one of the principal factors shaping Canadian federalism. It underlies such major social service schemes as family allowances,[18] the Canada Council,[19] and federal grants to universities,[20] to name a few, and it formed the legal basis for the tax-rental agreements.[21]

The federal parliament's power to lend is at least co-extensive with its power to spend.[22] Indeed, since loans do not involve the final expenditure of money, control may be maintained after the money has been parted with. To illustrate the importance of the lending power it is sufficient to mention the National Housing Act, 1954.[23]

In addition to grants of money, the Dominion has itself entered into many areas where it would not have jurisdiction except in some cases under the "Peace, Order, and Good Government" clause.[24] For example, it has been held that it can expend its money in establishing a Federal District Commission or a National Battlefield Commission.[25] If activities of this kind were the only ones in which the Dominion entered, the power would be of secondary importance. But it has gone into many other fields the economic and political implications of which are of the highest importance.[26] Thus it sells insurance[27] and is engaged through the Canadian

17/See D. V. Smiley, *Conditional Grants and Canadian Federalism* (Toronto, 1963).
18/R.S.C. 1952, c.109; amended (1957), 5 & 6 Eliz. II, c.14, s.10(Can.); (1966-67), 14, 15 & 16 Eliz. II, c.96, s.64.
19/(1957), 5 & 6 Eliz. II, c.3(Can.).
20/Federal Provincial Fiscal Arrangements Act (1960–61), 9 & 10 Eliz. II, c.58; amended (1962–63), 11 & 12 Eliz. II, c.14; (1965), 14 Eliz. II, c.18, s.30; (1966–67), 14, 15 & 16 Eliz. II, c.89(Can.).
21/See F. R. Scott, "The Constitutional Background of the Taxation Agreements" (1955), 2 *McGill L.J.*, p. 6; Scott, however, grounds the spending power in the prerogative.
22/This is the view expressed in Gouin and Claxton, *Legislative Expedients and Devices Adopted by the Dominion and Provinces*, A Study Prepared for the Royal Commission on Dominion-Provincial Relations (Ottawa, 1939).
23/(1953–54), 1 & 2 Eliz. II, c.23; amended (1956), 4 & 5 Eliz. II, c.9; (1957–58), 6 Eliz. II, c.18; (1958), 7 Eliz. II, c.3; (1959), 7 & 8 Eliz. II, c.6; (1960), 8 & 9 Eliz. II, c.10; (1960–61), 9 & 10 Eliz. II, cc.1, 61; (1962–63), 11 & 12 Eliz. II, c.17; (1964–65), 13 & 14 Eliz. II, c.15; (1965), 14 Eliz. II, c.3; (1966–67), 14 & 15 Eliz. II, c.58; (1967–68), 16 & 17 Eliz. II, c.39(Can.).
24/See *R.* v. *Red Line Ltd.* (1930), 54 C.C.C. 271; *Attorney-General of Canada* v. *Attorney-General of Ontario*, [1937] A.C. 355 (affirming *sub. nom., Reference re Employment and Social Insurance Act*, [1936] S.C.R. 427); *Angers* v. *Minister of National Revenue*, [1957] Ex. C.R. 83.
25/*R.* v. *Red Line Ltd.* (1930), 54 C.C.C. 271.
26/See R. E. Hodgetts, "The Public Corporation in Canada," in W. Friedman, *The Public Corporation, A Comparative Symposium* (Toronto, 1954), at 51 *et seq.*;

Wheat Board in the purchase and sale of wheat[28] and, through the Polymer Corporation, in the production and sale of synthetic rubber and allied products. In entering these fields, the Dominion has several important advantages over its competitors. It is free of provincial regulatory legislation because the provinces cannot legislate respecting Dominion public property,[29] and it is also exempt from provincial taxation, whether the property is owned directly or through a Crown corporation (as contrasted with an independent, government sponsored corporation).[30]

At the same time, in entering fields ordinarily within provincial competence the Dominion does not possess all the advantages it has regarding matters otherwise falling within the federal legislative sphere. Where a matter is justified by some other head of power it can exclude competitors or compel anyone to deal with it,[31] an advantage of which it cannot avail itself when a matter is within provincial competence. Again, though the Dominion may purchase whatever is necessary for any of its businesses it cannot expropriate except for purposes otherwise falling within federal legislative authority.[32]

Despite its paramount importance there are surprisingly few cases on the federal spending power. The most important is the *Unemployment Insurance* case.[33] There a Dominion statute provided for a system of unemployment insurance by means of the following scheme. A fund was created out of moneys provided in part from compulsory contributions by employers and employees in insured employments, and in part by appropriations from the Dominion treasury. The administration of the fund was entrusted to a board and unemployment benefits were payable by the board out of the fund to designated classes of unemployed persons under prescribed statutory conditions. The Dominion argued, *inter alia*, that an

B. Laskin, *Canadian Constitutional Law* (3rd ed., Toronto, 1966), at 563–64; F. R. Scott, "Our Changing Constitution" (1961), 55 *Proc. Royal Soc. of Can.*, 3rd ser., at 83.
27/Government Annuities Act, R.S.C. 1952, c.132; Crop Insurance Act, (1959), 7 & 8 Eliz. II, c.42; amended (1964–65), 13 & 14 Eliz. II, c.28; (1966–67) 14 & 15 Eliz. II, c.37(Can.).
28/Canadian Wheat Board Act, R.S.C. 1952, c.44; amended (1952–53), 1 & 2 Eliz. II, c.26; (1957), 5 & 6 Eliz. II, c.6; (1962), 10 & 11 Eliz. II, c.21; (1967–68), 16 & 17 Eliz. II, c.5(Can.).
29/See p. 190.
30/See pp. 134, 161–3, 190.
31/As it once did in the case of Air Canada and the Canadian Broadcasting Corporation.
32/See pp. 148–9.
33/*Attorney-General of Canada* v. *Attorney-General of Ontario*, [1937] A.C. 355; see also in the Supreme Court of Canada, *sub nom.*, *Reference re Employment and Social Insurance Act*, [1936] S.C.R. 427. The BNA Act, s.91(2A) as enacted by the BNA Act, 1940, 3 & 4 Geo. V, c.36(Imp.) now expressly authorizes the federal parliament to legislate respecting unemployment insurance.

obligation imposed on employers and employees was a mode of taxation, and that moneys so raised became public property; that being so the Dominion had complete legislative power to direct that such moneys should be applied in forming an insurance fund to be paid in accordance with the Unemployment Insurance Act. This argument found favour with Duff C.J. and Davies J. but a majority of the Supreme Court of Canada (Rinfret, Kerwin, Crocket, and Cannon JJ.) held that the Act was not in pith and substance an exercise of the powers of raising money by taxation and making laws for the disposal of public property, but dealt with the regulation of employment service and unemployment insurance.[34] The majority view was upheld in the Privy Council where the attitude of their Lordships was given as follows:

That the Dominion may impose taxation for the purpose of creating a fund for special purposes, and may apply that fund for making contributions in the public interest to individuals, corporations or public authorities, could not as a general proposition be denied. Whether in such an Act as the present compulsion applied to an employed person to make a contribution to an insurance fund out of which he will receive benefit for a period proportionate to the number of his contributions is in fact taxation it is not necessary finally to decide. It might seem difficult to discern how it differs from a form of compulsory insurance, or what the difference is between a statutory obligation to pay insurance premiums to the State or to an insurance company. But assuming that the Dominion has collected by means of taxation a fund, it by no means follows that any legislation which disposes of it is necessarily within Dominion competence.

It may still be legislation affecting the classes of subjects enumerated in s. 92, and, if so, would be ultra vires. In other words, Dominion legislation, even though it deals with Dominion property, may yet be so framed as to invade civil rights within the Province, or encroach upon the classes of subjects which are reserved to Provincial competence. It is not necessary that it should be a colourable device, or a pretence. If on the true view of the legislation it is found that in reality in pith and substance the legislation invades civil rights within the Province, or in respect of other classes of subjects otherwise encroaches upon the provincial field, the legislation will be invalid. To hold otherwise would afford the Dominion an easy passage into the Provincial domain. In the present case, their Lordships agree with the majority of the Supreme Court in holding that in pith and substance this Act is an insurance Act affecting the civil rights of employers and employed in each Province, and as such is invalid.[35]

While supporters of the constitutionality of the spending power have derived comfort from this quotation,[36] Quebec's Tremblay Commission has asserted that what the Privy Council had in mind was that the federal

34/*Reference re Employment and Social Insurance Act*, [1936] S.C.R. 427.
35/*Attorney-General of Canada* v. *Attorney-General of Ontario*, [1937] A.C. 355, at 366–67.
36/The different views on the subject are reviewed in Smiley, *Conditional Grants and Canadian Federalism* (Toronto, 1963), c.II.

parliament may create funds and expend them for purposes otherwise falling within federal power.[37] However, it seems reasonably clear that the passage asserts the federal parliament's competence to create funds by taxation and to distribute them by grants in any manner it sees fit, subject to the qualification that it must stop short of a scheme which in its true character is not an exercise of jurisdiction over public property but legislation in respect of a provincial matter. The act was held *ultra vires* because, and only because, it was in pith and substance an insurance Act affecting the civil rights of employers and employed in each province. This becomes evident on examination of the majority judgments of the Supreme Court of Canada with which the Privy Council agreed. The majority did not disagree with Duff C.J. and Davies J. that the federal parliament had a right to levy taxation and dispose of its money in any manner it saw fit in the exercise of its power over public property. They simply felt the impugned statute was not really legislation relating to public property at all, but was legislation respecting unemployment insurance. At one point, Kerwin J. (with whom Rinfret J. concurred) made it abundantly clear that parliament may expend its money in any way it pleases; he said:

... Parliament, by properly framed legislation may raise money by taxation and dispose of its public property in any manner that it sees fit. As to the latter point, it is evident that the Dominion may grant sums of money to individuals or organizations and that the gift may be accompanied by such restrictions and conditions as Parliament may see fit to enact. It would then be open to the proposed recipient to decline the gift or to accept it subject to such conditions. As to the first point, it is also undoubted, I conceive, that Parliament, by properly framed legislation may raise money by taxation, and this may be done either generally or for the specific purpose of providing the funds wherewith to make grants either before or after the conferring of the benefit.[38]

And Rinfret J. (with whom Kerwin and Crocket JJ. agreed) also noted that "... the benefits conferred on the employees by the Act are not gifts with conditions attached, which the employees are free to accept or not; the conditions attached to the benefits are made compulsory terms of all contracts in the specified employments ..."[39]

The Exchequer Court in *Angers* v. *Minister of National Revenue*[40] later upheld the validity of conditional grants – in that case, family allowances – even though not falling under other heads of section 91. Dumoulin J. found justification for his judgment in the "Peace, Order, and Good

37/*Report of the Royal Commission of Inquiry on Constitutional Problems* (Quebec, 1956), vol. II, at 216 *et seq.*
38/[1936] S.C.R. 427, at 457.   39/*Ibid.*, at 454–55.
40/[1957] Ex.C.R. 83. Old age pensions are specifically provided for by section 94A of the BNA Act, 1867, as enacted by the BNA Act, 1951, 14 & 15 Geo. VI, c.32(Imp.); note the declaratory form and the paramountcy of the province.

Government" clause, though it could have been based on section 91(1A). This line of reasoning, be it noted, parallels the approach taken respecting provincial public property. The provinces may attach conditions and restrictions to dispositions of their public property even though these may affect matters normally falling within federal legislative jurisdiction.[41]

The spending power seems inherent in Canadian federalism. Section 102 of the BNA Act, which provides that federal public moneys are "to be appropriated for the Public Service of Canada," cannot be narrowly construed. It must be read in the light of section 118 which provides for the payment of subsidies "by Canada to the several Provinces for the Support of their Governments and Legislatures"; lest the importance of this provision be underrated, it should be remembered that it originally accounted for nearly half the provincial revenues.[42] As Duff C.J. indicated, in the *Unemployment Insurance* case, section 102 in no way restricts parliament's discretion under section 91(1A) of determining which objects are and which are not within the scope of the words "for the Public Service of Canada."[43] The federal taxing power must also be looked at in this light.[44] It is written in very broad terms, providing for "The raising of Money by any Mode or System of Taxation." It is true that the Privy Council has stated that the federal taxing power does not extend to direct taxation for the raising of a provincial revenue (which is vested exclusively in the provinces)[45] and that it has left open the question whether Canada may impose indirect taxes for provincial purposes,[46] but these statements can hardly be expanded to prevent Canada from levying taxes to be distributed as subsidies or grants to the provinces because the BNA Act itself made provision for this and it is difficult to see how such payments can be distinguished from grants to individuals, organizations, and other public authorities. There seems no legal reason, then, for denying the power of the federal parliament to tax with a view to raising funds to be distributed as grants for such purposes as it may consider desirable.

41/See pp. 164–5.
42/See *Report of the Royal Commission of Inquiry on Constitutional Problems* (Quebec, 1956), vol. I, at 76.
43/*Reference re Employment and Social Insurance*, [1936] S.C.R. 427, *per* Duff C.J., Davis J. concurring (diss.), at 431. This is inherent in the majority judgments and in the judgment of the Privy Council, *Attorney-General of Canada* v. *Attorney-General of Ontario*, [1937] A.C. 355.
44/See G. V. La Forest, *The Allocation of Taxing Power under the Canadian Constitution* (Toronto, 1967), chap. II.
45/See *Citizens Insurance Co.* v. *Parsons* (1881–82), 7 A.C. 96; *Bank of Toronto* v. *Lambe* (1887), 12 A.C. 575; *Caron* v. *R.*, [1924] A.C. 999; *Forbes* v. *Attorney-General of Manitoba*, [1937] A.C. 47.
46/See *Caron* v. *R.*, [1924] A.C. 999.

The real legal issue regarding the federal parliament's power of making grants is the extent to which it can indirectly legislate by imposing conditions and restrictions on gifts. The *Unemployment Insurance* case[47] laid great stress on the compulsory nature of the scheme before it, but there may be circumstances where even a system of voluntary grants may be *ultra vires* because of the nature of the restrictions and conditions accompanying the grants. In *Angers* v. *Minister of National Revenue*[48] the appellant questioned the validity of the Family Allowances Act on the ground that, by making payment of the allowances for children of school age conditional on their attending school, the Act tended to establish compulsory school attendance and to reserve to itself the supervision or training of children, a matter which came within the provincial domain. But Dumoulin J. pointed out that this argument failed to distinguish between a mandatory law compelling an act, and a directory law offering aid on certain conditions. He added that the act made it clear that no interference with the provincial system of education was intended since the schools required to be attended were the ordinary provincial public schools or such other schools as might be approved by the provincial school authorities. He, therefore, held the allowances *intra vires* as falling within the "Peace, Order, and Good Government" clause. The judgment makes clear, however, that a completely different question would be raised if the Dominion sought by means of grants to introduce its own system of education in opposition to that provided by the provinces.

Despite the inability of the Dominion to enact legislation falling in substance within the provincial legislative area by means of its power to legislate respecting the expenditure of its money, parliament may nonetheless achieve its ends in these areas by co-operative arrangements with the provinces. This can be done by a federal statute authorizing the distribution of money to any province on condition that the province adopts legislation falling within the terms of the federal statute or regulations or a Dominion-provincial agreement under the statute.[49] Such schemes as allowances for blind[50] and disabled persons,[51] hospital insurance,[52] and the construction

47/*Attorney-General of Canada* v. *Attorney-General of Ontario*, [1937] A.C. 355.
48/[1957] Ex.C.R. 83.
49/See Gouin and Claxton, *Legislative Expedients and Devices Adopted by the Dominion and the Provinces*, A Study Prepared for the Royal Commission on Dominion-Provincial Relations (Ottawa, 1939), at 20 *et seq.*
50/R.S.C. 1952, c.17; amended (1955), 3 & 4 Eliz. II, c.26; (1957), 5 & 6 Eliz. II, c.14, s.11; (1957–58), 6 Eliz. II, c.4; (1962), 10 & 11 Eliz. II, c.2; (1963), 12 Eliz. II, c.26(Can.).
51/(1953–54), 2 & 3 Eliz. II, c.55; (1957), 5 & 6 Eliz. II, c.14, s.11; (1957–58), 6 Eliz. II, c.5; (1962), 11 Eliz. II, c.3; (1963), 12 Eliz. II, c.26(Can.).
52/(1957), 5 & 6 Eliz. II, c.28; (1957), 6 & 7 Eliz. II, c.6(Can.).

of the trans-Canada highway[53] may be mentioned.[54] Since much of the initiative for these schemes emanates from the federal authorities, it may be surmised that they exercise considerable influence in shaping them. It should perhaps also be noted that the offer of money for certain schemes may have the effect of diverting provincial resources to different areas than they otherwise would. These offers are usually conditional on the provinces' contributing half or some other proportion of the cost. It is difficult for the provinces to refuse grants of money, particularly for schemes for social services; but this may mean that other activities, which the provinces consider more important, may be neglected.[55]

EXECUTIVE POWER RESPECTING FEDERAL PROPERTY

Executive power in Canada follows the grant of legislative power.[56] Consequently the federal government (that is, the Crown acting on the advice of its federal ministers) has executive power over federal public property, and it has the same rights respecting its property as any other property owner.[57] There have been few cases on federal executive power over property, but the cases under the equivalent provincial power should be referred to.[58] Like the provincial power, it may possibly be subject to the limitation that the federal government may not transfer property to a province in the absence of legislation.[59]

Federal executive power respecting its public property cannot be interfered with by provincial legislation.[60] Indeed, it would appear that in exercising executive power relating to its public property the federal government may, under certain circumstances, override provincial legislation relating to private interests. In the *Spooner* case[61] Duff C.J. indicated that where a stipulation in a lease of federal property dealt with the very subject matter covered by provincial legislation, the stipulation in the lease must prevail.

53/R.S.C. 1952, c.269; amended (1956), 4 & 5 Eliz. II, c.12; (1959), 7 & 8 Eliz. II, c.10; (1960), 8 & 9 Eliz. II, c.22(Can.).
54/For other joint schemes, see D. V. Smiley, *Conditional Grants and Canadian Federalism* (Toronto, 1963).
55/See the brief of the province of New Brunswick to the Royal Commission on Banking and Finance.
56/*Liquidators of the Maritime Bank* v. *Receiver General of New Brunswick*, [1892] A.C. 437; *Mowat* v. *Casgrain* (1897), 6 Que. Q.B. 12.
57/See *R.* v. *Red Line* (1930), 54 C.C.C. 271.
58/See p. 167.
59/See pp. 19–20.
60/See p. 238.
61/*Spooner Oils Ltd.* v. *Turner Valley Gas Conservation Bd.*, [1933] S.C.R. 629.

Certain prerogative rights respecting Crown assets should be mentioned in this connection. Among these are the Crown's right of priority for non-commercial debts among creditors of equal degree.[62] This right may be exercised on behalf of either the Dominion[63] or the province,[64] so there is a possibility of conflicting claims. Until recently there was no authority on how the courts would dispose of these claims because in the cases where the question might have arisen the parties agreed to rank *pari passu*;[65] but it has been decided in a recent case that Dominion and provincial claims rank *pari passu* unless, according to one judge, the claims are to an object that cannot be shared, in which case the Dominion claim prevails.[66] In any event the federal parliament may, by legislation, give priority to the Crown in right of the federal government over the Crown in right of the provincial governments, though this must be done in express terms.[67] On the other hand, it is an open question whether a provincial legislature may legislate so as to affect federal prerogative rights;[68] it is certainly clear that it cannot do so except in express terms.[69] In any case,

62/See, *inter alia, R. v. Bank of Nova Scotia* (1885), 11 S.C.R. 1; *Liquidators of the Maritime Bank* v. *Receiver General of New Brunswick*, [1892] A.C. 437; *Crowther* v. *Attorney-General of Canada* (1959), 17 D.L.R. (2d) 437; *R. v. Hamilton* (1963), 37 D.L.R. (2d) 545; *R. v. Workmen's Compensation Board and City of Edmonton* (1963), 36 D.L.R. (2d) 166; *aff'd*: (1963), 42 W.W.R. 226; see a comment by Alan D. Reid (1964), 14 *U. of N.B. L.J.* 45.

63/See, *inter alia, R. v. Bank of Nova Scotia* (1885), 11 S.C.R. 1; *Crowther* v. *Attorney-General of Canada* (1959), 17 D.L.R. (2d) 437; *R. v. Hamilton* (1963), 37 D.L.R. 545.

64/See, *inter alia, Liquidators of the Maritime Bank* v. *Receiver General of New Brunswick*, [1892] A.C. 437; *R. v. Workmen's Compensation Board and City of Edmonton* (1963), 36 D.L.R. (2d) 166.

65/See *In re Silver Bros. Ltd.*, [1932] A.C. 514; see also *Exchange Bank of Canada* v. *R.* (1886), 11 A.C. 157.

66/*Re Walter's Trucking Service Ltd.* (1965), 50 D.L.R. (2d) 711; the qualification was made by McDermid J.A.

67/*Industrial Development Bank* v. *Valley Dairy Ltd. and MacDonald*, [1953] 1 D.L.R. 788; and see *In re Silver Bros. Ltd.*, [1932] A.C. 514; *Stroud* v. *Imperial Oil Ltd.* (1961), 28 D.L.R. (2d) 366; see also *Re McManus*, [1939] 4 D.L.R. 759; *R. v. Polycoating & Films Ltd.* (1965), 51 D.L.R. (2d) 673; *Re R. A. Nelson Construction Ltd.* (1965), 52 D.L.R. (2d) 189.

68/Cf. *Gauthier* v. *R.* (1917–8), 56 S.C.R. 176, per Fitzpatrick C.J. and Idington J.; *R. v. Lithwick* (1921), 20 Ex. C.R. 293; *Re Adams Shoe Co., Ex p. Penetanguishene*, [1923] 4D.L.R. 927; *Toronto and Toronto Electric Comm.* v. *Wade*, [1931] 4 D.L.R. 928; *R. v. Star Kosher Sausage Mfg. Co.*, [1940] 4 D.L.R. 365; *Bowers* v. *Hollinger*, [1946] 4 D.L.R. 186, at 196; *Re Mendelsohn* (1960), 22 D.L.R. (2d) 748; *Re Sternschein* (1965), 50 D.L.R. (2d) 762; and *R. v. Breton* (1968), 65 D.L.R. (2d) 76; with *Dominion Building Corporation* v. *R.*, [1933] A.C. 533; *Bank of Nova Scotia* v. *R.* (1961), 27 D.L.R. (2d) 120; *R. v. Murphy*, [1948] S.C.R. 357; see Gibson, "Interjurisdictional Immunity in Canadian Federalism," (1969), 47 *Can. Bar Rev.* 40.

69/*Gauthier* v. *R.* (1917–8), 56 S.C.R. 176; *R. v. Sandford*, [1939] 1 D.L.R. 374; *Re Mendelsohn* (1960), 22 D.L.R. (2d) 748.

if the prerogative touches federal property, the provinces cannot legislate respecting the matter, for the federal parliament has exclusive jurisdiction over such property. And the foregoing prerogative may be held to be related to property if the view of Duff C.J., that "public property" in section 91(1A) of the BNA Act refers to every kind of asset, is broadly construed.[70] However, if a right is created by a provincial statute, it should be possible to define the rights so as to prevent the federal Crown from benefitting from it.

One case relating to this prerogative, *Exchange Bank of Canada* v. *The Queen*,[71] has given rise to some difficulty. In that case the Crown claimed in right of Canada as well as in right of Quebec against the assets of a bank in process of liquidation. Canada and Quebec did not oppose each other; in fact they were jointly represented by counsel in seeking priority over other unsecured creditors. The Privy Council held that a Quebec statute dealt with the whole question of priorities and effectively barred the Crown's claim to priority. The case was later explained by the Privy Council in the *Liquidator's* case[72] as one which "negatived the preference claimed by the Dominion Government upon the ground that by the law of the province of Quebec the prerogative was limited to the case of the common debtor being an officer liable to the Crown for public monies collected or held by him." Since the Crown in right of the federal government was involved, this amounts to an assertion that in the circumstances of that case, the provincial statute bound the Crown in right of the federal government. As we have seen, however, the preponderance of authority has it that the province cannot bind the federal Crown.

It can, of course, be suggested that the Privy Council in the *Exchange* case overlooked the problem resulting from the fact that the federal Crown was involved, but the possibility of explaining the case as *per incuriam* disappeared with the remarks in the *Liquidator's* case. The explanation of the *Exchange* case appears to be that the provincial statute in question was a pre-Confederation statute which continued in force by virtue of section 129 of the BNA Act.[73] It is true that there is some authority for the view that a pre-Confederation provincial statute cannot affect the Crown in right of the Dominion on the ground that the federal Crown was

---

70/See *Reference re Employment and Social Insurance Act*, [1936] S.C.R. 427, *per* Duff C.J. and Davis J. (diss.), at 431; see also *R. v. Bell Telephone* (1935), 57 Que. K.B. 205, at 212.
71/(1886), 11 A.C. 157.
72/*Liquidators of the Maritime Bank* v. *Receiver General of New Brunswick*, [1892] A.C. 437, at 441.
73/See *Re D. Moore Co. Ltd.*, [1938] 1 D.L.R. 383, *per* Fisher J. and Masten J.A.; see also *Liquidators of Maritime Bank* v. *Receiver General of New Brunswick*

newly created by the BNA Act and could not be caught by a pre-Confederation statute,[74] but that argument seems at variance with the nature of executive government in Canada and the effect of the BNA Act, which was to divide, between the Dominion and the provinces, the legislative and executive subject matter over which each province had power. The executive in Canada is the Queen.[75] If, before Confederation, the Queen's prerogative was bound by a statute in a certain province, it continued to be bound there after Confederation, subject to the statute being repealed by the appropriate legislature after Confederation. (The statute involved in the *Exchange* case could have been repealed by the federal parliament in so far as it affected federal matters, but it was not.) Any other approach to pre-Confederation statutes would have meant that their operation would have continued (by section 129 of the BNA Act) but only in a highly truncated form, for many of the statutes affected prerogative and executive power.

Another explanation of the *Exchange* case is that in Quebec the prerogative is limited by the grant of civil law,[76] a view that was accepted in the Court of Appeal of Quebec in the case.[77] Of this point the Privy Council simply stated that the true effect of the Quebec Act probably was to introduce the law of property in the "Coutume de Paris" for most purposes as the law of Lower Canada from 1774 to 1867, but that at all events there had been a uniform current of decision to that effect in the colony at that time, dating back forty years or so before the date of the codes, which ought not now to be questioned.[78] Whatever explanation is accepted, it is clear that the privileges of the Crown in right of the Dominion to priority over other debtors is governed in Quebec by the pre-Confederation Civil Code of that province.

Another prerogative right affecting public property is that exempting public property from execution. This applies even when the execution

(1888–89), 17 S.C.R. 657; *Re La Chaussure Crescent; Ex Parte Trustee* (1926), 8 C.B.R. 92; *Re Colonial Piano Ltd.* (1926), 8 C.B.R. 266 (*aff'd* (1928), 10 C.B.R. 111). This was the explanation of Dorion C.J. (a judge with whose conclusion the Privy Council substantially agreed); see *R. v. Exchange Bank of Canada* (1885), M.L.R. 1 Q.B. 302.

74/See *Re D. Moore Co. Ltd.*, [1928] 1 D.L.R. 383, *per* Riddell and Middleton JJ.A.; *Re Mendelsohn* (1960), 22 D.L.R. (2d) 748; see also *Holmstead* v. *Minister of Customs and Excise*, [1927] Ex.C.R. 68; see also B. Laskin, *Canadian Constitutional Law* (3rd ed., Toronto, 1966), at 556.

75/BNA Act, 1867, 30 & 31 Vict., c.3, s.9.

76/See *Re Mendelsohn* (1960), 2 D.L.R. (2d) 748, citing *R. v. Bank of Nova Scotia* (1884), before Peters J. (unreported) and *Monk* v. *Ouimet* (1874), 19 L.C.J. 71.

77/*R. v. Exchange Bank of Canada* (1885), M.L.R. 1 Q.B. 302.

78/*Exchange Bank of Canada* v. *R.* (1885), 11 A.C. 157, at 164.

is directed at a third party. Thus, money owing by the Crown to an individual cannot be garnisheed, and a provincial statute could not provide that the federal Crown must comply with such an order.[79]

Finally, the Supreme Court of Canada has recently found a limitation to prerogative rights for the protection of Crown property inherent in the nature of Canadian federalism. In *British Columbia Power Corporation Ltd.* v. *British Columbia Electric Co. Ltd.*[80] it held that in a federal system where legislative power is divided, as are also the prerogatives of the Crown, it is not open to the Crown, either in right of Canada or of a province, to claim a Crown immunity based on an interest in property where its very interest in that property depends completely and solely on the validity of the legislation which it has itself passed, if there is a reasonable doubt of the constitutional validity of such legislation. In such a case the courts have the same jurisdiction to preserve assets whose title is dependent on the validity of the statute as it has to determine the validity of the legislation itself.

LEGISLATION RESPECTING PROVINCIAL PROPERTY

Under its legislative power under section 91, the Dominion may seriously affect provincial public property. Among the enumerated heads of that section under which Dominion laws are most likely to do so are trade and commerce, sea coast and inland fisheries, navigation and shipping, militia, military, and naval service and defence, Indians and lands reserved for Indians, and works and undertakings extending beyond the province; it may also seriously affect provincial property under such non-enumerated powers as that over aeronautics. Canada also exercises considerable powers over provincial public property by virtue of British Empire treaties implemented under section 132 of the BNA Act. An illustration of this is the control exercised by the federal authorities over international rivers, under the Boundary Waters Treaty of 1909.

In this chapter it is possible to examine only the basic principles governing the extent to which these powers may affect provincial property. First of all, the Dominion cannot in substance legislate respecting provincial public property under the guise of regulating a matter, such as fisheries, falling within section 91.[81] Yet if federal legislation affecting provincial

79/*Re Young*, [1955] 5 D.L.R. 225.
80/[1962] S.C.R. 642; cf. *Lovibond* v. *Grand Trunk Ry.*, [1930] A.C. 717; see Strayer, *Judicial Review of Legislation in Canada* (Toronto, 1968), at 82–8.
81/See *Attorney-General of Canada* v. *Attorney-General of British Columbia*, [1930] A.C. 111.

property truly falls within federal legislative power, it will prevail over provincial legislation respecting that property.[82] These statements, of course, are mere applications of general rules respecting the relation between Dominion and provincial legislation. But a special problem arises here: the conflict between federal legislative power and provincial proprietary rights. If either were to prevail entirely, the distributions of legislative power and property under the BNA Act would be frustrated. As Duff J. has said, it has never been suggested that the Dominion alone or a province alone is entitled to alter the terms of the arrangement in that act for the distribution of assets, liabilities, and sources of revenue.[83] However, under that arrangement the provinces were invested with the bulk of the public domain, and therefore effective federal legislation would often be impossible if the federal parliament were wholly incapable of affecting provincial property. The balance struck is best expressed in the *Fisheries* case[84] where the Dominion's power to affect both provincial and privately owned property was discussed. Here is what the Privy Council had to say about the matter:

... the power to legislate in relation to fisheries does necessarily to a certain extent enable the Legislature so empowered to affect proprietary rights. An enactment, for example, prescribing the times of the year during which fishing is to be allowed, or the instruments which may be employed for the purpose (which it was admitted the Dominion Legislature was empowered to pass) might very seriously touch the exercise of proprietary rights, and the extent, character, and scope of such legislation is left entirely to the Dominion Legislature. The suggestion that the power might be abused so as to amount to a practical confiscation of property does not warrant the imposition by the Courts of any limit upon the absolute power of legislation conferred. The supreme legislative power in relation to any subject-matter is always capable of abuse, but it is not to be assumed that it will be improperly used; if it is, the only remedy is an appeal to those by whom the Legislature is elected.[85]

There is no doubt, then, that the Dominion may very seriously affect provincial property by legislation. But legislative power is one thing, property, another; the Dominion cannot exercise, by legislation, what are virtually proprietary rights. Thus an attempt by the Dominion to give itself or an individual the exclusive right to fish in a provincial fishery would be *ultra vires*,[86] except, conceivably, under very special circumstances. This situation is closely akin to expropriation, the most acute form of conflict between legislative and proprietary rights. Before dealing with the federal

82/See pp. 170–3.
83/*Reference re Waters and Water-Powers*, [1929] S.C.R. 200, at 211, 212.
84/*Attorney-General of Canada* v. *Attorney-General of Ontario*, [1898] A.C. 700.
85/*Ibid.*, at 712–13.
86/*Ibid.*; see also *R.* v. *Robertson* (1882), 6 S.C.R. 52.

parliament's power to expropriate provincial property, something must be said of its power to expropriate generally.

EXPROPRIATION: GENERAL

The federal parliament may not authorize the expropriation of property for any purpose it deems fit. Its power appears to be limited to expropriation for purposes within the scope of its legislative authority.[87] This would seem to flow from *R. v. Robertson*[88] where a statute purporting to authorize a grant of an exclusive fishery to a person in waters where the bed was owned by another person was held *ultra vires*. The purported authorization of exclusive rights of fishery on privately owned lands was not an exercise of legislative power over fisheries (which involved the power of regulating, protecting, and improving fisheries) but related to property and civil rights. In that case, of course, the grant of an exclusive fishery could in no way be related to the regulation of fisheries. A different result might follow if it were necessary in the development or conservation of a particular type of fishery for the federal government to have sole control of that type of fishing in an area.

The power of expropriation of privately owned lands would appear to by inherent in most heads of power under section 91 of the BNA Act,[89] as well as expropriation consequent upon a declaration of a work to be for the general advantage of Canada under section 92(10)(c) of that Act.[90] This might possibly include power to expropriate land by virtue of section 91(1A) for the more convenient use of public property, but this would be narrowly construed; the head could not be used as a colourable device for appropriating land for purposes falling outside Dominion legislative power.[91] The federal power of expropriation is by no means limited to purposes coming under enumerated heads of power; expropriation by virtue of the general power to legislate respecting peace, order, and good government is also valid. The Supreme Court of Canada has recently upheld section 13 of the National Capital Act, which authorizes the compulsory taking of land for the development of a National Capital Region on this ground.[92] Finally, there seems no constitutional impediment to the

87/See *Reference re Waters and Water-Powers*, [1929] S.C.R. 200, at 218–19.
88/(1882), 6 S.C.R. 52; see also *Steadman* v. *Robertson* (1879), 18 N.B.R. 580 (reversing the decision in *Robertson* v. *Steadman* (1876), 16 N.B.R. 621) and *Attorney-General of Canada* v. *Attorney-General of Ontario*, [1898] A.C. 700.
89/See *R.* v. *O'Halloran*, [1934] Ex.C.R. 67.
90/*Re Ontario Power Co. of Niagara Falls and Hewson* (1903), 6 O.L.R. 11; aff'd 8 O.L.R. 88; 36 S.C.R. 596.
91/Cf., B. Laskin, *Canadian Constitutional Law* (3rd ed., Toronto, 1966), at 566.
92/*Munro* v. *National Capital Commission*, [1966] S.C.R. 663.

federal parliament expropriating private property without compensation, however undesirable this may be.[93]

We must now review the cases dealing with the federal power of expropriating property owned by the provinces. The cases relating to provincial fisheries, already mentioned, make it clear that while the Dominion may seriously affect proprietary rights in legislating respecting "Sea Coast and Inland Fisheries," it cannot confer upon itself or others proprietary rights to provincial or privately owned fisheries, either directly or by the conferment of exclusive rights of fishery.[94] Nor can it give the right to affix fishing apparatus to the solum where it is owned by the province.[95] A similar view was taken in respect of the power to legislate respecting "Indians and Lands reserved for Indians." In *Ontario Mining Co.* v. *Seybold*[96] the Privy Council stated that the Dominion had no power to appropriate, as reserves for Indians, lands vested in the province, even when the Indians' usufructuary title to such lands had been surrendered to the Crown partly in consideration of reserves being set up on the surrendered lands.

These cases may, at first sight, appear to deny to the Dominion a power to expropriate provincial lands but other cases make that conclusion untenable as a general proposition. Thus it is clear that parliament, in legislating respecting railways under the power given by the combined effect of sections 91(29) and 92(10), may expropriate, or give power to others to expropriate, provincial Crown lands.[97] The same is true of the power to build interprovincial and international canals.[98] Thus in *Lazare*

93/*Fort George Lumber Co.* v. *Grand Trunk Pacific Ry.* (1915), 24 D.L.R. 527, at 528; this also seems to flow from the remarks of Duff J. in *Reference re Waters and Water-Powers*, [1929] S.C.R. 200, who was troubled by remarks of the Privy Council that the Dominion might be compelled to pay compensation when expropriating provincially owned land under an ancillary power; see also *Attorney-General of British Columbia* v. *Canadian Pacific Ry.* (1904–5), 11 B.C.R. 289, per Martin J., at 304. The point has been decided in so far as the provinces are concerned: see p. 173.
94/*R.* v. *Robertson* (1882), 6 S.C.R. 52; *Attorney-General of Canada* v. *Attorney-General of Ontario*, [1898] A.C. 700.
95/*Attorney-General of British Columbia* v. *Attorney-General of Canada*, [1914] A.C. 153; *Attorney-General of Canada* v. *Attorney-General of Quebec*, [1921] 1 A.C. 413.
96/[1903] A.C. 73. This was inherent also in *St. Catherine's Milling and Lumber Co.* v. *R.* (1889), 14 A.C. 46.
97/*Attorney-General of British Columbia* v. *Canadian Pacific Ry.*, [1906] A.C. 204; *Attorney-General of Quebec* v. *Nipissing Central Ry.*, [1926] A.C. 715.
98/*Reference re Waters and Water-Powers*, [1929] S.C.R. 200; *Lazare* v. *St. Lawrence Seaway Authority*, [1957] Que. S.C. 5.

v. *St. Lawrence Seaway Authority*,[99] the Authority was held competent to expropriate lands in an Indian reserve notwithstanding that the underlying title may be vested in the province. Again, the *Montreal Harbour*[100] case decided that the Dominion may expropriate provincial property where the needs of navigation require it.

It should also be noted that provincial quasi-proprietary rights may be effectively taken away from a province by the exercise of a Dominion legislative power or by the mere grant of that power. Thus in the *Fines* case[101] the Privy Council held that the Dominion could vest the right to collect fines in a municipality even if the collection of fines was a "royalty" vested in the province under section 109 of the BNA Act, for this royalty extended only to fines not otherwise appropriated. And, in the *International and Inter-provincial Ferries Reference*,[102] it was held, in effect, that the Crown's power to grant exclusive rights of ferries, though a royalty, was not vested in the provinces under section 109 because the power to grant the right to run an interprovincial or international ferry was obviously vested in the Dominion under section 91(13) which gives it legislative power over "Ferries between a Province and any British or Foreign country or between two Provinces."

The apparent conflict in the cases was dealt with in *Reference re Waters and Water Powers*.[103] Duff J., giving the judgment of the court, expressed the view that different considerations applied to different heads of power. He appears to have thought that the Dominion could not expropriate provincial lands under its legislative power over Indians and fisheries, but that it could do so for the construction of railways or canals. The distinction, he intimated, was justifiable because, under the conditions prevailing in this country, the federal legislative power over railways and canals could not effectively be exercised without power to expropriate provincial Crown lands but that this was not true of legislation respecting fisheries and Indians.[104]

Although the remarks of Duff J. are, as always, entitled to great respect, it should not be forgotten that they were made in a reference, and one, moreover, in which satisfactory answers were virtually impossible. Consequently, his judgment was more an attempt to restate the result of the

99/*Ibid.*; see also *Point* v. *Diblee Construction Co.*, [1934] 2 D.L.R. 785.
100/*City of Montreal* v. *Montreal Harbour Commissioners*, [1926] A.C. 299; Clement, J., had thought otherwise: *Fort George Lumber Co.* v. *Grand Trunk Pacific R. Co.* (1915), 24 D.L.R. 527.
101/*Toronto* v. *R.*, [1932] A.C. 98.
102/(1905), 36 S.C.R. 206.
103/[1929] S.C.R. 200.
104/See also *In re s.189 Ry. Act*, [1926] S.C.R. 163.

earlier cases than to reformulate principle. Actually the cases are susceptible of a different interpretation. The limitation on the Dominion power expressed in the early cases must be looked at in the context of situations where the Dominion sought in substance to legislate respecting property and civil rights or some other head of provincial power rather than to effect some scheme falling within its legislative sphere. Thus, as appears from *R*. v. *Robertson*,[105] the giving by the Dominion of exclusive power to its licensees to fish on provincial land could not in pith and substance be characterized as legislation respecting fisheries. It was not as if, for instance, it was necessary to take provincial lands to conserve a fishery. It was rather an attempt to control provincial lands, a matter falling under section 92(5) of the BNA Act. The same may be said of the attempted dealing, in *Ontario Mining Co*. v. *Seybold*,[106] with provincial lands for the benefit of Indians without regard to the province's title. Cases may well arise where it is necessary to expropriate provincial lands to create an Indian reserve. It would seem open to the courts to hold valid any federal law expropriating provincial property if it is clearly required for a scheme falling squarely within any federal legislative power. This seems to be consistent with the language of the Privy Council in *Attorney-General for Quebec* v. *Nipissing Central Ry*.[107] Speaking of the passage in the *Fisheries* case where it is stated that the legislative power under section 91 does not authorize the Dominion to transfer the property of the province to itself or others, their Lordships emphasized the qualification to the passage that the power to legislate necessarily enabled proprietary rights to be affected and continued, "... it may be added that where (as in this case) the legislative power cannot be effectually exercised without affecting the proprietary rights both of individuals in a Province and of the Provincial Government, the power so to affect those rights is necessarily involved in the legislative power."[108] As can be seen, their Lordships made no distinction between one head of power and another. The sole question was whether the taking was necessary to an effectual exercise of the power. However, the approach of Duff J. appears valid to the extent that a siuation giving rise to the necessity of expropriating is more likely to arise under some heads of power than under others.

105/(1882), 6 S.C.R. 52; see also *Attorney-General of Canada* v. *Attorney-General of Ontario*, [1898] A.C. 700.
106/[1903] A.C. 73; see also *City of Montreal* v. *Montreal Harbour Commissioners*, [1926] A.C. 299.
107/[1926] A.C. 715.
108/*Ibid.*, at 724; see *City of Montreal* v. *Montreal Harbour Commissioners*, [1926] A.C. 299, at 313, where the Privy Council does not appear to make any distinction in this regard between legislative power over fisheries and navigation.

There are further *dicta* in the Supreme Court of Canada drawing a distinction between expropriation in respect of matters strictly and necessarily falling within the legislative heads in section 91 and ancillary matters which, though not necessarily falling within those heads, are implied to permit the Dominion to fully exercise its legislative functions.[109] This distinction was made to explain the Privy Council's statement, in the *Montreal Harbour* case,[110] that the Dominion legislative power over navigation and shipping is not so extensive as to authorize the compulsory acquisition of provincial lands without paying compensation. In both the *Nipissing*[111] and the *Water Powers*[112] references, the Supreme Court thought the statement was limited to a situation like that in the *Montreal Harbour* case, an attempted vesting of provincially owned harbour property in harbour commissioners, which the Supreme Court believed amounted to an exercise of mere ancillary power. The views of Duff J. in the *Water Powers* reference may thus be summarized: legislation pursuant to ancillary powers will override competent legislation on the same matter in its provincial aspects, but the power to legislate "notwithstanding anything in this [the BNA] Act" applies only to matters necessarily falling within the enumerated heads and not to ancillary powers. Legislation falling squarely within an enumerated head would consequently include the power to take property vested in the province under section 109 of the BNA Act if necessary to execute the power, and there is no obligation to pay compensation. But, apart from the observations in the *Montreal Harbours and Nipissing* cases, there is no authority showing that provincial land could be taken in exercise of an ancillary power, and if the power exists those cases indicate that it can only be exercised by paying compensation.

It is possible, however, to view the observations in the *Montreal Harbours* case in another light. The Privy Council did not necessarily intend to draw a distinction for this purpose between legislation falling squarely within a head of power and an ancillary power.[113] Their Lordships may simply have meant that whenever it is necessary for the federal parliament

---

109/*Reference re s.189 Railway Act*, [1926] S.C.R. 163 (on appeal to the Privy Council, their Lordships expressed their complete agreement with the Supreme Court's judgment: *Attorney-General of Quebec* v. *Nipissing Central Ry.*, [1926] A.C. 715, at 724); *Reference re Waters and Water-Powers*, [1929] S.C.R. 200.
110/*City of Montreal* v. *Montreal Harbour Commissioners*, [1926] A.C. 299, at 313.
111/[1926] S.C.R. 163.
112/[1929] S.C.R. 200.
113/Mr. Justice Laskin believes the ancillary doctrine is heading for eclipse; see B. Laskin, "Occupying the Field: Paramountcy in Penal Legislation" (1963), 41 *Can. Bar Rev.* 234, at 241; see also B. Laskin, *Canadian Constitutional Law* (3rd ed., Toronto, 1966), at 101–04.

in legislating within its powers to completely appropriate provincial land, it cannot do so unless it recognizes the province's property rights under section 109 of the BNA Act by paying compensation. On the other hand the statement requiring the payment of compensation might be interpreted – as was a similar statement in the *St. Catherine's* case[114] – as referring simply to the honourable, as opposed to legal, obligation owing between governments.[115] In any case it is to be hoped that the view that only enumerated powers carry the right to expropriate provincial land will not prevail. For it might on occasion seriously impair the Dominion's ability to legislate on matters of national concern, such as aeronautics.[116]

In the *Water-Powers* reference,[117] Duff J. also asserted that the extent of interference with provincial property must be justifiable under the power exercised; for example, if only surface rights are required for a federal project, the Dominion would not be warranted in taking the subsoil and minerals in provincial lands. He put it this way:

> But although the Dominion may, by legislation enacted in exercise of its exclusive powers relating to railways and canals, authorize the construction through the property of a province of a railway or canal, to which its jurisdiction extends, this does not involve the right to appropriate the whole beneficial interest of the site of the work (including the minerals, for example), for the purpose of making it available as an asset or source of revenue for the benefit of the Dominion or of the Dominion's grantees, where that site is vested in His Majesty and is, by the B.N.A. Act, subject to the administration and control of the Provincial legislature.
>
> Apart from the fact that such legislation would not be legislation exclusively competent to the Dominion, it would transcend the ambit of Dominion authority touching railways or canals, which was not intended to enable the Dominion to take possession of sources of revenue assigned to the provinces, and by assuming the administration of them, to appropriate to itself a field of jurisdiction belonging exclusively to the provinces.[118]

This fragmentation of ownership seems highly inconvenient from a practical standpoint. There is nothing in other cases indicating that the federal power of expropriation is limited in this manner;[119] nor does it seem essential to protect provincial sources of revenue. It is one thing for the courts to prevent colourable attempts by the Dominion to appropriate

114/(1889), 14 A.C. 46.
115/See *Dominion of Canada* v. *Province of Ontario*, [1910] A.C. 637.
116/See *Johanneson* v. *West St. Paul*, [1952] 1 S.C.R. 292; the decision of Duff J., of course, preceded the wide application of the "peace, order, and good government" clause in this case; see also *In re Regulation and Control of Radio Communication in Canada*, [1932] A.C. 304.
117/[1929] S.C.R. 200.   118/*Ibid.*, at 218.
119/The tenor of the judgments in *Attorney-General of Canada* v. *C.P.R. and C.N.R.*, [1958] S.C.R. 285 clearly indicates the judges in that case saw no such limitation.

provincial sources of revenue. It is quite another to unreasonably restrict the scope of federal legislative power when fairly directed at implementing a legitimate federal project. It may also be added that some of the reasoning of Duff J. would seem equally applicable to the taking of privately owned lands. By taking possession of such lands, the Dominion equally displaces the province's power to legislate; the province can no longer legislate over "property and civil rights" regarding the lands under its power because the land becomes the "public property of Canada".[120]

Finally, under section 117 of the BNA Act the Dominion has the right to assume any lands and public property required for fortifications or the defence of the country. This has been held to be an executive and not a legislative power.[121] There is no doubt that under section 91(7) the Dominion may pass laws to effect the same purpose.[122]

TIDAL FISHERIES

There are two types of provincial property where the nature of the federal legislative power is such that the provinces have little or no legislative control over them: tidal fisheries and lands reserved for Indians.

Tidal fisheries were discussed by the Privy Council in the *British Columbia Fisheries* case[123] where their Lordships pointed out that the ownership of the bed of any body of water, whether tidal or non-tidal, carries with it the exclusive right to fish there in the absence of severance by grant or prescription. But in tidal waters, whether on the foreshore, in creeks, or tidal rivers the exclusive character of this right is qualified by the paramount right of the public to fish no matter who owns the bed. This public right, which dates from immemorial antiquity, is subject to some exceptions in England, for the king once had power to grant exclusive fisheries in tidal waters to the owner of the solum. But the king's power was removed by Magna Charta and consequently no private fishery in tidal waters can be granted in Canada in the absence of statute (at least where the fishing does not require use of the solum, a situation that will be discussed later). The right to fish in tidal waters is therefore, a public, not a property, right. It can be regulated, but this comes within "Sea Coast and Inland Fisheries." There is nothing left for the provinces to legislate upon.

At one point in the judgment their Lordships state that no right of property or control of tidal fisheries remained in the provinces because of the

120/See p. 190.
121/*Attorney-General of Quebec* v. *Nipissing Central Ry.*, [1926] A.C. 715; see also p. 24.
122/*L'Union St. Jacques de Montreal* v. *Bélisle* (1874), 6 P.C. 31.
123/*Attorney-General of British Columbia* v. *Attorney-General of Canada*, [1914] A.C. 153.

wide nature of the Dominion's powers of legislation over sea coast and inland fisheries and navigation and shipping. Yet at another point they indicate that ownership of the solum, even in lands underlying tidal waters, carries with it an exclusive proprietary right to fish in the waters above it. This right, it is true, is qualified by the paramount public right to fish in tidal waters, but their Lordships do not say that the private right is destroyed, merely qualified. The possible conflict between the two statements may have practical results in relation to the grant of exclusive fisheries. If the province retains an underlying proprietary right to fish in tidal waters where it owns the soil, the grant by the Dominion to a third person of an exclusive right to fish might well be construed as an interference with the provincial property right rather than a regulation of the fisheries (as has been the case with non-tidal waters).[124] On the whole, however, it would appear that their Lordships held that complete control of ordinary tidal fisheries was in the Dominion.

The public right of fishing in tidal waters did not, however, encompass fishing requiring the use of the solum. Though fishing by means of kiddles, weirs, or other engines involving the use of the soil may be regulated by the Dominion, the province, like any other landowner, has proprietary jurisdiction over the soil. Consequently if fishing requires the use of land belonging to a province, provincial permission to do so would be required.[125]

The foregoing reasoning is based on English law and is consequently applicable to all the provinces governed by the common law. But it does not apply to Quebec. To determine the position in that province, a number of questions were submitted to the Court of King's Bench of the province by the Lieutenant-Governor in council in 1917.[126] When the case came before the Privy Council,[127] their Lordships found it unnecessary to examine the early French law on the subject because that law had been altered by a series of pre-Confederation statutes, which, as interpreted by the Privy Council, established a public right of fishing in tidal waters similar to that existing under English law. Under these statutes, the public has the right to fish in "such fisheries as were either 'deep sea', or so accessible from the sea as to make them natural adjuncts to these fisheries."[128] The fisheries to be regarded as so adjoining would not,

124/*R.* v. *Robertson* (1882), 6 S.C.R. 52.
125/*Attorney-General of British Columbia* v. *Attorney-General of Canada,* [1914] A.C. 153; see also *Attorney-General of Canada* v. *Attorney-General of Quebec,* [1921] 1 A.C. 413.
126/*Re Quebec Fisheries* (1917), 35 D.L.R. 1.
127/*Attorney-General of Canada* v. *Attorney-General of Quebec,* [1921] 1 A.C. 413.
128/*Ibid.,* at 429.

accordingly, include either the fishing in inland lakes or in non-navigable waters. All navigable tidal waters would thus be included.

Unlike the situation under English law since Magna Charta, the last of the pre-Confederation statutes establishing a public right of fishing in Quebec also gave power to commissioners of Crown lands to grant leases and licenses for fisheries, where the exclusive right of fishing did not reside in private persons. Before Confederation such a provision was within the competence of the provincial legislature because it had plenary powers to legislate respecting fisheries. In their Lordships' opinion the provision was of a regulative as well as of a proprietary character. In so far as it was regulative of the fisheries, it passed to the Dominion parliament. In so far as it was proprietary, it passed to the province. Consequently, the Board decided, the power no longer exists in its entirety since the province could not grant exclusive rights to fisheries in tidal waters, because this would affect the public right; and the federal government could not do so on provincial or privately owned land because it would amount to a proprietary right. The Board pointed out, however, that exclusive rights actually granted before 1867 were another matter and would require separate consideration.

The law regarding fishing by kiddles, weirs, and other instruments was held to be the same as English law.[129]

INDIAN LANDS

The Dominion, under section 91(24) of the BNA Act, has exclusive authority to legislate respecting "Indians, and Lands reserved for the Indians." The term "Lands reserved for the Indians" is used in a very broad sense. It was argued in the *St. Catherine's*[130] case that the expression "Indian reserves" was used to designate certain lands in which the Indians had, after the royal proclamation of 1763, acquired a special interest by treaty or otherwise, and not lands occupied by them in virtue of the proclamation. But the Privy Council rejected this contention, stating that the words "... are, according to their natural meaning, sufficient to include all lands reserved, upon any terms or conditions, for Indian occupation. It appears to be the plain policy of the Act that, in order to ensure uniformity of administration, all such lands, and Indian affairs generally, shall be under the legislative control of one central authority."[131]

There seems little doubt that under this heading the Dominion can make any legislation affecting Indian reserves, except that it cannot alter

129/See p. 156.
130/*St. Catherine's Milling and Lumber Co.* v. *R.* (1889), 14 A.C. 46.
131/*Ibid.*, at 59.

the terms of the property arrangements under the BNA Act by, for example, depriving the provinces of their title to Indian lands,[132] or legislate respecting provincial matters under the guise of legislating respecting lands reserved for Indians. As to the former point, however, federal expropriation of provincial lands for the creation of Indian reserves may well be justifiable in certain circumstances.[133]

The extent of the federal legislative power over Indian lands can be seen by looking at the various provisions of the Indian Act,[134] which, either directly or by incorporation of provincial laws, deal with all legal aspects of Indian reserves. There seems little doubt that the federal parliament could abolish the Indian title, and it has done so on at least one occasion.[135] That this is a valid exercise of power seems obvious from *Logan* v. *Styres*,[136] where it was held that, under section 91(24), the Dominion has power to provide for the surrender of reserved Indian lands even though the method provided interferes with the system of internal government of Indian bands. More recently the Supreme Court of Canada has held Indians to have been properly convicted of violating a regulation under the Migratory Birds Convention Act, 1917, prohibiting the shooting of ducks out of season notwithstanding that they acted in reliance on the terms of a treaty permitting them to do so.[137] In *Daniels* v. *White and the Queen*,[138] the Supreme Court of Canada further held that this was so in the Prairie provinces notwithstanding that a provision in each of the resources agreements[139] contains express provisions for securing Indian rights. In the majority's view, that was limited to provincial laws; it did not apply to federal legislation. Moreover Pigeon J. held, as had the court

132/*St. Catherine's Milling and Lumber Co.* v. *R.* (1889), 14 A.C. 46; *Ontario Mining Co.* v. *Seybold*, [1903] A.C. 73; *Reference re Waters and Water-Powers*, [1929] S.C.R. 200.

133/See p. 151.

134/R.S.C., 1952, c.149; for a recent discussion of federal power under section 91(24), see K. Lysyk, "The Unique Constitutional Position of the Canadian Indian" (1967), 45 *Can. Bar Rev.* 513.

135/See The British Columbia Indian Lands Settlement Act (1920), 10 & 11 Vict., c.51(Can.); see also (1960), 8 & 9 Eliz. II, c.20(Can.).

136/(1960), 20 D.L.R. (2d) 416; see also *Point* v. *Diblee Construction Co.*, [1934] 2 D.L.R. 785.

137/*Sikyea* v. *R.*, [1964] S.C.R. 642; affirming *R.* v. *Sikyea* (1964), 43 D.L.R. (2d) 150; *R.* v. *George*, [1966] S.C.R. 267; this set to rest a number of recent cases suggesting limitations on the power of abridging Indian rights: *R.* v. *Sikyea* (1962), 40 W.W.R. 494; see also *Re Noah Estate* (1961–62), 36 W.W.R. 577; *R.* v. *Koonungnak* (1963), 45 W.W.R. 282; *R.* v. *George*, [1963] 3 C.C.C. 109; aff'd: *Attorney-General of Canada* v. *George* (1964), 45 D.L.R. (2d) 709; *Kallooar* v. *R.* (1964), 50 W.W.R. 602; for a discussion, see Schmeiser "Indians, Eskimos and the Law" (1968), 33 *Sask. L.R.* 19.

138/[1968] S.C.R. 517; aff'ing: (1966), 57 D.L.R. (2d) 365.

139/This paragraph is discussed at pp. 180–2.

below, that the Migratory Birds Convention Act, having been enacted
to implement an international treaty, must, in the absence of clear words
to the contrary, prevail over Indian rights even if this involved a breach
of an obligation to the Indians embodied in an Indian treaty. Some support
for this position is also evident in the majority judgment.

The abolition of the Indian right to hunt on Crown lands pursuant to
treaty would not appear to violate the provisions of the Canadian Bill
of Rights.[140] But, when *R.* v. *Sikyea*[141] came before the Territorial Court
of the Northwest Territories, Sissons J. held that it did. The case arose
from the following circumstances. In 1960, following *R.* v. *Kogogolak*[142]
in which the same judge had held a Northwest Territories game ordnance
ineffective to curtail hunting and fishing by Eskimos, the Dominion
parliament enacted an amendment to the Northwest Territories Act[143]
providing that territorial ordnances were, subject to certain exceptions,
applicable to Indians and Eskimos. But, in *R.* v. *Sikyea*, Sissons J. held
the amendment ineffective as violating the Canadian Bill of Rights. He
pointed out that the Bill declared that all acts of parliament must be so
construed as not to infringe upon any rights or freedoms mentioned in
the Bill unless there is a provision in an act that it is to operate notwithstanding the Bill of Rights. The only possible rights the learned judge
could have alluded to in this context are the right of the individual to the
enjoyment of property and the right not to be deprived thereof except by
due process of law which are set forth in section 1 of the Bill. One must
assume that the Indian and Eskimo privileges of hunting and fishing were
not regarded as the enjoyment of property because nothing is said about
it in the higher courts.[144] It might be thought that a different result would
follow from the interference with the Indians' right to reserved lands,
but it is difficult to believe that the termination of such privilege pursuant
to the instrument creating it can be looked upon as an arbitrary revocation
of it. The privilege under the 1763 proclamation was expressly accorded
the Indians (and Eskimos) "for the present, and until our [i.e. the sovereign's] further Pleasure be Known."[145] As the Privy Council put it in the

140/(1960), 8 & 9 Eliz. II, c.44(Can.).
141/(1962), 40 W.W.R. 494; reversed: (1964), 43 D.L.R. (2d) 150, which was
affirmed by *Sikyea* v. *R.*, [1964] S.C.R. 642.
142/(1959), 28 W.W.R. 376; see also *Kallooar* v. *R.* (1964), 50 W.W.R. 602.
143/(1960), 8 & 9 Eliz. II, c.20(Can.); see also a similar amendment to the Yukon
Act (1960), 8 & 9 Eliz. II, c.24(Can.).
144/*R.* v. *Sikyea* (1964), 43 D.L.R. (2d) 150; aff'd: [1964] S.C.R. 642; *Sigeareak
El-53* v. *R.*, [1966] S.C.R. 645.
145/R.S.C., VI, 6127, at 6130; see *Attorney-General of Canada* v. *George* (1964),
45 D.L.R. (2d) 709, per Gibson J.A. (diss.); the majority view was reversed by the
Supreme Court of Canada in *R.* v. *George*, [1966] S.C.R. 267.

St. Catherine's Milling case,[146] the right is dependent on the good will of the sovereign. Responsibility for the exercise of the sovereign's functions in this field is now vested in the federal authorities. Indian and Eskimo rights over the former Hudson's Bay Company territory is of the same character.[147] Apart from the requirements of the Indian Act, the privilege could in all probability also be abrogated by a federal order in council without recourse to parliament.

It should be noted that the administration and control of Indian lands is included in the grant of legislative power.[148] This includes the right of the Crown in right of the Dominion to recover possession of reserved lands improperly in the possession of an individual,[149] and, except as modified by statute, possibly the power of abrogating the Indian title.

OBLIGATIONS AND LIMITATIONS RESPECTING
FEDERAL PROPERTY

Brief mention should be made of a number of obligations respecting federal property. Several charges are imposed on the Dominion consolidated revenue fund by the BNA Act, 1867, and by section 106 these charges must be met before money is appropriated for the public service of Canada. The first charge is the costs, charges, and expenses incident to the collection, management, and receipt of revenues;[150] the second is the annual interest on the public debts of the various provinces for which Canada was made liable at Confederation, subject to reimbursement by the provinces for the excess set forth in the BNA Act;[151] the third charge is for the governor general's salary.[152] Canada is also liable under the constitution for the payment of the salaries and allowances of the lieutenant governors and superior and county judges.[153] In addition by various constitutional instruments Canada must pay subsidies to the various provinces.[154] Apart from financial obligations of this kind several provisions provide for the construction and maintenance of public works. Thus, sec-

146/*St. Catherine's Milling and Lumber Co.* v. *R.* (1889), 14 A.C. 46, at 53–4.
147/See pp. 123–4.
148/*St. Catherine's Milling and Lumber Co.* v. *R.* (1889), 14 A.C. 46, at 59; *Mowat* v. *Casgrain* (1897), 6 Que. Q.B. 12.
149/ *R.* v. *McMaster*, [1926] Ex.C.R. 68.
150/BNA Act, 1867, 30 & 31 Vict., c.3, s.103(Imp.).
151/*Ibid.*, ss.104, 111–15.
152/*Ibid.*, s.105.
153/*Ibid.*, ss.60, 100; see also term 5 of the terms of union with British Columbia (R.S.C. 1952, VI, at 6262); those with Prince Edward Island (R.S.C. 1952, VI, at 6274); term 33 of those with Newfoundland (see Schedule to the BNA Act, 1949, 12 & 13 Geo. VI, c.22(Imp.)).
154/See *supra* note 15.

tion 145 of the BNA Act, 1867, imposed a duty on the government and parliament of Canada to construct the Intercolonial Railway; the terms of union with British Columbia provide for its extension to the Pacific coast,[155] and further guarantees mail service between Victoria and San Francisco, and Victoria and Olympia.[156] Those with Prince Edward Island provide that efficient steam services for the conveyance of mail and passengers are to be established and maintained between the island and the mainland so as to place the island in continuous communication with the Intercolonial Railway and railway system of the Dominion; there is a similar obligation to maintain telegraphic communication between the island and the mainland.[157] Similarly, term 32 of the terms of union with Newfoundland provides that Canada is to maintain, in accordance with the traffic offering, a freight and passenger steamship service between North Sydney and Port aux Basques which, on completion of a motor highway between Corner Brook and Port aux Basques, will include suitable provision for the carriage of motor vehicles.[158] There are also various constitutional provisions expressly imposing obligations upon the federal treasury for services within its legislative sphere,[159] and there are other obligations of a transitional nature.[160] As Duff J. pointed out in the *Reference re Waters and Water-Powers*,[161] the Dominion could not unilaterally legislate to divest itself of these obligations which, therefore, constitute limitations on the Dominion executive and legislative power respecting public property.

The agreements validated by the BNA Act, 1930,[162] also imposed a number of limitations on Canada's legislative and executive powers respecting its public property. Thus it undertook certain obligations respecting Indian reserves, and agreed to continue and to administer the parks described therein as national parks and to retransfer them to the provinces when no longer required for the purpose. These and other provisions affecting the Dominion's legislative and executive power over its property are discussed in other connections.[163]

155/Term 11; see R.S.C. 1952, VI. at 6263.
156/Term 4; see *ibid.*, at 6262.
157/See *ibid.*, at 6274.
158/See BNA Act, 1949, 12 & 13 Geo. VI, c.22(Imp.).
159/See terms 5 and 13 of the terms of union with British Columbia (see R.S.C. 1952, VI, at 6262, 6264); terms of union with Prince Edward Island (see R.S.C. VI, at 6274); terms of union with Newfoundland in Schedule to BNA Act, 1949, *ibid.*, s.31.
160/See term 6 of the terms of union with British Columbia, *ibid.*; terms 28 and 29 of the terms of union with Newfoundland, *ibid.*
161/[1929] S.C.R. 200.
162/21 Geo. V, c.26(Imp.).   163/See pp. 35–45, 129–30.

EXEMPTION OF PUBLIC PROPERTY FROM TAXATION

Section 125 of the BNA Act, 1867, exempts property of the Dominion and the provinces from taxation by the other. The section reads as follows:

125   No Lands or Property belonging to Canada or any Province shall be liable to taxation.

The section prevents indirect control of provincial property – a term including every type of asset or interest[164] – by means of the federal taxing power.[165] It also protects federal property, but this is in any event a concomitant of the doctrine of paramountcy.[166]

Since the provision has been fully examined elsewhere,[167] it suffices here to mention only a few of the most salient points. And, for convenience, the limitation on both the federal and provincial taxing power will receive attention.

Despite the broad terms of the section, it does not prevent federal taxation of federal property or taxation by a province of its property.[168] It merely prevents the federal parliament from taxing provincial property, and the provinces from taxing federal property and, probably, property of another province.[169] And by federal and provincial property is here meant property belonging to the Dominion or province in the sense elsewhere described in this work[170] or to a Crown corporation.[171] In other words, property owned by a private person does not belong to a province merely because it is located there. In fact, private interests in an asset are taxable even though the Crown may also have a partial interest in the asset. For example, in *Smith* v. *Vermillion Hills Rural Council*[172] a lessee of federal land was held liable to pay a provincial tax in respect of his interest. And it does not matter that, because of arrangements between the Dominion and the taxpayer, the Dominion ultimately has to repay him the amount of the tax.[173]

The exemption in section 125 is restricted to the power to tax property;

164/See *R.* v. *Bell Telephone Co.* (1935), 59 Que. K.B. 205, at 210.
165/See *Attorney-General of British Columbia* v. *Attorney-General of Canada* (1922), 64 S.C.R. 377, at 385.
166/See p. 190.
167/See G. V. La Forest, *The Allocation of Taxing Power under the Canadian Constitution* (Toronto, 1967), chap. VIII.
168/*Re Taxation of University of Manitoba Lands*, [1940] 1 D.L.R. 579.
169/See B. Laskin, *Canadian Constitutional Law* (3rd ed., Toronto, 1960), at 769.
170/See pp. 17–18.
171/*City of Halifax* v. *Halifax Harbour Commissioners*, [1935] S.C.R. 215.
172/[1916] 2 A.C. 569.
173/*City of Montreal* v. *Attorney-General of Canada*, [1923] A.C. 136.

it does not apply to legislative power under other provisions of the BNA Act or to other types of taxation. Thus, in *Attorney-General of British Columbia* v. *Attorney-General of Canada*,[174] a province was held liable to pay customs duties under a federal act in respect of liquor imported into the province. A customs duty falls not only under the taxing power but also under the trade and commerce clause. Moreover a customs duty is not a property tax, even though it may affect a province's use of its property.[175]

A province, however, could not levy a tax against the federal government, whether categorized as a property tax or not; the paramountcy doctrine prevents this.[176] However, if the federal government accepts provincial or municipal goods or services, whether in respect of its property or otherwise, it will be subject to a reasonable charge. Thus in *Minister of Justice* v. *Levis*,[177] the Dominion was held liable to pay a fair and reasonable charge for water supplied by a city council under a provincial statute. However, the courts will not permit a province to impose what is in substance a tax under the guise of a regulatory charge.[178]

174/[1924] A.C. 222.
175/See *per* Duff J. in the case in the Supreme Court of Canada: (1922), 64 S.C.R. 377.
176/See p. 190.
177/[1919] A.C. 505.
178/*Société centrale d'Hypothèques* v. *Cité de Québec*, [1961] Que. K.B. 661.

CHAPTER NINE

Provincial Legislative and Executive Power

LEGISLATION RESPECTING
PROVINCIAL PROPERTY

By section 92(5) of the British North America Act each province is given exclusive power to make laws respecting "The Management and Sale of the Public Lands belonging to the Province and of the Timber and Wood thereon." By lands "belonging to the province" is meant lands vested in Her Majesty, but over which the legislature has power of appropriation.[1] Such a power would probably exist by implication; the provinces are certainly empowered to deal with and dispose of their other assets either under head 13 or 16 of section 92 of the BNA Act or by virtue of the prerogative.[2]

The wide ambit of section 92(5) can perhaps best be demonstrated by an examination of *Smylie* v. *R.*[3] where the Ontario Court of Appeal held intra vires an act of that province providing that timber cut under a provincial licence of Crown lands should be manufactured in Canada. It had been argued that the act infringed on section 91(2) of the BNA Act (which gives the Dominion legislative power over trade and commerce) by indirectly prohibiting export to foreign countries, but the contention was rejected on the ground that the act was merely dictating the terms on which the province would dispose of its public property. As Osler J.A. put it, a major source of provincial revenues consists of minerals and timber land; to hold that such legislation relates to trade and commerce would constitute a serious restriction on the province's right to dispose of its property to the advantage of the general interests of the province. Moss J.A. looked at the statute as one of an administrative and directory character addressed to the officials of the Crown Lands Department. He could see no reason why the legislature could not, in respect of this property, do what any other proprietor might do when proposing to dis-

1/See *St. Catherine's Milling and Lumber Co.* v. *R.* (1889), 14 A.C. 46, at 56.
2/B. Laskin in *Canadian Constitutional Law* (3rd ed., Toronto, 1960), at 553 relies on s.91(3), (13), and (16). F. R. Scott believes the provinces have power to expend money by virtue of the prerogative; see F. R. Scott, "The Constitutional Background of the Taxation Agreements" (1955), 2 *McGill L.J.*, at 6; Scott, "Our Changing Constitution" (1961), 55 *Proc. Royal Soc. of Can.*, 3rd ser., at 83.
3/(1900), 27 O.A.R. 172.

pose of property, that is, attach conditions to the grant. There can be no doubt of the correctness of these views since the Privy Council decision in *Brooks-Bidlake and Whittall Ltd.* v. *Attorney-General of British Columbia.*[4] There a provincial act validating a term in licences to cut provincial timber which stipulated that no Chinese or Japanese labour was to be hired in connection therewith was held intra vires. Though legislation respecting "naturalization and aliens" was vested in the Dominion, the act was nonetheless valid under section 92(5).

The provinces have been held to have similar powers to legislate by virtue of section (92(5) in respect of their fisheries, even though the Dominion has extensive powers to legislate respecting "Sea Coast and Inland Fisheries" under section 92(12) of the BNA Act. Indeed, as was pointed out in the *Fisheries*[5] case, a province may legislate on the proprietary aspects not only of provincially owned but also of privately owned fisheries in the province, by virtue of section 92(13) of the BNA Act which gives the provinces power to legislate in relation to property and civil rights. Their Lordships mentioned, as proper subjects of legislation under this head, modes of conveying or disposing of, and the rights of succession to, fisheries. In addition the provinces, under section 92(5), have power to make laws respecting "The Management and Sale of Public Lands," and under this head or section 92(13) they may prescribe the terms upon which provincially owned fisheries may be granted, leased, or otherwise disposed of, and the rights which, consistently with any Dominion regulations respecting fisheries, may be conferred therein.

Their Lordships instanced as good illustrations of valid provincial legislation sections 1375, 1376, and 1377(1) of the Revised Statutes of Quebec. These provisions would, if applicable to all fisheries, ordinarily be regarded as legislation respecting fisheries, but they were expressly restricted to waters within the legislative jurisdiction of the province and so would only apply to provincially owned fisheries. They provided *inter alia* that line fishing and rod and line fishing were alone permitted, that non-residents were not permitted to fish except pursuant to licences valid for the time, places, and persons therein indicated, and that the minister might grant leases to fish in non-navigable waters.

Ontario provisions (similarly restricted to waters in respect of which the province had legislative authority) were also in question in the *Fisheries* case. Though their Lordships did not give any definite answer concerning their validity, the Supreme Court of Canada did.[6] All the judges of that court, except Gwynne J., declared the Ontario provisions, as well

4/[1923] A.C. 450.
5/*Attorney-General of Canada* v. *Attorney-General of Ontario*, [1898] A.C. 700.
6/*Re Provincial Fisheries* (1895), 26 S.C.R. 444.

as articles 1375 to 1378 of the Revised Statutes of Quebec, intra vires except in so far as they might be overridden by valid Dominion legislation. The Ontario provisions regulated *inter alia* the sizes of fish that might be caught, the places where fishing was permitted, the nature of the instruments to be used, and provided for closed seasons. However, one must be cautious in accepting the views expressed in the Supreme Court because the Privy Council expressly disagreed with the approach taken by some of the judges who thought the provinces had jurisdiction over fisheries, subject to the overriding power of the Dominion. Nonetheless the Board did make it clear that a province can deal with provincially owned fisheries as property by, for example, defining the rights which may, consistently with Dominion legislation, be conferred on grantees, lessees, and other persons permitted to use the fisheries by the province. That this gives a province considerable scope to regulate its fisheries is evident from the principles followed in *Smylie* v. *R.*[7] and *Brooks-Bidlake and Whittall* v. *Attorney-General of British Columbia.*[8] Provincial power over provincially owned fisheries is also emphasized by the statement of Strong J. in *R.* v. *Robertson*[9] that "the provincial governments may, without legislation and in exercise of their right of property, restrict their use in any manner which may seem expedient just as freely as private owners might do." In *R.* v. *Wagner,*[10] however, a majority of the Manitoba Court of Appeal held that the establishment of closed seasons was wholly ultra vires the province, but the dissent of Robson J. seems justified; the imposition of a closed season seems to be simply a method of defining the privileges accorded by the province to those to whom it permits the use of its property.

The foregoing remarks must be limited to non-tidal fisheries. In tidal fisheries the public right to fish overrides the proprietary right flowing from the ownership of the subsoil and the Dominion has exclusive legislative capacity to regulate this public right.[11] Even here, however, if use of the solum belonging to the province is required, provincial permission must be obtained; consequently the province may by legislation establish conditions under which this permission might be granted.[12]

Some provinces have special provisions regarding legislative power over fisheries. Each of the resources agreements with Manitoba, Alberta, and Saskatchewan has a paragraph reading as follows:

7/(1900), 27 O.A.R. 172.   8/[1923] A.C. 450.
9/(1882), 6 S.C.R. 52, at 136.   10/[1932] 3 D.L.R. 679.
11/*Attorney-General of British Columbia* v. *Attorney-General of Canada*, [1914] A.C. 153, dealing with the common law provinces; *Attorney-General of Canada* v. *Attorney-General of Quebec*, [1921] 1 A.C. 413, dealing with Quebec. For a more detailed discussion, see pp. 155–7.
12/*Ibid.*

10 Except as herein otherwise provided, all rights of fishery shall, after the coming into force of this agreement, belong to and be administered by the Province, and the Province shall have the right to dispose of all such rights of fishery by sale, licence or otherwise, subject to the exercise by the Parliament of Canada of its legislative jurisdiction over sea-coast and inland fisheries.[13]

This paragraph does not, however, appear to make any distinction between the laws of these provinces and others. Since the resources agreements were in terms entered into to put these provinces on a footing of equality with the others,[14] they should be so interpreted where the terminology permits it. In Newfoundland, term 22 of the terms of union provides for the continuance of Newfoundland fishery laws for a transitional period of five years,[15] but the Dominion's legislative powers in that province would now appear to be the same as in other provinces.[16]

EXECUTIVE POWER RESPECTING PROVINCIAL PUBLIC PROPERTY

Provincial legislative power over its property carries with it the power of administration and control by the provincial executive.[17] This means that a provincial government may, without legislation, exercise in respect of its property the same rights as a private owner, and consequently attach such restrictions as it deems fit when it makes grants by lease or licence.[18] The power to administer and control probably includes power to sell to private individuals or to transfer to the Dominion, but there is some doubt about this.[19] In any case the power of sale is generally controlled by statute.[20]

The provincial power of administration and control of its lands does not apply to lands reserved for Indians. While these lands are vested in the province, they are subject to the Indian's usufructuary title, and since the right to legislate respecting such lands is vested in the Dominion by section 91(24) of the BNA Act, the Dominion government has the management and control thereof.[21]

13/Para. 10, Manitoba agreement; para. 9, Alberta and Saskatchewan agreements; validated by the BNA Act, 1930, 21 Geo. V, c.26(Imp.). The paragraph was briefly discussed in *R.* v. *Wagner*; *R.* v. *Tommasson*, [1932] 3 D.L.R. 679.
14/See the preamble and article 1 of each of these agreements and the preamble to the BNA Act, 1930, *ibid*.
15/Confirmed by the BNA Act, 1949, 12 & 13 Geo. VI, c.22.
16/Term 3, confirmed by *ibid*.
17/See *R.* v. *Robertson* (1882), 6 S.C.R. 52, *per* Strong J., at 136; *Smylie* v. *R.* (1900), 27 O.A.R. 172, *per* Moss J.
18/*Ibid*.
19/The problem is discussed at pp. 157–60.
20/See, for example, the Crown Lands Act, R.S.N.B. 1952, c.53.
21/See p. 114.

Provincial executive power includes a number of prerogative rights and privileges respecting its assets, such as a right of priority over creditors. The Dominion has the same rights and privileges; these have already been discussed.[22]

SIGNIFICANCE OF PROVINCIAL POWER RESPECTING ITS PROPERTY

Smylie v. *R.*[23] illustrates that the provinces' power to control their public property gives them a most effective weapon for controlling their economic destiny. Thus laws such as the one in question in that case have had the effect of developing the pulp and paper industry in Canada, and preventing the export of the material in its raw state for manufacture in the United States.[24] It has also given the provinces some control in areas that otherwise would have been totally within federal competence. Thus there is little question that a provincial statute forbidding a private landowner from exporting timber out of Canada would be ultra vires as dealing with trade and commerce, just as a statute preventing the hiring of Chinese in privately owned coal mines was found ultra vires[25] even though similar prohibitions respecting provincially owned mines are valid.[26]

The provinces have not failed to act to retain or extend this power. For example, since 1884, New Brunswick reserves, in every grant of land, the beds and a strip adjoining the banks of certain rivers so as to have control of the fisheries; it then leases the fishing rights subject to such conditions as it sees fit, and retains in addition valuable water rights.[27] To extend their control over natural resources some of the provinces have declared that all petroleum, minerals, and many other natural resources belong to the provinces; they then control exploration, drilling, and production by means of permits, leases, and licences.[28] Moreover, the provinces can

22/See pp. 143–7.
23/(1900), 27 O.A.R. 172.
24/See Hugh G. J. Aitken, "The Changing Structure of the Canadian Economy," in *The American Economic Impact on Canada* (Durham, N.C., 1959), 1, esp. at 13–15.
25/*Union Colliery Co.* v. *Bryden*, [1899] A.C. 580.
26/*Brooks-Bidlake and Whittall Ltd.* v. *Attorney-General of British Columbia*, [1923] A.C. 450.
27/See G. V. La Forest, "Rights of Landowners in New Brunswick respecting Water in Streams on or Adjoining their Land" (1957), 10 *U. of N.B. L.J.*, 21, at 28–9; *sub nom* "Riparian Rights in New Brunswick" (1960), 3 *Can. Bar. J.*, pp. 135, 178, at 142–43, 180.
28/For the situation in some of the western provinces, see J. B. Ballem, "Constitutional Validity of Provincial Oil and Gas Legislation" (1963), 41 *Can. Bar Rev.* 199. In other provinces, see, *inter alia*, Mining Act (1961), 10 & 11 Eliz. II, c.45, s.8(N.B.); Oil and Natural Gas Act, R.S.N.B. 1952, c.162, ss.2, 1(a); Petroleum

purchase property or expropriate it, even without compensation[29] and, like the Dominion, they have gone into numerous business activities, either directly or through Crown corporations. Among the commercial operations conducted by provincial Crown corporations are telephone systems, power utilities, liquor boards, marketing agencies, and manufacturing establishments.[30] The activities of a provincial Crown corporation are not limited to the confines of the provinces,[31] and it may even enter fields normally within federal jurisdiction (for example, airways), though in such fields its operations would be subject to federal regulatory control.[32] In operating business enterprises, a province has advantages similar to those of the Dominion. Thus, the property of the provinces and provincial Crown corporations is exempt from taxation by the Dominion and probably by other provinces.[33] The provinces do not, however, have the power to create a provincial government monopoly by prohibiting Dominion corporations or Dominion Crown corporations from conducting certain activities in the province.[34]

Like the Dominion, the provinces have made use of their money as a lever for promoting policies they consider desirable.[35] They too, for example, have made use of their spending power to make grants to individuals and public bodies. And there seems no constitutional impediment to prevent the provinces from encouraging schemes falling largely within

and Natural Gas Act, R.S.N.S. 1954, c.215, ss.2, 1(b); Lands and Forests Act, R.S.N.S. 1954, c.145, ss.18, 19; The Oil, Natural Gas and Minerals Act (1957), 6 Eliz. II, c.24, ss.27, 28(P.E.I.). In New Brunswick such a policy was followed from the founding of the province, the governor being instructed not to reserve minerals; see *Gesner* v. *Gas Co.* (1853), 2 N.S.R. 72; these reservations are given a broad meaning under the Mining Act, R.S.N.B. 1952, c.146, s.8; see also the powers of vesting other minerals in the province under an Act Respecting Ownership of Minerals (1953), 2 Eliz. II, c.10(N.B.).

29/See *Municipality of Cleveland* v. *Municipality of Melbourne and Brompton Gore* (1881), 4 L.N. 277; *Florence Mining Co. Ltd.* v. *Cobalt Lake Mining Co.* (1908), 18 O.L.R. 274, *per* Riddell J., at 279; aff'd by the Ontario Court of Appeal and the Privy Council (1918), 43 O.L.R. 474.

30/See A. E. Blakeney, "Saskatchewan Crown Corporations" in W. Friedman (ed.), *The Public Corporation* (Toronto, 1954), at 93.

31/See *Bonanza Creek Gold Mining Co. Ltd.* v. *R.*, [1916] 1 A.C. 566.

32/See A. E. Blakeney, "Saskatchewan Crown Corporations," in W. Friedman (ed.), *The Public Corporation* (Toronto, 1954), at 93. Newfoundland controls an airline company operating throughout the whole Atlantic region of Canada.

33/By virtue of s.125 of the BNA Act: see pp. 161–3. For a more detailed discussion, see G. V. La Forest, *The Allocation of Taxing Power under the Canadian Constitution* (Toronto, 1967), at 150–60.

34/*La Compagnie Hydraulique de St. François* v. *Continental Heat and Light Co.*, [1909] A.C. 194. See also 190–5. In so far as Dominion Crown corporation are concerned, this would be legislation respecting Dominion property.

35/See F. R. Scott, "Our Changing Constitution," (1961), 55 *Proc. Royal Soc. of Can.*, 3rd ser., at 83.

federal regulatory control in the absence of inconsistent federal legislation. The provinces have made grants to bodies outside the province; for example, the province of Quebec has contributed to the Maison canadienne in Paris. F.R. Scott justifies such activities under the Queen's prerogative rights over property independent of legislative power,[36] but they can as easily be explained as legislation respecting the property and civil rights of the Queen in right of the province. A theoretical difficulty arises in connection with grants given outside a province, for a province is limited to taxation in order to the raising of a revenue for provincial purposes but, as Duff C.J. pointed out in the *Reference re Employment and Social Insurance Act*,[37] "the words 'for provincial purposes' mean neither more nor less than this: the taxing power of the legislature is given to them for raising money for the exclusive disposition of the legislature." The provinces have also made extensive use of their lending power. An important aspect of this has been the assistance in developing industries, either by direct loans or by underwriting securities of private corporations. Such activities are limited only by the amount of money capable of being raised by the provinces.

RELATION TO FEDERAL LEGISLATIVE POWER

In the *Smylie*,[38] *Brooks-Bidlake*,[39] and *Fisheries*[40] cases we saw that provincial legislation respecting its property may incidentally affect matters falling within section 91 of the BNA Act. But such legislation must be strictly limited to the control of property; it cannot invade the federal sphere. For example, while a provincial act prescribing the width of tires to be used by vehicles travelling on provincial highways may be intra vires as coming, *inter alia*, within section 92(5) of the BNA Act,[41] this does not enable the province to regulate interprovincial or international traffic under the guise of legislating respecting its roads.[42] Similarly, in *Attorney-General of British Columbia* v. *Attorney-General of Canada*[43] the Privy Council pointed out that an act such as that in question in the *Brooks-Bidlake* case probably could not go beyond providing conditions of renewals.

36/*Ibid.*; see also F. R. Scott, "The Constitutional Background of the Taxation Agreements" (1955), 2 *McGill L.J.*, at 6.
37/[1936] S.C.R. 427, at 434.
38/*Smylie* v. *R.* (1900), 27 O.A.R. 172.
39/*Brooks-Bidlake and Whittall* v. *Attorney-General of British Columbia*, [1923] A.C. 450.
40/*Attorney-General of Canada* v. *Attorney-General of Ontario*, [1898] A.C. 700.
41/*R.* v. *Howe* (1890), 2 B.C.R. 36.
42/*Attorney-General of Ontario* v. *Israel Winner*, [1954] A.C. 541.
43/[1924] A.C. 203.

There is a considerable area over which federal and provincial legislation may overlap, where both may legislate on the same matter under different aspects; for example the Dominion may legislate respecting fisheries *qua* fisheries, while the provinces may pass legislation regarding their fisheries *qua* land. In such a case, where the Dominion has not legislated in the field, provincial legislation will be effective but it must give way to valid Dominion legislation. Thus the legislation in the *Brooks-Bidlake* case was subsequently overridden by Dominion legislation under the Empire treaty clause, section 132 of the BNA Act.[44] Section 132, of course, is a special provision but legislation under section 91 also prevails over section 92. This raises the complicated doctrine of federal legislative paramountcy.[45]

The doctrine has been expressed in various forms, but perhaps the most quoted exposition is that of Lord Tomlin in the *Fish Canneries*[46] case, which reads as follows: "There can be a domain in which provincial and Dominion legislation may overlap, in which case neither legislation will be ultra vires if the field is clear, but if the field is not clear and the two legislations meet the Dominion legislation must prevail." This apparently simple statement bristles with difficulty. It is certain, however, that where federal and provincial legislation conflict, the provincial legislation must give way;[47] for example, a province could not permit fishing in its waters during a closed season established by the Dominion. The same result would probably follow if the federal legislation was obviously intended to cover the whole field, even though there was no actual conflict.[48] Apart from this, however, what is the situation where the provincial legislation is simply more stringent than the federal legislation, as for example, where the closed season in provincial waters for a certain fish is shorter under the provincial than under the federal legislation? Authorities in other fields suggest that both federal and provincial legislation are valid[49]

44/*Attorney-General of British Columbia* v. *Attorney-General of Canada*, [1924] A.C. 203.
45/For discussions of this problem, see B. Laskin, *Canadian Constitutional Law* (3rd ed., Toronto, 1966), at 104 *et seq.*; B. Laskin, "Occupying the Field: Paramountcy in Penal Legislation" (1963), 41 *Can. Bar. Rev.*, at 234; W. R. Lederman, "The Concurrent Operation of Federal and Provincial Laws in Canada," (1962–63), 9 *McGill L.J.*, at 185.
46/*Attorney-General of Canada* v. *Attorney-General of British Columbia*, [1930] A.C. 111, at 118.
47/See *Attorney-General of Ontario* v. *Attorney-General of Canada*, [1896] A.C. 343; *Smith* v. *R.*, [1960] S.C.R. 776, at 800.
48/See W. R. Lederman, "The Concurrent Operation of Federal and Provincial Laws in Canada" (1962–63), 9 *McGill L.J.* 185, at 191–92.
49/See *Provincial Secretary of Prince Edward Island* v. *Egan and Attorney-General of Prince Edward Island*, [1941] S.C.R. 396; *Lord's Day Alliance* v. *Attorney-General of British Columbia*, [1959] S.C.R. 497; *R.* v. *Yolles* (1959), 19 D.L.R.

and this seems consistent with cases like *Smylie* v. *R.*[50] and *In re Provincial Fisheries*[51] which asserted that the provinces have the same rights regarding their property as a private owner.

Sometimes provincial legislation is neither in conflict with, nor more stringent than, federal legislation but is identical or substantially so. A situation of this kind is discussed in *R.* v. *Wagner.*[52] There a Manitoba statute prohibited the possession of fish caught during a time prohibited by law. The same statute adopted by reference certain federal regulations establishing, *inter alia*, a closed season for sturgeon in Manitoba. Wagner was found unlawfully in possession of fish under the Manitoba statute, but an appeal by way of stated case was taken to the Manitoba Court of Appeal to determine whether the accused was rightly convicted under the Manitoba statute while the federal regulations were in force. The reasoning of the judges is not too helpful. Prendergast C.J.M. took the view that the establishment of a closed fishing season was wholly ultra vires the province whether there was Dominion legislation or not, a wholly untenable proposition in view of the authorities already examined. Dennistoun J.A. seems to have shared the view but he did deal with the question of paramountcy. He appears to have thought that whenever the Dominion had occupied the field by legislating on the subject matter, provincial legislation was inoperative; he makes no distinction between conflicting, supplementary, or identical legislation. However, this broad view of paramountcy would, as we have seen, not now be followed. Richards J.A. agreed with both judgments. Robson J.A. dissented on the ground that the provincial legislation, not being in conflict with the federal regulations, was valid as dealing with the management of provincial property. While there is much to be said for the approach of Robson J.A., the authorities have, until recently, favoured the view that where federal and provincial provisions were substantially identical the federal legislation should displace the provincial.[53] However, a recent statement by Martland J. in *Smith* v. *R.*[54] appears to support the opinion of Robson J.A.

Finally, it should be noted that the full development of some provincial

(2d) 19; *O'Grady* v. *Sparling*, [1960] S.C.R. 804; *Mann* v. *R.*, [1966] S.C.R. 238; *McIver* v. *R.*, [1966] S.C.R. 254.
50/(1900), 27 O.A.R. 172.
51/(1895), 26 S.C.R. 444.
52/[1932] 3 D.L.R. 679.
53/See *Lymburn* v. *Mayland*, [1932] A.C. 318, at 326–27; *Home Insurance Co.* v. *Lindal & Beattie*, [1934] S.C.R. 33, at 40; W. R. Lederman in "The Concurrent Operation of Federal and Provincial Laws in Canada" (1962–63), 9 *McGill L.J.* 185, at 196, suggests the avoidance of wasteful duplication of legislation justifies this approach.
54/[1960] S.C.R. 776, at 800.

resources cannot be achieved without the co-operation of the federal and provincial authorities.[55] Only a few examples need be mentioned. Fishing operations requiring the use of the subsoil come within federal legislative jurisdiction respecting fisheries, but where the subsoil belongs to a province its permission to use it must be obtained.[56] Similarly the development of underwater gas wells in navigable waters where the bed is owned by the province is subject to provincial jurisdiction but the developers must comply with federal regulations for the protection of navigation.[57] Again, the development of rivers forming or crossing the international boundary may have to conform to federal and provincial legislation.[58]

EXPROPRIATION

A province may, in the exercise of its legislative power over property and civil rights, expropriate or authorize the expropriation of property, and it may even do so without paying compensation.[59] But there are limits to the power. First of all, the province could not expropriate federal property because legislation respecting such property is within the exclusive competence of parliament.[60] Further, it cannot interfere with federal legislation or mutilate federal undertakings. An example of the courts' resistance to attempts to do this is *Bourgoin* v. *Compagnie du Chemin de Fer de Montreal, Ottawa et Occidental.*[61] There the respondent company had originally been incorporated by a Quebec statute but was subsequently declared to be a work for the general benefit of Canada by a Dominion statute and became a federal railway subject to the Canadian

55/B. Laskin, "Jurisdictional Framework for Water Management" in *Resources for Tomorrow*, Background Papers (Ottawa, 1961), vol. 1, at 211.
56/See *Attorney-General of Canada* v. *Attorney-General of Ontario*, [1898] A.C. 700.
57/*Underwater Gas Developers Ltd.* v. *Ontario Labour Relations Board* (1960), 21 D.L.R. (2d) 345; see also *Normand* v. *St. Laurent River Navigation Co.* (1879), 5 Q.L.R. 215.
58/The federal government has enacted many statutes governing the use of such waters; see, *inter alia*, the International Boundary Waters Treaty Act (1911), 1 & 2 Geo. V, c.28; amended (1914), 4 & 5 Geo. V, c.5; (1952), 1 Eliz. II, c.43; International River Improvements Act (1955), 3 & 4 Eliz. II, c.47(Can.).
59/See *Municipality of Cleveland* v. *Municipality of Melbourne and Brompton Gore* (1881), 4 L.N. 277; *Florence Mining Co. Ltd.* v. *Cobalt Lake Mining Co.* (1908), 18 O.L.R. 274, *per* Riddell J., at 279; affirmed by the Ontario Court of Appeal and the Privy Council (1918), 43 O.L.R. 474; *Nelson* v. *Pacific Great Eastern Ry.*, [1918] 1 W.W.R. 597.
60/See pp. 134–5.
61/(1879–80), 5 A.C. 66; see also *Attorney-General of Alberta* v. *Attorney-General of Canada*, [1915] A.C. 363; *Spooner Oils Ltd.* v. *Turner Valley Conservation Board*, [1933] S.C.R. 629, *per* Duff C.J., at 647. (see pp. 190–5); *Campbell-Bennett Ltd.* v. *Comstock Midwestern Ltd. and Trans-Mountain Pipe Line Co.*, [1954] S.C.R. 207.

Railway Act. The company then purported to convey all its assets and liabilities to the Quebec government by deed and agreed to dissolve itself as soon as the transfer could be perfected. A Quebec statute then confirmed the deed, combined the enterprise of the company and that of another which had made a similar transfer, and dissolved the respondent company. The Privy Council held the deed invalid since the company did not have power to make it and provincial legislation could not validate it and do the other things provided by the Act; a federal statute was required. The recent decision of Lett C.J. in *British Columbia Power Corporation* v. *Attorney-General of British Columbia*[62] asserts a far more serious limitation on the provincial power of expropriation. There British Columbia purported to vest in the province all the shares of a provincially incorporated power company, which was, to the knowledge of the legislature, virtually a wholly owned subsidiary of, and having the same directors and officers as, the plaintiff, a holding company incorporated by the Dominion. The shares constituted the bulk of the assets of the plaintiff, and the legislation had the effect under the circumstances of making it impossible for the plaintiff to carry on a like business. Lett C.J. held that the legislation was specifically aimed at the company and had the effect of destroying the status and powers conferred on it by the Dominion within the reasoning of the Privy Council in *John Deere Plow Co.* v. *Wharton*,[63] *Great West Saddlery Co.* v. *R.*,[64] and *Attorney-General of Manitoba* v. *Attorney-General of Canada*.[65]

These cases undoubtedly offer strong support for the opinion of Lett C.J., but the authorities are certainly open to another interpretation. A later Privy Council case, *Lymburn* v. *Mayland*,[66] indicates that a Dominion company constituted with powers to carry on a particular business is subject to competent legislation of the province as to that business, even if this means that the company's special activities are completely paralyzed. Control over water power within a province ordinarily comes within provincial jurisdiction, and this would include the power of expropriating the property of individuals for the purpose. The mere fact that some, or even all, of this property is owned by a Dominion company or companies is a mere coincidence. The legislation does not on that account cease to be legislation respecting property and civil rights and become legislation respecting companies. Unless this view is adopted, the provinces could be seriously hindered in legislating on a matter that is in substance provincial, by the mere device of incorporating a company under

62/(1963), 44 W.W.R. 65.   63/[1915] A.C. 330.
64/[1921] 2 A.C. 91.   65/[1929] A.C. 260.   66/[1932] A.C. 318.

Dominion law. This could, in the words of Lord Atkin in the *Unemployment Insurance* case,[67] "afford the Dominion an easy passage into the Provincial domain." And, as that case and others show, the courts have shown a strong disinclination to interpret the constitution in this manner, because it would "undermine the constitutional safeguards of Provincial constitutional autonomy."[68] If the judgment of Lett C.J. is accepted, however, the provinces could use the device employed by the province of Quebec in nationalizing the electric-power facilities, namely, purchase of the shares of the companies. It should also be noted that the judgment indicates that a different result might follow if the legislation applied generally and was not specifically aimed at a federal company.

There was another ground of decision in the *British Columbia Power* case:[69] that the company expropriated was an undertaking extending beyond the limits of the province within section 92(10)(a) of the BNA Act and consequently fell within the exclusive jurisdiction of parliament by virtue of section 91(29) of that Act. It is beyond the scope of this work to examine the characteristics of such undertakings and whether or not the company fell within that category.[70] However, assuming that the company was an extra provincial company within section 92(10)(a), it should be noted that the case went further than previous decisions. In other cases where provincial legislation has been held void as infringing upon the legislative power of parliament over extraprovincial undertakings, the legislation either interfered with federal legislation[71] or sought to regulate the undertaking.[72] Here it was simply the property that was transferred. True the province would thereby acquire the control over the undertaking as owner and could also legislate regarding it as its property, but Dominion legislation regarding the undertaking would have to be respected. This point was raised but received only passing attention, the judgment on this part of the case being largely concerned with the question whether the undertaking did fall within section 92(10)(a). The learned judge

67/[1937] A.C. 355, at 367.
68/*Attorney-General of Canada* v. *Attorney-General of Ontario*, [1937] A.C. 326, at 352; see also *Caron* v. *R.*, [1924] A.C. 999, at 1006; *Forbes* v. *Attorney-General of Manitoba*, [1937] A.C. 260.
69/*British Columbia Power Corp.* v. *Attorney-General of British Columbia* (1963), 44 W.W.R. 65.
70/For a discussion of extra-provincial undertakings, see J. B. Ballem, "Constitutional Validity of Provincial Oil and Gas Legislation" (1963), 41 *Can. Bar Rev.* 199, at 219 *et seq.*
71/See, for example, *Campbell-Bennett Ltd.* v. *Comstock Midwestern Ltd. and Trans Mountain Pipe Line Co.*, [1954] S.C.R. 207.
72/See *Toronto Corporation* v. *Bell Telephone Co. of Canada*, [1905] A.C. 52; *Attorney-General of Ontario* v. *Israel Winner*, [1954] A.C. 541.

obviously came to the conclusion that the legislation was in pith and substance legislation relating to an extraprovincial undertaking and not of property and civil rights. It may well be that legislation expropriating extraprovincial companies goes beyond the threshold of permissible provincial action in a federation, but before the decision is accepted its implications should be more carefully weighed. Would, for example, a province be prevented from expropriating lands covered with water because of the legislative jurisdiction of the Dominion over fisheries, and would the situation be different if its purpose was to produce electric power, or operate a mill, or develop the fisheries? The extraprovincial aspects do not altogether change the situation. There seems little doubt that a province may purchase and operate undertakings falling within federal regulatory control and that it may expropriate the shares of a corporation having purely provincial purposes even though the corporation owns considerable assets outside the province.

LEGISLATION RESPECTING INDIAN LANDS

Since the underlying title to lands reserved for Indians belongs to the provinces,[73] legislative power over these lands would in the absence of other provisions vest in the provinces by virtue of their power to legislate respecting public lands belonging to the provinces. But the power to legislate respecting Indians and lands reserved for Indians is, by section 91(24) of the BNA Act, vested in the Dominion, so provincial power in this domain must necessarily be confined within a very narrow compass. A province has power to legislate respecting its underlying title, but is perhaps limited to legislation that transfers title[74] or is based on the assumption of a surrender of the Indian title.

The real problem in this field is to determine the extent to which the provinces may affect persons and activities on Indian lands by virtue of their power to legislate under other heads of section 92, especially heads 13 and 16 which give legislative power respecting property and civil rights and local and private matters. It is clear that the provinces cannot legislate respecting Indians *qua* Indians or Lands reserved for Indians *qua* lands reserved for Indians.[75] At the same time an Indian reserve remains part of

73/*St. Catherine's Milling and Lumber Co.* v. *R.* (1889), 14 A.C. 46.
74/See, for example (1958), 7 Eliz. II, c.4(N.B.); see also pp. 26–7.
75/See *R.* v. *McLeod* (1930), 54 C.C.C. 107; *R.* v. *Smith,* [1935] 3 D.L.R. 703; see also *R.* v. *Hill* (1908), 15 O.L.R. 406. For a recent discussion of many of the following problems, see K. Lysyk, "The Unique Constitutional Position of the Canadian Indian" (1967), 45 *Can. Bar Rev.* 513.

the province,[76] and consequently persons on the reserve are subject to the general laws of the province.[77] Thus in *Carter* v. *Nichol*[78] it was held that a person on an Indian reserve was bound to take the precautions regarding threshing engines required by the Prairie Farm Ordinance. So, too, in *R.* v. *Gullberg*,[79] Lees D.C.J. held that a white man on a reserve is subject to the general laws of the province, and must, therefore, obtain a licence to operate a restaurant on the reserve under the Alberta Restaurant Act. Again in *R.* v. *Morley*[80] the accused was convicted of killing a pheasant in contravention of the British Columbia Game Act. He appealed on the ground that he was on an Indian reserve at the time of the killing, and that the Act was ultra vires in so far as it sought to legislate respecting offences on Indian reserves. The appeal was rejected; the court held that the Act was one of general application and did not infringe on section 91(24) of the BNA Act. It could be justified under section 92(13) or (16) of that Act. Though it might affect persons on Indian reserves, it was not legislation *qua* Indian reserves.

So far the cases have dealt with white men on reserves. In *R.* v. *Groslouis*,[81] Pettigrew J. held that an Indian who resides in an Indian reserve and operates a retail store there must comply with the Quebec Retail Sales Act on a sale to a white man and *semble* to anyone outside the reserve. Sales to Indians on the reserve were exempt but that was by virtue of a section in the Indian Act. The case, it is submitted, was properly decided. For in the absence of inconsistent federal legislation, it is difficult to understand why general provincial legislation should not apply to Indians on a reserve merely because the Dominion has legislative jurisdiction over lands reserved for Indians under section 91(24) of the BNA Act. The case is in accord with the many cases holding that Indians off a reserve are bound by general provincial laws in the absence of conflicting federal legislation.[82]

There are, however, several cases where it has been held that provincial games acts were inapplicable to Indians on a reserve. Thus in *R.* v. *Jim*[83]

76/See *R.* v. *Groslouis* (1943), 81 C.C.C. 167.
77/*R.* v. *Rodgers*, [1923] 3 D.L.R. 414, *per* Dennistoun J. (diss.); *R.* v. *McLeod* (1930), 54 C.C.C. 107; *R.* v. *Commanda*, [1939] 3 D.L.R. 635; *R.* v. *Groslouis* (1943), 81 C.C.C. 167; and see the other cases discussed in this section.
78/[1911] 1 W.W.R. 392, *per* Lamont J.   79/(1933), 62 C.C.C. 281.
80/[1932] 4 D.L.R. 483; see also *R.* v. *McLeod* (1930), 54 C.C.C. 107 where the accused was an Indian agent.
81/(1943), 81 C.C.C. 167.
82/See, for example, *R.* v. *Hill* (1908), 15 O.L.R. 406; *R.* v. *Martin* (1917), 39 D.L.R. 635.
83/(1915), 26 C.C.C. 236.

the accused, an Indian, had killed a deer for his own use and was convicted of violating the provincial Game Act. On appeal Hunter C.J.B.C. quashed the conviction. One ground of decision was that the subject matter was dealt with in the Indian Act, and there is no doubt that this is a valid ground for the decision; for it is clear that the Dominion, in legislating respecting Indians and lands reserved for Indians, may override provincial legislation.[84] But Hunter C.J. held the legislation invalid simply because it entered into the field of Indian legislation. The case was followed in *R.* v. *Hill*[85] and a similar approach was taken by the Manitoba Court of Appeal in *R.* v. *Rodgers.*[86]

These cases, however, are not really inconsistent with *R.* v. *Groslouis* though there are remarks by Lane Co. Ct. J. in *R.* v. *Hill* and Prendergast C.J.M. in *R.* v. *Rodgers* indicating that these judges believed that no provincial legislation applied to Indians on a reserve. The fact is that game and fishing laws are distinguishable from other provincial legislation. The 1763 proclamation, which has the force of statute, gave a usufructuary right to Indians to certain lands, a right that would certainly include hunting and fishing rights.[87] The right under the proclamation is a right peculiar to Indians, and consequently legislation altering it is legislation respecting Indians which only the federal parliament may enact. The same reasoning applies to reserves created by other instruments. Support for this approach may be found in the fact that Hunter C.J.B.C. in *R.* v. *Jim* and Perdue C.J.A. in *R.* v. *Rodgers* appear to limit their judgment strictly to hunting and fishing rights.

One case, *R.* v. *Commanda*[88] before Greene J. of the Ontario High Court, does not accord with the foregoing reasoning. The appellant, an Ojibway Indian, was convicted of being in possession of parts of two moose and a deer in contravention of the Ontario Game and Fisheries Act. He contended that the legislation was invalid in so far as it included Ojibways hunting in territories surrendered under the Robinson Treaty of 1850, which granted the Indians the privilege of hunting in that territory. This privilege, the appellant averred, was a trust or interest in the land other than that of the province and so was preserved by section 109 of the BNA Act. Greene J. rejected this view, but he added that even if the privilege fell within section 109, the Game and Fisheries Act was not legislation respecting Indians, but related to matters falling within section 92(13) and (16) of the BNA Act. Reasons have already been advanced in support

84/See *R.* v. *Rodgers*, [1923] 3 D.L.R. 414, *per* Dennistoun J.A. (diss.); *R.* v. *Groslouis* (1943), 81 C.C.C. 167.
85/(1958), 101 C.C.C. 343.   86/[1923] 3 D.L.R. 414.
87/See pp. 112–13.   88/[1939] 3 D.L.R. 635.

of the view that the right to hunt and fish on surrendered lands is an interest preserved by section 109. The second ground of decision is no more convincing. The right to hunt and fish is a special privilege given to Indians *qua* Indians either by statute or by executive act.[89] Consequently it can only be repealed by legislation respecting Indians, a matter absolutely vested in the federal parliament.[90]

It should perhaps be mentioned that while the provinces are unable to regulate Indian rights, there is nothing to prevent them from giving Indians special privileges in respect of provincial property, such as permitting them to hunt and fish on provincial lands while prohibiting other persons from doing so, or giving them grants.[91]

The foregoing cases must now be read in the light of section 87 of the Indian Act,[92] which reads as follows:

> **87** Subject to the terms of any treaty and any other Act of the Parliament of Canada, all laws of general application from time to time in force in any province are applicable to and in respect of Indians in the province, except to the extent that such laws are inconsistent with this Act or any order, rule, regulation or by-law made thereunder, and except to the extent that such laws made provision for any matter for which provision is made by or under this Act.

The section makes clear that the provincial laws apply to Indians,[93] and there is no doubt that it extends to Indians on a reserve. The laws made applicable must, however, be general laws; the section does not validate provincial laws that would otherwise be invalid as dealing with Indians.[94] The section also makes clear that treaty provisions must now take priority over provincial laws. It is not so clear, however, what is meant by the last exception,[95] but it would appear that provincial laws are inapplicable in

89/See *R.* v. *Strongquill* (1935), 8 W.W.R. (N.S.) 247.

90/See *ibid.*, at 265, 271; *R.* v. *White and Bob* (1965), 50 D.L.R. (2d) 613, *per* Norris J.A.

91/See, for example, an order of the Lieutenant-Governor of Quebec in council, dated 16 January 1932, reproduced in *Annual Report of the Department of Indian Affairs* for 1936 (Ottawa, 1937), prohibiting hunting and fishing in certain areas to all but Indians.

92/R.S.C. 1952, c.149; see *R.* v. *Shade* (1952), 102 C.C.C. 316; see also *R.* v. *Little Bear* (1958), 25 W.W.R. 580; *aff'd*: (1958), 26 W.W.R. 335; *R.* v. *White and Bob* (1965), 50 D.L.R. (2d) 613; *aff'd*: (1966), 52 D.L.R. (2d) 481; *R.* v. *Discon and Baker* (1968), 67 D.L.R. (2d) 619. For a recent discussion of this section and other problems in this part, see K. Lysyk, "The Unique Constitutional Position of the Canadian Indian" (1967), 45 *Can. Bar Rev.* 513; see also K. Lysyk, "Indian Hunting Rights: Constitutional Considerations and the Role of Indian Treaties in British Columbia" (1966), 2 *U.B.C. L.R.* 401.

93/R. v. *George*, [1966] S.C.R. 267, makes it clear that the provision does not apply to federal laws; see also *R.* v. *Cooper* (1969), 1 D.L.R. (2d) 113.

94/See *R.* v. *Strongquill* (1953), 8 W.W.R. (N.S.) 247, at 265, 271.

95/See *R.* v. *Simon* (1958), 124 C.C.C. 110.

respect of any matter that is dealt with in the Indian Act. It must not be thought that the section has made the cases we have discussed entirely obsolete; they would be relevant to cases involving Eskimos, since the Indian Act does not apply to Eskimos.[96]

Finally, the resources agreements with Manitoba, Saskatchewan, and Alberta[97] have special constitutional provisions respecting Indian lands that impose limitations on provincial legislative power. Most of these are more germane to the nature of the Indian title and have already been discussed.[98] But one provision (paragraph 12 of the Saskatchewan and Alberta agreements, paragraph 13 of the Manitoba agreement) requires discussion here. It reads:

> **12**   In order to secure to the Indians of the Province the continuance of the supply of game and fish for their support and subsistence, Canada agrees that the laws respecting game in force in the Province from time to time shall apply to the Indians within the boundaries thereof, provided, however, that the said Indians shall have the right, which the Province hereby assures to them, of hunting, trapping and fishing game and fish for food at all seasons of the year on all unoccupied Crown lands and on any other lands to which the said Indians may have a right of access.

The effect of the provision is to give the Indians a constitutional right as against the provinces to hunt and fish on unoccupied Crown lands; it cannot be unilaterally altered by the provinces.[99] It appears to have been inserted to protect similar rights accorded by the various treaties under which the Indians surrendered the territory now comprising the Prairie provinces,[100] and it has been held to be quite proper to look at these treaties for assistance in determining the meaning of the provision.[101]

In interpreting the provision the courts have been torn between giving the Indian right a liberal application and the need for conservation, but the Indian right has generally prevailed. In *R. v. Wesley*[102] the conviction of an Indian for killing a male deer having antlers less than four inches in length, contrary to the Alberta Game Act, was quashed by the Appellate

---

96/R.S.C. 1952, c.149, s.4(1).

97/Confirmed by the BNA Act, 1930, 21 Geo. V, c.26; for a discussion of the cases under this provision, see A. H. Jakeman, "Indian Rights to Hunt for Food" (1963), 6 *Can. Bar J*. 223; K. Lysyk, "The Unique Constitutional Position of the Canadian Indian" (1967), 45 *Can. Bar Rev*. 513.

98/See pp. 129–30.

99/*R. v. Smith*, [1935] 3 D.L.R. 703; *R. v. Strongquill* (1953), 8 W.W.R. (N.S.) 247; the Dominion is not subject to the paragraph, however: see *Daniels* v. *White and the Queen*, [1968] S.C.R. 517.

100/*R. v. Wesley*, [1932] 2 W.W.R. 337.

101/*R. v. Smith*, [1935] 3 D.L.R. 703; *R. v. Strongquill* (1953), 8 W.W.R. (N.S.) 247.

102/[1932] 2 W.W.R. 337.

Division of the Supreme Court of Alberta on the ground that the Indian was protected by the provision. The court explained that the word "game" in the provision was used in the broadest sense and that Indians could, without licence, hunt for food on any unoccupied Crown land at any season, regardless of the provisions of the Game Act. In the recent case of *R. v. Prince*,[103] however, the Manitoba Court of Appeal by a majority of three to two refused to follow *R. v. Wesley*, stating that the court in that case had overlooked the important principle of conservation implicit in the provision which obviously contemplated the maintenance of sufficient game for the continuance of the Indian right in perpetuity. The majority, therefore, held the accused liable for hunting with the assistance of night lights even though he was an Indian. Though having the right to hunt at any time of year, an Indian was restricted to the methods provided by the Game Act. On appeal to the Supreme Court of Canada,[104] however, that court upheld the approach in *R. v. Wesley*. The Indians, it held, could hunt without regard to the restrictions imposed on non-Indians.

The balancing of the Indian's right to hunt against the need for conservation can also be seen in two cases before the Saskatchewan Court of Appeal, *R. v. Smith*[105] and *R. v. Strongquill*.[106] In the *Smith* case an Indian was charged with violating an absolute prohibition against carrying firearms on a game preserve. The point was whether the game preserve was "unoccupied Crown lands" as used in the resources agreement. The court held that that term referred to Crown lands not appropriated by the Crown for some definite purpose; game preserves, having been appropriated by the Crown, were not unoccupied. To the suggestion that the earlier treaties should be examined, the court pointed out that under those treaties Indians were not permitted to hunt on lands used for settlement, mining, lumbering, or other purposes. "Other purposes" was not subject to the *ejusdem generis* rule and was capable of including lands set apart as game preserves; while the parties to the treaties probably did not have this in contemplation, it was a purpose for which the land might reasonably be expected to be used as the territory became settled. It was further argued that the Indians had a right of access to the land, but the court held that their right of access was no different from that of the public generally, that is, a right of access *without firearms*. In *R. v. Strongquill*, an Indian was charged with shooting moose in an area used as a forest reserve and a fur conservation area. The area was uninhabited Crown land to which the

103/(1962), 40 W.W.R. 234.
104/*Prince and Myron v. R.*, [1964] S.C.R. 81.
105/[1935], 3 D.L.R. 703; see also *R. v. Little Bear* (1958), 25 W.W.R. 580.
106/(1953), 8 W.W.R. (N.S.) 247.

public had access and on which visiting hunters could hunt for animals other than moose on obtaining a licence. The court, Martin C.J.S. dissenting, held that the accused was protected under the resources agreement. The majority distinguished the *Smith* case on the ground that in that case no one was entitled to access to the game preserve while carrying firearms. Here the Indians, in common with other members of the public, had a right of access, and moreover the area was open to hunting for visitors.

There is some suggestion in *R. v. Smith*[107] that the Indian right to hunt and fish under the resources agreements is limited to Crown lands on a reserve or at least to Crown lands on which they have a right of access peculiar to themselves, but this is not in accord with the terms of the agreement. *R. v. Wesley*[108] and *R. v. Strongquill*[109] show that the protection applies to any "unoccupied" land, and the latter case adds that it would also apply to occupied Crown lands to which the Indians have a right of access. *R. v. Little Bear*[110] holds that the application of the provision is not limited to Crown lands. There the appellant, an Indian, was convicted of shooting a deer for food out of season on land belonging to a white man who had given the Indian permission to hunt there. On appeal, Turcotte D.C.J. quashed the conviction, holding that the Indian had a right of access thereto under paragraph 12 of the Alberta agreement. In *R. v. Prince*[111] the Manitoba Court of Appeal went somewhat further. In that case there was a prohibition against hunting on any land for which a notice had been given by posting signs, as prescribed, prohibiting hunting within the boundaries of the land. The court held that unless such notices were posted, any person (including an Indian) would have access thereto for hunting.

Finally, the declaration in the provision that provincial laws are to apply to Indians is limited to general laws. Consequently a specific provision seeking to regulate an Indian right would be ultra vires.[112]

OBLIGATIONS AND LIMITATIONS RESPECTING PROVINCIAL PROPERTY

In addition to the paragraph just studied, the resources agreements with the four western provinces contain several other provisions imposing constitutional limitations or obligations on provincial legislative and execu-

107/[1935] 3 D.L.R. 703, *per* Turgeon J.A., at 707; see *R. v. Little Bear* (1958), 25 W.W.R. 580.
108/[1932] 2 W.W.R. 337.   109/(1953), 8 W.W.R. (N.S.) 247.
110/1958), 25 W.W.R. 580; *aff'd*: (1958), 26 W.W.R. 335.
111/(1962), 40 W.W.R. 234; in the Supreme Court of Canada the right of access was admitted: *Prince and Myron v. R.*, [1964] S.C.R. 81.
112/*R. v. Strongquill* (1953), 8 W.W.R. (N.S.) 247; *R. v. White and Bob* (1965), 50 D.L.R. (2d) 613, *per* Norris J.A.

tive power respecting public property.[113] Unless otherwise noted, these provisions have province-wide application in Manitoba, Alberta, and Saskatchewan; in British Columbia, however, the provisions are generally restricted to the Railway Belt and the Peace River block.

The first of these limitations requiring examination appears in paragraph 2 of the agreements with the Prairie provinces and in paragraph 3 of the British Columbia agreement. Under the provision the province agreed to carry out contracts to purchase or lease Crown lands, mines, or minerals and any other arrangement giving a person an interest therein against the Crown. In the agreements with the Prairie provinces, those provinces further agreed not to affect or alter any term of such contract or agreement by legislation or otherwise, subject to certain exceptions to be examined later. The provision as it appears in the latter agreements reads as follows:

> 2 The Province will carry out in accordance with the terms thereof every contract to purchase or lease any Crown lands, mines or minerals and every other arrangement whereby any person has become entitled to any interest therein as against the Crown, and further agrees not to affect or alter any term of any such contract to purchase, lease or other arrangement by legislation or otherwise, except either with the consent of all the parties thereto other than Canada or in so far as any legislation may apply generally to all similar agreements relating to lands, mines or minerals in the Province or to interests therein, irrespective of who may be the parties thereto.

This provision has been discussed in several cases. In *In re Refund of Dues Under Timber Regulations*,[114] the meaning of "arrangement" as used in the paragraph was discussed. The facts briefly were these. While the lands of the western provinces were vested in the Dominion the Dominion Lands Act provided that settlers could be granted "entry for homestead" on parcels of land in the western provinces. If after three years a settler had complied with certain conditions, he might be granted the land. Under timber regulations made under another part of the Dominion Lands Act, it was provided that the holder of an entry for homestead should pay dues on timber cut by him and sold to persons who were not actual settlers, but it was further provided that, on such a holder being granted the land by the Crown, the dues should be refunded to him. The question for determination was whether the obligation to refund the dues was an arrangement within article 2. The Privy Council, affirming the Supreme Court of Canada, held that it was;[115] consequently the province was liable for the

113/Confirmed by the BNA Act, 1930, 21 Geo. V, c.26.
114/[1935] A.C. 184; affirming [1933] S.C.R. 616.
115/For a similar interpretation of "arrangement" under para. 3 of the resources agreements, see *Huggard Assets Ltd.* v. *Attorney-General of Alberta*, [1953] A.C. 420; see pp. 41–2.

dues. The court went further and held that under the circumstances under which the 1930 agreements were made, the paragraph constituted a statutory novation,[116] and the obligation of the Dominion to refund these dues had ceased. The settlers had, therefore, lost their right against the Dominion, but could obtain redress against the province.

The type of agreement protected by the paragraph also received attention in *Re Taxation of University of Manitoba Lands*.[117] There provincial and municipal taxes were levied against university lands not directly used for educational purposes. It was argued, *inter alia*, that the taxes were invalid by virtue of the paragraph because the land had been conveyed by the Dominion to the university in trust to apply the proceeds for educational purposes and the taxes would impair or nullify the trust. The majority of the Manitoba Supreme Court rejected the argument, Trueman J.A. dissenting. They held that the conveyance to the university was absolute, subject to a collateral covenant that the land should revert to the Crown on its ceasing to be used for university purposes. The paragraph had no application to lands completely transferred before the resources agreement. In any case any trust or obligation was in favour of the Crown; it was not (as in the *Spooner* case to be discussed below) a contractual licence to a third party which the province could not reduce because of the paragraph.

As already mentioned, under the agreements with the Prairie provinces those provinces agreed not to alter or affect arrangements transferred to them under the agreements. The meaning of "affect" was considered in *Spooner Oils Ltd.* v. *Turner Valley Gas Conservation Board*.[118] There, before the transfer agreements were entered into in 1930, a lease had been granted by the Dominion giving the right to the lessee to work the land leased for petroleum and natural gas for a renewable term of twenty-one years. Under the lease and the regulations pursuant to which it was issued, the lessee was given the right to conduct his working of the land "in such manner only as is usual and customary in skilful and proper mining operations ... conducted by proprietors ... on their own land." Since there was no adequate market for naphtha gas, the method of operation customarily followed, and actually followed by the lessee, was to burn the gas. In 1932 Alberta passed an Act for the purpose of reducing the gas so burned, and a board was set up for the purpose of conserving it. The Supreme Court of Canada held that the Act affected the lease in a substantial way. Under the lease the lessees were entitled to work their lands in the ordinary skilful

116/See also *Anthony* v. *Attorney-General of Alberta*, [1943] S.C.R. 320; *Huggard Assets Ltd.* v. *Attorney-General of Alberta*, [1953] A.C. 420.
117/[1940] 1 D.L.R. 579.   118/[1933] S.C.R. 629.

manner with a view to exploiting the property in a profitable way. But the 1932 Act provides that wells are to be exploited in accordance with general rules laid down in the Act pursuant to a policy of conserving natural gas in the general public interest with little regard to the usual and customary manner of landowners in skilfully working their land for profit. The Act did not, therefore, apply to the lease. As will be seen, however, the Alberta agreement was subsequently modified to permit the province to carry out schemes of the kind discussed in this case.

Despite the agreement not to alter or affect arrangements transferred to them, the Prairie provinces may certainly vary an agreement when the Dominion could make such variations under the terms of an arrangement. The extent to which this can be done was discussed in *Anthony* v. *Attorney-General of Alberta*.[119] There the Dominion, when the public lands of Alberta were vested in it, had granted a timber licence to the appellants. The licence was renewable annually on certain terms, among them the payment of such dues as might be fixed by regulations in force at the time of the renewal. Following the transfer of resources to Alberta the same provisions were carried forward by the province. Under the regulations of both the Dominion and Alberta the annual renewal dues were never more than $1.00 per 1,000 feet, until 1941 when the province increased them to $1.75. It was now proposing to increase them further to $2.50 and $3.00. The court held that the increase to $1.75 was intra vires. The Dominion possessed power to vary dues and this power had passed to the province under the resources agreement which constituted a statutory novation. The increase did not violate paragraph 2 of the resources agreement but there is a limit on the amount to which those dues might be increased. If the increase were so great as to nullify the licence indirectly, it would not be valid. There was no adequate evidence that the increase here had that intent, although there was some suspicion of the motives behind it.

Finally in *West Canadian Collieries* v. *Attorney-General of Alberta*[120] the exceptions in the paragraph as it appears in the agreements with the Prairie provinces were discussed. In those agreements, the provision that previous arrangements and contracts will not be altered is subject to two exceptions: (1) when the consent of all parties thereto other than Canada are obtained, and (2) when and in so far as any legislation may apply generally to all similar agreements relating to lands, mines, minerals, and royalties in the province irrespective of who may be the parties thereto. In 1948 Alberta passed a statute substantially increasing royalties payable under agreements entered into with the Crown. The Privy Council held

119/[1943] S.C.R. 320.   120/[1953] A.C. 453.

that this Act was invalid under the paragraph unless the exceptions were applicable. The first exception, they held, did not apply because the necessary agreement was lacking. The second exception posed more difficulty because the Act applied generally to all Crown leases, but their Lordships held that the exception referred only to legislation applicable generally whoever the parties may be, not where the legislation was limited to cases where the Crown was a party. The statute was not severable so as to make it apply to Crown grants made by the province because the court could not presume the legislature would have passed it in this truncated form; it was, therefore, ultra vires.

Further exceptions to paragraph 2 were added to the Alberta and Manitoba agreements in 1938 and 1948, respectively. The Alberta agreement permits that province to establish oil and gas conservation schemes by excluding from the terms of the agreement:

> ... legislation relating to the conservation of oil resources or gas resources or both by the control or regulation of the production of oil or gas or both, whether by restriction or prohibition and whether generally or with respect to any specified area or any specified well or wells or by repressuring of any oil field, gas field or oil-gas field, and, incidentally thereto, providing for the compulsory purchase of any well or wells.[121]

By virtue of the 1948 agreement,[122] paragraph 2 of the Manitoba agreement was modified by adding a complicated series of exceptions intended to give the province a free hand in the development of electric power in the province. The agreement excepts from the operation of the paragraph legislation regarding almost every conceivable aspect of power development, including legislation relating to the development, transmission, and marketing of electricity and the control of the flow of waters for generating power or purposes connected therewith. It further permits provincial legislation for acquisition by purchase or expropriation of the rights of any person relating to the flow of water and of any installations or devices for the development or transmission of electric power.

A number of provisions in the resources agreements impose obligations on the provinces to convey lands to private persons and corporations. Thus each agreement provides that the provinces will perform every obligation of Canada, arising by virtue of any statute, order in council, or regulation in respect of the public lands transferred to the provinces by the agreement, to any person entitled to a grant by way of subsidy for the construction of railways or otherwise or to any railway company for grants of land for

121/(1938), 2 Geo. VI, c.36(Can.); (1938), 2 Geo. VI (1st sess.), c.14(Alta.).
122/(1947–48), 11 & 12 Geo. VI, c.60(Can.); (1948) 12 Geo. VI, c.1(Man.).

rights of way, road beds, stations, station grounds, workshops, buildings, yards, ballast, pits, or other appurtenances.[123] Further, under paragraph 12 of the agreement with British Columbia the province is bound to grant and assure to the Canadian Pacific Railway Company a registered fee-simple title free from encumbrance of the lands occupied or required by it to construct and operate its railway in that part of the Railway Belt known as the Sumas Dyking Lands. Again, by virtue of paragraph 5 of the respective agreements, the Prairie provinces are to carry out the terms and conditions of the Deed of Surrender of Rupert's Land from the Hudson's Bay Company dated 19 November 1869 (as modified by the Dominion Lands Act and an agreement of 19 December 1924),[124] grant any lands in each province that the company is entitled to select under the 1924 agreement, and release and discharge the reservation for public roads, canals, and other public works in patents referred to in clause 3 of that agreement. Since the rights of the company are not to be in any way prejudiced or diminished by the resources agreement or modifications of it, it seems probable that this paragraph would not constitute a statutory novation like paragraph 2 of the agreements; if so, the Dominion continues to be bound by this agreement vis-à-vis the Company.

Special provisions respecting the legislative power of the four western provinces over national parks were also made by the resources agreements. After stipulating that certain national parks shall continue to belong to Canada,[125] the agreements provide as follows:

15   The Parliament of Canada shall have exclusive legislative jurisdiction within the whole area included within the outer boundaries of each of the said parks, notwithstanding that portions of any such area may not form part of the park proper, and the laws now in force within such areas shall continue so in force only until changed by the Parliament of Canada or under its authority, provided, however, that all laws of the Province now or hereafter in force, which are not repugnant to any law or regulation made applicable within the said areas or any of them by or under the authority of the Parliament of Canada, shall extend to and be enforced within the same, and that all general taxing acts passed by the Province shall apply within the same unless expressly excluded from application therein by or under the authority of the Parliament of Canada.[126]

123/Para. 4. Manitoba, Alberta and Saskatchewan agreements; para. 3, British Columbia agreement.
124/The agreement appears in the *Canada Gazette* of 7 February 1925, vol. 58, no. 32.
125/For this and other provisions relating to natural parks, see pp. 38–9.
126/Para. 16, Manitoba and British Columbia agreements; para. 15, Saskatchewan and Alberta agreements.

The exclusive legislative power over the parks given the Dominion by this paragraph is much wider than the ordinary power to legislate respecting its public property alone. Under the latter power it could not invalidate provincial laws relating to the civil rights of individuals that did not affect the property. The paragraph ensures that provincial laws apply in the parks only if not repugnant to federal laws or, in the case of taxing measures, until expressly repealed by parliament.

The paragraph has been considered in several cases. In *Cherry* v. *Smith*,[127] Doak D.C.J. held that the Saskatchewan Land Titles Act did not apply to premises in a national park. Although the paragraph under discussion provides for the application in those parks of provincial laws not repugnant to Dominion laws, the paragraph did not apply the provincial Land Titles Act to the parks because under the terms of that Act it was effective only when land was brought under its provisions and a certificate of title had been issued for it. Since the Act could not apply to the fee simple, which was vested in the Crown, it equally did not apply to a sub-lease from a lessee of that land. In *R.* v. *Hughes*,[128] the accused was charged with driving without due care and attention in violation of the Alberta Vehicles and Highway Traffic Act even though there was a provision in the National Parks Highway Regulations providing that no person shall operate a vehicle otherwise than in accordance with provincial laws. This latter provision seems to have been intended to incorporate the provincial laws as part of the federal regulations, and the Ontario Court of Appeal has recently held that an almost identical section had this effect.[129] But Farthing D.C.J. held that it was no more than an indication that the regulations were not intended to cover the whole field of law. He did, however, deal with the argument that the provincial enactment is repugnant to the federal regulations on the ground that the penalty for violating the provincial Act is more severe than that for violating the regulations, and held that there was no repugnancy.

In *Re Rush and Tompkins Construction Co.*[130] Hutcheson J., of the Supreme Court of British Columbia, relied on the paragraph in holding that the provincial sales tax applied to a contractor in respect of building materials used in performing a construction contract with the federal government. Finally, in *Re Regina* v. *McMahon*,[131] Kirby J., of the Alberta Supreme Court, held that a magistrate appointed under a provincial statute had jurisdiction to hear a charge of a criminal offence

127/[1933] 1 W.W.R. 205.
128/(1958), 122 C.C.C. 198.
129/*R.* v. *Glibbery* (1963), 36 D.L.R. (2d) 548.
130/(1961), 28 D.L.R. (2d) 441.   131/(1964), 44 D.L.R. (2d) 752.

alleged to have been committed in a national park even though a federal statute authorized the governor in council to appoint magistrates for national parks, since the governor in council had not appointed a magistrate for the park.

In the agreements with Saskatchewan, Alberta, and British Columbia there is another provision stipulating that the province will not, by works outside any of the parks, reduce the flow of water in any of the rivers or streams within the parks to less than that deemed by the minister of the interior necessary to preserve the scenic beauty of the park.[132]

The agreements with the four western provinces also contain a paragraph providing that each province will not dispose of any historic site of which it is notified by Canada and which Canada undertakes to maintain as a historic site.[133] The paragraph further provides that each province will continue and preserve the bird sanctuaries and shooting grounds already established and will set aside such additional bird sanctuaries and shooting grounds as may hereafter be established between the minister of the interior and the appropriate provincial minister. However, by later agreements with Alberta and Saskatchewan it was provided that these provinces might discontinue any such bird sanctuary or shooting ground on agreement between the federal and provincial authorities.[134]

Before concluding this examination of these limitations, it should perhaps be noted that federal legislation relating to the lands transferred by the resources agreements continued to apply to these lands on the transfer of administration thereof to the provinces, but it was expressly provided that the provinces could at any time legislate otherwise.[135] On the other hand, the British Columbia Railway Belt agreement provided that the Belt would become subject to provincial laws, but such provision was not to affect any right or interest granted or agreed to be granted by Canada.[136]

Finally there are a number of other provisions limiting provincial powers that are germane to other issues that are discussed in other parts of this work.[137]

132/Para. 16, Saskatchewan and Alberta agreements; para. 18, British Columbia agreement; in Alberta, this was made conditional on the Dominion's excluding certain areas from the parks.
133/Para. 19, Manitoba and Alberta agreements; para. 20, Saskatchewan agreement; para. 22, British Columbia agreement.
134/Para. 19A, Alberta agreement, validated by (1945), 9 & 10 Geo. VI, c.10(Can.); (1946), 11 Geo. VI, c.2(Alta.); para. 20A, Saskatchewan agreement, validated by (1947), 11 Geo. VI, c.45(Can.); (1947), 11 Geo. VI, c.17(Sask.).
135/Para. 1, Manitoba, Saskatchewan, Alberta agreements.
136/Paras. 1 and 5, British Columbia agreement.
137/See pp. 37, 40, 127–30.

LEGISLATION AFFECTING FEDERAL PROPERTY

A provincial legislature can neither deal directly with Dominion public property,[138] nor take away or abridge any proprietary right or privilege of the Crown in right of the Dominion whether arising out of prerogative or statute.[139] This flows from the Dominion's paramount power to legislate respecting its public property, and in the field of taxation there is an express exemption of federal property in section 125 of the BNA Act 1867.[140]

The exemption of federal property from provincial legislation may be exemplified by *Deeks, McBride Ltd.* v. *Vancouver Associated Contractors Ltd.*[141] There the Dominion registered land under the British Columbia Registry Act and obtained an indefeasible title. Had the land belonged to a private person it would have been subject to a lien under the provincial Mechanics Lien Act; the trial judge held that the land in question was subject to the Act even though it was owned by the Crown. But the British Columbia Court of Appeal reversed the decision, holding that the Dominion has exclusive jurisdiction respecting Dominion public property by virtue of section 91(1A) of the BNA Act, and this excluded provincial jurisdiction.[142] Similarly in *City of Ottawa* v. *Shore and Horwitz Construction Co. Ltd.*[143] a construction company engaged by a federal Crown agency to erect a building on federal property, under a contract by which the control of the work was in a minister of the Crown and the ownership of all tools and equipment was vested in the minister, was held not to be obliged to obtain a building permit or comply with other requirements of a municipal by-law regulating the structure of buildings on the ground that Dominion public property falls within section 91(1A) and so is beyond provincial competence. Since the property was exempt, the contractor was equally exempt. It was further held that a clause in the contract requiring the contractor to comply with all federal, provincial, and municipal regulations could not be regarded as a waiver of federal immunity.

In the cases where provincial legislation was held inapplicable to federal

138/*Attorney-General of Alberta* v. *Attorney-General of Canada*, [1928] A.C. 475.
139/*R.* v. *Powers*, [1923] Ex.C.R. 131. See also *R.* v. *Anderson* (1930), 54 C.C.C. 321, and *R.* v. *Rhodes*, [1934] 1 D.L.R. 251 which appear to be based partly on this principle; see also *Prudential Trust Co. Ltd.* v. *Registrar, Humboldt*, [1957] S.C.R. 658; *Attorney-General of Canada* v. *Toth* (1959), 17 D.L.R. (2d) 273. For the conflicting views on provincial power over federal prerogative rights generally, see p. 144.
140/Section 125 is briefly discussed at pp. 161–3. For a detailed discussion, see G. V. La Forest, *The Allocation of Taxing Power under the Canadian Constitution* (Toronto, 1967), chap. VIII.
141/[1954] 4 D.L.R. 844.
142/See also *Bain* v. *Director, Veterans' Land Act*, [1947] O.W.N. 917.
143/(1960), 22 D.L.R. (2d) 247.

property, the legislation substantially continued to function in other respects. A different question might arise if a provincial statute, not specifically aimed at federal property, would be substantially nullified by a rigid application of the principle that provincial legislation must not take away federal proprietary rights. It seems inconceivable, for example, that a general statute abolishing riparian rights, or one providing for a large hydro-electric power development, would be frustrated by the fact that the Dominion owned lands on a river which would inevitably be affected.

In any event, Dominion property may be subject to a provincial act that is invoked by the federal government, for when the Crown invokes an act it must accept it as a whole, taking qualified benefits as qualified.[144] In *Reid* v. *Canadian Farm Loan Board*,[145] however, the court went much beyond this principle. There the board sought to foreclose two mortgages, one based on common law principles, the other on a provincial statute. The Debt Adjustment Act of Manitoba required a permit before a foreclosure order could be obtained and the board had not obtained one. The court held that the board could not obtain the foreclosure. While the case may well be correct in that the special act of the board may require conformity with provincial law and there may possibly be doubt whether the board is an emanation of the Crown, the reasons given are certainly open to question. The court held that the board, having taken advantage of provincial legislation, must take the obligations under it with the benefits. Whatever validity this reasoning may have with respect to the statutory mortgage, it seems clearly inapplicable to the common law mortgage, where the board was not resorting to a statutory remedy but was invoking the equitable jurisdiction of the court. As to the statutory mortgage, the reasoning appears doubtful for another reason. The Debt Adjustment Act was a quite separate statute from the Registry Act invoked. It seems doubtful whether the federal government, by following the requirements of a provincial registry act in respect of a piece of land, makes the land subject to every provincial statute affecting property. The judgment then adds that though the Dominion has power to legislate respecting its property, the power may be subject to provincial legislation – a wholly untenable conclusion.

Land does not, by becoming federal property, cease to be part of the province,[146] and provincial legislation may well affect activities on such

144/*Deeks McBride Ltd.* v. *Vancouver Contractors, Ltd.*, [1954] 4 D.L.R. 844, at 845.
145/[1937] 4 D.L.R. 248; this case is criticized in *Deeks McBride Ltd.* v. *Vancouver Associated Cement Ltd.*, [1954] 4 D.L.R. 844.
146/In addition to the cases in the text, see *Attorney-General of British Columbia* v. *Attorney-General of Canada* (1889), 14 A.C. 295; *Burrard Power Co.* v. *R.*, [1911] A.C. 87.

land. Thus in *Coté* v. *Quebec Liquor Commission*,[147] the appellants were held properly convicted of transporting liquor in contravention of a Quebec statute notwithstanding that the offence occurred on a federally owned wharf. Again in *R.* v. *Smith*[148] a soldier was held guilty of violating provincial game laws although he was hunting within a military camp owned by the federal government. The soldier had no property in the soil and no permission to hunt. The case might have been decided differently if the soldier had had permission to hunt from the federal authorities, for the right to hunt is associated with the ownership of the soil, and provincial laws cannot interfere with federal property rights. *Re Sturmer and Town of Beaverton*[149] provides another example. There it was held that a municipal by-law could extend to a public harbour. So, too, provincial legislation may competently be enacted to provide for a municipal ferry that traverses water and touches land – a public harbour which is owned by the federal Crown.[150] At times such legislation may indirectly affect the federal government, for example, by increasing its costs under a cost-plus contract. An example is *Re Rush and Tomkins Construction Ltd.*[151] where contractors, in carrying on a construction contract with the federal government in a national park, were held liable to pay the provincial sales tax in respect of goods imported into the province for use in connection with the contract. Again, in *In re Stone*[152] it was held that the province, in legislating respecting property and civil rights, could validly make laws providing that illegitimate children could succeed to property on intestacy, even though this might on occasion defeat the Crown's right of escheat on intestacy, then vested in the Dominion. When, however, the province attempted to deprive the Dominion of escheats by making the University of Alberta the ultimate heir in case of intestacy, the Act was declared ultra vires.[153] As Fitzpatrick C.J. stated in *Trusts and Guarantee Co.* v. *R.*:[154] "... Lands escheat to the Crown for defect of heirs and this has nothing to do with the question who are a person's heirs. But altering the law of inheritance is one thing and appropriating the right of the Dominion on failure of heirs is quite another thing." These cases no longer

147/[1931] 4 D.L.R. 137.
148/[1942] 3 D.L.R. 764.
149/(1911), 24 O.L.R. 65; see also *Re Vancouver Charter, Re Wheatley, Re Kodak and Marsh* (1958), 24 W.W.R. 323; *R.* v. *Karchaba* (1965), 52 D.L.R. (2d) 438.
150/*Owen Sound Transportation Co.* v. *Tackaberry*, [1936] 3 D.L.R. 272; *Toronto Transit Commission* v. *Aqua Taxi Ltd.* (1957), 6 D.L.R. (2d) 721.
151/(1961), 28 D.L.R. (2d) 441.
152/[1924] S.C.R. 682.
153/*Attorney-General of Alberta* v. *Attorney-General of Canada*, [1928] A.C. 475; see also *Trusts and Guarantee Co.* v. *R.* (1917), 54 S.C.R. 107.
154/*Ibid.*, at 110.

apply to the Prairie provinces, but they do apply to the Yukon and North-west territories because the councils of the territories may make ordinances respecting property and civil rights and the federal government, of course, owns the lands.[155]

It should also be noted that while provincial legislation does not apply *proprio vigore* to federal public lands, it may well be adopted by federal legislation or regulations requiring that provincial legislation be complied with. This can be seen from *R. v. Glibbery*[156] where a person was held liable to a penalty imposed by federal regulations prohibiting anyone from operating a motor vehicle on federal property otherwise than in accordance with the laws of the province.

A question of considerable difficulty arises where the federal government has a partial interest in property in which a private person also has an interest. The province may certainly legislate respecting the interest of the private person – for example, by levying taxes on, or imposing a duty in respect of the interest,[157] but such legislation cannot affect the Dominion interest, for example, by authorizing a sale involving the Dominion interest. Such a situation might arise where the Dominion held a lease or other partial interest from a private person. But the more difficult cases occur where the Dominion has, pursuant to statutory regulations, granted a lease or other particular interest to an individual. For, in those cases, the particular interest being the creature of federal legislation respecting public property, provincial legislation respecting the interest may easily amount to a nullification of the federal legislation, and this is beyond the capacity of a province.

Such a situation arose in *Spooner Oils Ltd. v. Turner Valley Gas Conservation Board.*[158] In that case the Dominion issued a lease of its lands to a lessee pursuant to statutory regulations under which the lessee was empowered to work the land for petroleum and natural gas in such manner as is usual and customary in skilful and proper mining operations conducted by proprietors on their own land. In working the land, the lessee would burn most of the naphtha gas extracted, this being the usual practice since there was no market for it. In 1932 Alberta passed an act for the purpose of reducing the amount of gas burned, and a board was set up for conserving the gas. When this Act was enacted the Dominion interest in

155/Northwest Territories Act, R.S.C. 1952, c.331, s.13(h); Yukon Act, (1952–53), 1 & 2 Eliz. II, c.53, s.16(h).
156/(1963), 36 D.L.R. (2d) 548; see also *R. v. Hughes* (1958), 122 C.C.C. 198; *R. v. Johns* (1962), 39 W.W.R. 49.
157/See, *inter alia, City of Montreal v. Attorney-General of Canada*, [1923] A.C. 136; see p. 162.
158/[1933] S.C.R. 629.

the land had been transferred to Alberta, and the case turned on the meaning of a provision in the natural resources agreement, but it was also necessary to deal with the case on the basis of the situation that would have existed had the land remained in the Dominion. On this basis the Supreme Court of Canada held that the provincial statute would have altered the right granted by the Dominion lease and would consequently have nullified the effect of the Dominion legislation under which it was issued. That being so, the provincial legislation was inapplicable to the lessee's interest. Duff C.J. observed that it is difficult, in this connection, to draw an abstract line between provincial legislation and Dominion legislation under section 91(1A) and the ancillary powers thereto. He instanced provincial laws in respect of nuisances which impose a duty on occupiers generally, subject to a personal penalty. These will usually be valid against occupiers of Dominion lands. But he pointed out that provincial legislation empowering an administrative board to prescribe rules in relation to such matters with respect to any individual tract, including Dominion public property, might possibly be subject to different considerations, and he added that where the regulations under which a Dominion lease to the land is issued, or the lease itself, contain provisions on the same subject matter, such provisions must, in case of conflict, prevail over the provincial legislation. He also observed that, while an occupant of Dominion lands may be taxed respecting his occupancy, it does not necessarily follow that such taxation can in every case be enforced by remedies involving the sale or appropriation of the occupant's right without regard to the nature of that right.

There are, however, rare cases where a tax may be enforced by sale or expropriation of property even though the Crown has an interest in it. An example is *Calgary and Edmonton Land Co.* v. *Attorney-General of Alberta*.[159] There a Dominion act authorized the granting of aid for the construction of a railway by a subsidy of federal Crown lands, and by section 2 of the act it was declared that such grants should be "free grants" subject only to payment, on the issue of letters patent therefor, of the costs of the survey and incidental expenses at the rate of ten cents per acre. Part of this land was conveyed to the appellant before letters patent were issued to the company and consequently before the payment above described was made. While this situation obtained, the land was rated for taxes and condemned for arrears under a provincial statute. The Supreme Court of Canada held that the condemnation was valid.

The Crown had the bare legal title only, the whole beneficial interest being vested in the appellant. Such a seizure in no way nullified the effect

159/(1911), 45 S.C.R. 170.

of the Dominion statute; if it had, the provisions of the provincial statute could not have applied to it.

Finally, Duff C.J. dealt with the question of confiscation (which he defined as the taking of land by a special law dealing with a particular case) by a province of a partial interest of an individual in federal property. Of this he stated that it might be difficult to hold that a statute specifically appropriating to the province the interest of a lessee in Dominion lands was not legislation dealing with Dominion public property. He added that it might also be difficult in most cases to escape the conclusion that an attempt to substitute the Crown in right of the province as lessee in place of a lessee who acquired under federal legislation might not be repugnant to such legislation.

Major Constitutional Provisions Respecting Natural Resources and Public Property

THE BRITISH NORTH AMERICA ACT, 1867[1]

30 & 31 Vict., c. 3 (Imp.)

91 It shall be lawful for the Queen, by and with the Advice and Consent of the Senate and House of Commons, to make Laws for the Peace, Order, and good Government of Canada, in relation to all Matters not coming within the Classes of Subjects by this Act assigned exclusively to the Legislatures of the Provinces; and for greater Certainty, but not so as to restrict the Generality of the foregoing Terms of this Section, it is hereby declared that (notwithstanding anything in this Act) the exclusive Legislative Authority of the Parliament of Canada extends to all Matters coming within the Classes of Subjects next herein-after enumerated; that is to say ...

1[2] The Public Debt and Property.

And any Matter coming within any of the Classes of Subjects enumerated in this Section shall not be deemed to come within the Class of Matters of a local or private Nature comprised in the Enumeration of the Classes of Subjects by this Act assigned exclusively to the Legislatures of the Provinces.

24 Indians, and Lands reserved for the Indians.

92 In each Province the Legislature may exclusively make Laws in relation to Matters coming within the Classes of Subjects next herein-after enumerated; that is to say ...

5 The Management and Sale of the Public Lands belonging to the Province and of the Timber and Wood thereon.

102 All Duties and Revenues over which the respective Legislatures of Canada, Nova Scotia, and New Brunswick before and at the Union had and have Power of Appropriation, except such Portions thereof as are by this Act reserved to the respective Legislatures of the Provinces, or are raised by them in accordance with the special Powers conferred on them by this Act, shall form One Consolidated Revenue Fund, to be appropriated for the Public Service of Canada in the Manner and subject to the Charges in this Act provided.

107 All Stocks, Cash, Banker's Balances, and Securities for Money belonging to each Province at the Time of the Union, except as in this Act mentioned, shall be the Property of Canada, and shall be taken in Reduction of the Amount of the respective Debts of the Provinces at the Union.

1/The following sections of the BNA Act, 1867, were extended (sometimes with modifications) to the provinces entering Confederation after 1867 by general provisions making these sections applicable; see chap. three.

2/As renumbered by the BNA (No. 2) Act, 1949, 13 Geo. VI, c.81(Imp.).

108 The Public Works and Property of each Province, enumerated in the Third Schedule to this Act, shall be the Property of Canada.

109 All Lands, Mines, Minerals, and Royalties belonging to the several Provinces of Canada, Nova Scotia, and New Brunswick at the Union, and all Sums then due or payable for such Lands, Mines, Minerals, or Royalties, shall belong to the several Provinces of Ontario, Quebec, Nova Scotia, and New Brunswick in which the same are situate or arise, subject to any Trusts existing in respect thereof, and to any Interest other than that of the Province in the same.

110 All Assets connected with such Portions of the Public Debt of each Province as are assumed by that Province shall belong to that Province.

113 The Assets enumerated in the Fourth Schedule to this Act belonging at the Union to the Province of Canada shall be the Property of Ontario and Quebec conjointly.

117 The several Provinces shall retain all their respective Public Property not otherwise disposed of in this Act, subject to the Right of Canada to assume any Lands or Public Property required for Fortifications or for the Defence of the Country.

125 No Lands or Property belonging to Canada or any Province shall be liable to Taxation.

126 Such Portions of the Duties and Revenues over which the respective Legislatures of Canada, Nova Scotia, and New Brunswick had before the Union Power of Appropriation as are by this Act reserved to the respective Governments or Legislatures of the Provinces, and all Duties and Revenues raised by them in accordance with the special Powers conferred upon them by this Act, shall in each Province form One Consolidated Revenue Fund to be appropriated for the Public Service of the Province.

142 The Division and Adjustment of the Debts, Credits, Liabilities, Properties, and Assets of Upper Canada and Lower Canada shall be referred to the Arbitrament of Three Arbitrators, One chosen by the Government of Ontario, One by the Government of Quebec, and One by the Government of Canada; and the Selection of the Arbitrators shall not be made until the Parliament of Canada and the Legislatures of Ontario and Quebec have met; and the Arbitrator chosen by the Government of Canada shall not be a Resident either in Ontario or in Quebec.

THE THIRD SCHEDULE

Provincial Public Works and Property to be the Property of Canada

1 Canals, with Lands and Water Power connected therewith
2 Public Harbours
3 Lighthouses and Piers, and Sable Island
4 Steamboats, Dredges, and public Vessels
5 Rivers and Lake Improvements
6 Railways and Railway Stocks, Mortgages, and other Debts due by Railway Companies
7 Military Roads

8 Custom Houses, Post Offices, and all other Public Buildings, except such as the Government of Canada appropriate for the Use of the Provincial Legislatures and Governments
9 Property transferred by the Imperial Government, and known as Ordnance Property
10 Armouries, Drill Sheds, Military Clothing, and Munitions of War, and Lands set apart for general Public Purposes

THE FOURTH SCHEDULE

Assets to be the Property of Ontario and Quebec conjointly

Upper Canada Building Fund
Lunatic Asylums
Normal School
Court Houses ⎫
    in   ⎬ Lower Canada
Aylmer
Montreal
Kamouraska ⎭
Law Society, Upper Canada
Montreal Turnpike Trust
University Permanent Fund
Royal Institution
Consolidated Municipal Loan Fund, Upper Canada
Consolidated Municipal Loan Fund, Lower Canada
Agricultural Society, Upper Canada
Lower Canada Legislative Grant
Quebec Fire Loan
Temiscouata Advance Account
Quebec Turnpike Trust
Education – East
Building and Jury Fund, Lower Canada
Municipalities Fund
Lower Canada Superior Education Income Fund

THE BRITISH NORTH AMERICA ACT, 1930[3]
21 Geo. V, c. 26 (Imp.)

1 The agreements set out in the Schedule to this Act are hereby confirmed and shall have the force of law notwithstanding anything in the British North America Act, 1867, or any Act amending the same, or any Act of the Parliament of Canada, or in any Order in Council or terms or conditions of union made or approved under any such Act as aforesaid.

2 The agreement relating to the Province of Alberta which is confirmed by this Act shall be construed and have effect for all purposes as if it contained a provision to the following effect, namely, that the said Province shall, in addition to the rights accruing to it under the said agreement as originally executed, be entitled to such further rights, if any, with respect to the subject matter of the said agreement as are required to be vested in the Province in order that it may enjoy rights equal to those conferred upon, or reserved to, the Province of Saskatchewan under the agreement relating to that Province which is confirmed by this Act.

SCHEDULES

MANITOBA, MEMORANDUM OF AGREEMENT

Made this fourteenth day of December, 1929.

Between

The Government of the Dominion of Canada, represented herein by the Honourable Ernest Lapointe, Minister of Justice, and the Honourable Charles Stewart, Minister of the Interior,

Of the First Part,

and

The Government of the Province of Manitoba, represented herein by the Honourable John Bracken, Premier of Manitoba, and the Honourable Donald G. McKenzie, Minister of Mines and Natural Resources,

Of the Second Part.

Now Therefore This Agreement Witnesseth:

Transfer of Public Lands Generally

1 In order that the Province may be in the same position as the original Provinces of Confederation are in virtue of section one hundred and

3/The schedules listing national parks, British Columbia wharf locations, and an agreement between Canada, Ontario and Manitoba regarding the control of the upper waters of the Winnipeg River, though dealing with public property, are omitted.

nine of the British North America Act, 1867, the interest of the Crown in all Crown lands, mines, minerals (precious and base) and royalties derived therefrom within the Province [and the interest of the Crown in the waters and water-powers within the Province under the *Irrigation Act*, being chapter sixty-one of the Revised Statutes of Canada, 1906, as amended by chapter thirty-eight, 7–8 Edward VII, and chapter thirty-four, 9–10 Edward VII, and under the *Dominion Water Power Act*],[4] and all sums due or payable for such lands, mines, minerals or royalties [or for interests or rights in or to the use of such waters or water-powers], shall, from and after the coming into force of this agreement, and subject as therein otherwise provided, belong to the Province, subject to any trusts existing in respect thereof, and to any interest other than that of the Crown in the same, and the said lands, mines, minerals and royalties shall be administered by the Province for the purposes thereof, subject, until the Legislature of the Province otherwise provides, to the provisions of any Act of the Parliament of Canada relating to such administration; any payment received by Canada in respect of any such lands, mines, minerals or royalties before the coming into force of this agreement shall continue to belong to Canada whether paid in advance or otherwise, it being the intention that, except as herein otherwise specially provided, Canada shall not be liable to account to the Province for any payment made in respect of any of the said lands, mines, minerals or royalties before the coming into force of this agreement, and that the Province shall not be liable to account to Canada for any such payment made thereafter.

2 The Province will carry out in accordance with the terms thereof every contract to purchase or lease any Crown lands, mines or minerals and every other arrangement whereby any person has become entitled to any interest therein as against the Crown, and further agrees not to affect or alter any term of any such contract to purchase, lease or other arrangement by legislation or otherwise, except either with the consent of all the parties thereto other than Canada or in so far as any legislation may apply generally to all similar agreements relating to lands, mines or minerals in the Province or to interest therein, irrespective of who may be the parties thereto [or except in so far as any legislation

a is legislation relating to the control and regulation of the generation, development, transformation, transmission, utilization, distribution, supply, delivery, dealing in, sale and use of electrical power and energy

4/The words in brackets were added by an agreement between Canada and Manitoba, dated 5 March 1938, validated by The Natural Resources Transfer (Amendment) Act, 1938, 2 Geo. VI, c.36(Can.); (1937–38), 1 & 2 Geo. VI, c.27(Man.). The agreement further provided that "... the amendments to said paragraph 1 hereinbefore provided shall have effect, and said paragraph 1 shall be read and construed as if it contained the said amendments, as from the coming into force of the said Natural Resources Transfer Agreement, subject nevertheless to the other provisions of the said Natural Resources Transfer Agreement and to the exception of all such interests in or rights to the use of the waters and water-powers within the Province as continue, in virtue of such provisions, to belong to or to be administrable by the Crown in the right of Canada, and of all sums due or payable for such interests or rights."

in Manitoba, and of the flow and right to the use, for the generation and development of such power and energy, or any other purpose connected therewith, of the water at any time in any river, stream, watercourse, lake, creek, spring, ravine, canyon, lagoon, swamp, marsh or other body of water within the Province and the taking, diversion, storage or pondage of such water for any of the said purposes, whether by restriction, prohibition or otherwise and whether generally or with respect to any specified area therein;

or

b   is legislation providing for the taking, acquisition and purchase by agreement or compulsorily or otherwise or by expropriation of any indentures, agreements, arrangements, permits, interim permits, final licences, licences, interim licences, leases, interim leases, rights, liberties, privileges, easements, benefits, advantages or other concessions of any person of whatever nature, in relation to the flow and right to the use of the said water or the taking, diversion, storage or pondage thereof for the generation and development of electric power and energy, the utilization, transmission, distribution and sale of such power and energy, the occupation and use of Crown lands of the Province for the maintenance and operation of hydro-electric and other works of any person and any other rights, liberties, privileges, easements, benefits, advantages and concessions connected therewith or incidental or appurtenant thereto;

or

c   is legislation providing for the taking, acquisition and purchase by agreement or compulsorily or otherwise or by expropriation of any property, works, plant, lands, easements, rights, privileges, machinery, installations, materials, devices, fittings, apparatus, appliances and equipment of any person constructed, acquired or used in the generation, development or transmission of such power and energy or in the taking, use, diversion, storage or pondage of said water, and whether generally in the said Province or in any specified area therein.][5]

3   Any power or right, which, by any such contract, lease or other arrangement, or by any Act of the Parliament of Canada relating to any of the lands, mines, minerals or royalties hereby transferred, or by any regulation made under any such Act, is reserved to the Governor in Council or to the Minister of the Interior or any other officer of the Government of Canada, may be exercised by such officer of the Government of the Province as may be specified by the Legislature thereof from time to time, and until otherwise directed, may be exercised by the Minister of Mines and Natural Resources of the Province.

4   The Province will perform every obligation of Canada arising by virtue of the provisions of any statute or Order in Council or regulation in respect of the public lands to be administered by it hereunder to any person entitled to a grant of lands by way of subsidy for the construction of railways or otherwise or to any railway company for grants of land

5/The words in brackets were added by an agreement between Canada and Manitoba, dated 19 April 1948, validated by The Manitoba Natural Resources Transfer (Amendment) Act, 1948, (1947–48), 11 & 12 Geo. VI, c.60(Can.); (1948), 12 Geo. VI, c.1(Can.).

for right of way, road bed, stations, station grounds, workshops, buildings, yards, ballast pits or other appurtenances.

5 The Province will further be bound by and will, with respect to any lands or interests in lands to which the Hudson's Bay Company may be entitled, carry out the terms and conditions of the Deed of Surrender from the said Company to the Crown as modified by the Dominion Lands Act and the Agreement dated the 23rd day of December, 1924, between His Majesty and the said Company, which said Agreement was approved by Order in Council dated the 19th day of December, 1924 (P.C. 2158), and in particular the Province will grant to the Company any lands in the Province which the Company may be entitled to select and may select from the lists of lands furnished to the Company by the Minister of the Interior under and pursuant to the said Agreement of the 23rd day of December, 1924, and will release and discharge the reservation in patents referred to in clause three of the said agreement, in case such release and discharge has not been made prior to the coming into force of this agreement. Nothing in this agreement, or in any agreement varying the same as hereinafter provided, shall in any way prejudice or diminish the rights of the Hudson's Bay Company or affect any right to or interest in land acquired or held by the said Company pursuant to the Deed of Surrender from it to the Crown, the Dominion Lands Act or the said Agreement of the 23rd day of December, 1924.

School Lands Fund and School Lands

6 Upon the coming into force of this agreement, Canada will transfer to the Province the money or securities constituting that portion of the school lands fund, created under sections twenty-two and twenty-three of the Act to amend and consolidate the several Acts respecting Public Lands of the Dominion, being chapter thirty-one of forty-two Victoria, and subsequent statutes, which is derived from the disposition of any school lands within the Province or within those parts of the District of Keewatin and of the Northwest Territories now included within the boundaries of the said Province.

7 The School Lands Fund transferred to the Province under the terms hereof, and such of the school lands specified in section 37 of the Dominion Lands Act, chapter 113 of the Revised Statutes of Canada, 1927, as passed to the administration of the Province under the terms hereof, shall be administered or disposed of in such manner as the Province may determine.[6]

6/This paragraph formerly read as follows: "The School Lands Fund to be transferred to the Province as aforesaid and such of the school lands specified in section thirty-seven of the Dominion Lands Act, being chapter one hundred and thirteen of the Revised Statutes of Canada, 1927, as pass to the administration of the Province under the terms hereof, shall be set aside and shall continue to be administered by the Province in accordance, *mutatis mutandis*, with the provisions of sections thirty-seven to forty of the Dominion Lands Act, for the support of schools organized and carried on therein in accordance with the law of the Province." By agreement between Canada and Manitoba, dated 11 June, 1951, validated by the Manitoba Natural Resources Transfer (Amendment) Act, 1951, 15 Geo. VI (1st sess.),

Water

8   The Province will pay to Canada, by yearly payments on the first day of January in each year after the coming into force of this agreement, the proportionate part, chargeable to the development of power on the Winnipeg River within the Province, of the sums which have been or shall hereafter be expended by Canada pursuant to the agreement between the Governments of Canada and of the Provinces of Ontario and Manitoba, made on the 15th day of November, 1922, and set forth in the Schedule hereto, the Convention and Protocol relating to the Lake of the Woods entered into between His Majesty and the United States of America on the 24th day of February, 1925, and the Lac Seul Conservation Act, 1928, being chapter thirty-two of eighteen and nineteen George the Fifth, the annual payments hereunder being so calculated as to amortise the expenditures aforesaid in a period of fifty years from the date of the coming into force of this agreement and the interest payable to be at the rate of five per cent. per annum.

9   Canada agrees that the provision contained in section four of the Dominion Water Power Act, being chapter two hundred and ten of the Revised Statutes of Canada, 1927, that every undertaking under the said Act is declared to be a work for the general advantage of Canada, shall stand repealed as from the date of the coming into force of this agreement in so far as the same applies to such undertakings within the Province; nothing in this paragraph shall be deemed to affect the legislative competence of the Parliament of Canada to make hereafter any declaration under the tenth head of section ninety-two of the British North America Act, 1867.

Fisheries

10   Except as herein otherwise provided, all rights of fishery shall, after the coming into force of this agreement, belong to and be administered by the Province, and the Province shall have the right to dispose of all such rights of fishery by sale, licence or otherwise, subject to the exercise by the Parliament of Canada of its legislative jurisdiction over sea-coast and inland fisheries.

Indian Reserves

11   All lands included in Indian reserves within the Province, including those selected and surveyed but not yet confirmed, as well as those confirmed, shall continue to be vested in the Crown and administered by the Government of Canada for the purposes of Canada, and the Province will from time to time, upon the request of the Superintendent General of Indian Affairs, set aside, out of the unoccupied Crown lands hereby

c.53(Can.); (1952), 16 Geo. VI & 1 Eliz. II, c.44(Man.), this paragraph was amended but by further agreement dated 13 July, 1961, validated by The Natural Resources Transfer (School Lands) Amendment Act, 1961, (1960–61), 9 & 10 Eliz. II, c.62(Can.); (1963), 12 Eliz. II c.53(Man.), the paragraph as amended was deleted and the one in the text substituted therefor.

transferred to its administration, such further areas as the said Superintendent General may, in agreement with the Minister of Mines and
Natural Resources of the Province, select as necessary to enable Canada
to fulfil its obligations under the treaties with the Indians of the Province,
and such shall thereafter be administered by Canada in the same way in
all respects as if they had never passed to the Province under the provisions hereof.

12 The provisions of paragraphs one to six inclusive and of paragraph eight
of the agreement made between the Government of the Dominion of
Canada and the Government of the Province of Ontario on the 24th
day of March, 1924, which said agreement was confirmed by statute of
Canada, fourteen and fifteen George the Fifth chapter forty-eight, shall
(except so far as they relate to the Bed of Navigable Waters Act) apply
to the lands included in such Indian reserves as may hereafter be set
aside under the last preceding clause as if the said agreement had been
made between the parties hereto, and the provisions of the said paragraphs shall likewise apply to the lands included in the reserves heretofore selected and surveyed, except that neither the said lands nor the
proceeds of the disposition thereof shall in any circumstances become
administrable by or be paid to the Province.

13 In order to secure to the Indians of the Province the continuance of the
supply of game and fish for their support and subsistence, Canada agrees
that the laws respecting game in force in the Province from time to time
shall apply to the Indians within the boundaries thereof, provided, however, that the said Indians shall have the right, which the Province hereby
assures to them, of hunting, trapping and fishing game and fish for food
at all seasons of the year on all unoccupied Crown lands and on any
other lands to which the said Indians may have a right of access.

Soldier Settlement Lands

14 All interests in Crown lands in the Province upon the security of which
any advance has been made under the provisions of the Soldier Settlement Act, being chapter 188 of the Revised Statutes of Canada, 1927,
and amending Acts, shall continue to be vested in and administered by
the Government of Canada for the purposes of Canada.

National Park

15 The lands specified as included in the Riding Mountain Forest Reserve,
as such reserve is described in the schedule to the Dominion Forest
Reserves and Parks Act, being chapter seventy-eight of the Revised
Statutes of Canada, 1927, as amended by eighteen and nineteen George
the Fifth chapter twenty, shall be established as a national park, and the
said lands, together with the mines and minerals (precious and base)
in such area and the royalties incident thereto shall continue to be vested
in and shall be administered by the Government of Canada for the
purposes of a national park, but in the event of the Parliament of
Canada at any time declaring that the said lands or any part thereof
are no longer required for such purposes, the lands, mines, minerals

(precious and base) and the royalties incident thereto, specified in any such declaration, shall forthwith upon the making thereof belong to the Province, and the provisions of paragraph three of this agreement shall apply thereto as from the date of such declaration.

16   The Parliament of Canada shall have exclusive legislative jurisdiction within the whole area included within the outer boundaries of the said park, notwithstanding that portions of such area may not form part of the park proper; the laws now in force within the said area shall continue in force only until changed by the Parliament of Canada or under its authority, provided, however, that all laws of the Province now or hereafter in force which are not repugnant to any law or regulation made applicable within the said area by or under the authority of the Parliament of Canada, shall extend to and be enforceable within the same, and that all general taxing acts passed by the Province shall apply within the same unless expressly excluded from application therein by or under the authority of the Parliament of Canada.

Seed Grain, Etc., Liens

17   Every lien upon any interest in any unpatented land passing to the Province under this agreement, which is now held by Canada as security for an advance made by Canada for seed grain, fodder or other relief, shall continue to be vested in Canada, but the Province will, on behalf of Canada, collect the sums due in respect of such advances, except so far as the same are agreed to be uncollectible, and upon payment of any such advance, any document required to be executed to discharge the lien may be executed by such officer of the Province as may be authorized by any provincial law in that behalf; the Province will account for and pay to Canada all sums belonging to Canada collected hereunder, subject to such deduction to meet the expenses of collection as may be agreed upon between the Minister of the Interior and the Minister of Mines and Natural Resources or such other Minister of the Province as may be designated in that behalf under the laws thereof.

General Reservation to Canada

18   Except as herein otherwise expressly provided, nothing in this agreement shall be interpreted as applying so as to affect or transfer to the administration of the Province (a) any lands for which Crown grants have been made and registered under the Real Property Act of the Province and of which His Majesty the King in the right of His Dominion of Canada is, or is entitled to become the registered owner at the date upon which this agreement comes into force, or (b) any ungranted lands of the Crown upon which public money of Canada has been expended or which are, at the date upon which this agreement comes into force, in use or reserved by Canada for the purpose of the federal administration.

Historic Sites, Bird Sanctuaries, Etc.

19   The Province will not dispose of any historic site which is notified to it by Canada as such and which Canada undertakes to maintain as an

historic site. The Province will further continue and preserve as such the bird sanctuaries and public shooting grounds which have been already established and will set aside such additional bird sanctuaries and public shooting grounds as may hereafter be established by agreement between the Minister of the Interior and the Minister of Mines and Natural Resources, or such other Minister of the Province as may be specified under the laws thereof.

Financial Terms

[Paragraphs 20 to 22 provide for a subsidy sufficient to put the province in a position of equality with other provinces as of its establishment. For a discussion, see pp. 40-1.]

Records

23 Canada will, after the coming into force of this agreement, deliver to the Province from time to time at the request of the Province the originals or complete copies of all records in any department of the Government of Canada relating exclusively to dealings with Crown lands, mines and minerals, and royalties derived therefrom within the Province, and will give to the Province access to all other records, documents or entries relating to any such dealings and permit to be copied by the Province any of the documents required by it for the effective administration of the Crown lands, mines, minerals and royalties.

Amendment of Agreement

24 The foregoing provisions of this agreement may be varied by agreement confirmed by concurrent statutes of the Parliament of Canada and the Legislature of the Province.

When Agreement Comes Into Force

25 This agreement is made subject to its being approved by the Parliament of Canada and by the Legislature of the Province of Manitoba, and shall take effect on the fifteenth day of July, 1930, if His Majesty has theretofore given His Assent to an Act of the Parliament of the United Kingdom of Great Britain and Northern Ireland confirming the same, and if He has not given such Assent before the said day, then on such date as may be agreed upon.

ALBERTA, MEMORANDUM OF AGREEMENT

Made this fourteenth day of December, 1929.

[Most of the provisions of the Alberta agreement are the same or substantially the same as those in the Manitoba agreement and it suffices to reproduce those that are substantially different. Paragraph 1 is identical with paragraph 1, Manitoba agreement. As in the case of the Manitoba agreement it did not originally include the words in brackets but these were added by an agreement between Canada and Alberta, dated 5 March 1938, validated by the Natural Resources Transfer (Amendment) Act, 1938, 2 Geo. VI, c.36 (Can.); (1938), 2 Geo. VI. (1st sess.), c.14 (Alta.). The provision quoted *supra* note 4 was also made. Paragraph 2 is reproduced below. Paragraphs 3 to 6 are substantially the same as paragraphs 3 to 6, Manitoba agreement. Paragraph 7 is identical with the present paragraph 7, Manitoba agreement. Originally the paragraph was identical with the original Manitoba paragraph appearing in *supra* note 6, but by agreement between Canada and Alberta, dated 31 March 1951, validated by The Alberta Natural Resources Transfer (Amendment) Act, 1951, 15 Geo. VI, c.37 (Can.); (1951), 15 Geo. VI, c.3 (Alta.), it was amended, and by further agreement dated 13 July 1961, validated by the Natural Resources Transfer (School Lands) Amendment Act, 1961 (1960–61), 9 & 10 Eliz. II, c.62 (Can.); (1962), 11 Eliz. II, c.57 (Alta.), the paragraph as amended was deleted and substituted by the present one. Paragraphs 8 to 13 are substantially the same as paragraphs 9 to 14, respectively, of the Manitoba agreement. It should also be mentioned in relation to paragraph 13 that by agreement dated 25 September 1945, validated by The Alberta Natural Resources Transfer (Amendment) Act, 1945, 9 & 10 Geo. V, c.10 (Can.); (1946), II Geo. V, c.2 (Alta.), differences between the Dominion and the province regarding water powers on the Bow River within or adjacent to the Stony Indian Reserve were settled. Paragraphs 14 and 15 are similar to paragraphs 15 and 16, Manitoba agreement, respectively. It should be noted that by agreement between Canada and Alberta, dated 28 March 1941, validated by The Natural Resources Transfer (Amendment) Act, 1941, 4 & 5 Geo. VI, c.22 (Can.); (1941), 5 Geo. VI, c.72 (Alta.), authority was granted the Calgary Power Co. Ltd. to proceed with certain works in Banff National Park. Paragraph 16 is reproduced below. Paragraphs 17 to 19 are identical with paragraphs 17 to 19, Manitoba agreement. Paragraph 19a is reproduced below. Paragraphs 20 to 22 provide for a subsidy and financial adjustments to put the province in a position of equality with other provinces as of its establishment. For a discussion, see pp. 40-1. Paragraphs 23 and 24 are identical with paragraphs 23 and 24, Manitoba agreement. Paragraph 25 is reproduced below.]

2 The Province will carry out in accordance with the terms thereof every contract to purchase or lease any Crown lands, mines or minerals and every other arrangement whereby any person has become entitled to any interest therein as against the Crown, and further agrees not to affect or alter any term of any such contract to purchase, lease or other arrangement by legislation or otherwise, except either with the consent of all the parties thereto other than Canada or in so far as any legislation may apply generally to all similar agreements relating to lands, mines or minerals in the Province or to interests therein, irrespective of who may be the parties thereto [or is legislation relating to the conservation of oil resources or gas resources or both by the control or regulation of the production of oil or gas or both, whether by restriction or prohibition and whether generally or with respect to any specified area or any specified well or wells or by repressuring of any oil field, gas field or

oil-gas field, and, incidentally thereto, providing for the compulsory purchase of any well or wells.][7]

16 The Government of Canada will introduce into the Parliament of Canada such legislation as may be necessary to exclude from the parks aforesaid certain areas forming part of certain of the said parks which have been delimited as including the lands now forming part thereof which are of substantial commercial value, the boundaries of the areas to be so excluded having been heretofore agreed upon by representatives of Canada and of the Province, and the Province agrees that upon the exclusion of the said areas as so agreed upon, it will not, by works outside the boundaries of any of the said parks, reduce the flow of water in any of the rivers or streams within the same to less than that which the Minister of the Interior may deem necessary adequately to preserve the scenic beauties of the said parks.

19a The Province may discontinue any bird sanctuary or public shooting ground which was transferred to the Province by virtue of this Agreement or which has since been established by the Province or which may hereafter be established by the Province pursuant to this Agreement in any case in which an agreement is entered into between the Minister of Mines and Resources of Canada and the Minister of Lands and Mines of Alberta approved by the Governor in Council and the Lieutenant Governor in Council respectively, providing for the discontinuance of any such bird sanctuary or public shooting ground.[8]

When Agreement Comes Into Force

25 This agreement is made subject to its being approved by the Parliament of Canada and by the Legislature of the Province of Alberta, and shall take effect on the first day of the calendar month beginning next after the day upon which His Majesty gives His Assent to an Act of Parliament of the United Kingdom of Great Britain and Northern Ireland confirming the same.[9]

SASKATCHEWAN, MEMORANDUM OF AGREEMENT

Made this 20th day of March, 1930.

[Most of the provisions of the Saskatchewan agreement are the same or substantially the same as those in the Manitoba agreement and it suffices

7/Para. 2 was originally identical with para. 2 of the original Manitoba agreement. The words in brackets in the Manitoba agreement were never added to the Alberta agreement. Instead by para. 2 of an agreement of 5 March 1938, validated by the Natural Resources Transfer (Amendment) Act, 1938, 2 Geo. VI, c.36(Can.), (1938), 2 Geo. VI (1st sess.) c.14(Alta.) the words in brackets above were added.
8/This paragraph was added by an agreement between Canada and Alberta, dated 26 September 1945, validated by the Alberta Natural Resources Transfer (Amendment) Act, 1945, 9 & 10 Geo. VI, c.10; (1946), 11 Geo. V, c.2(Alta).
9/By agreement between Canada and Alberta dated 29 July 1930, validated by The Alberta Natural Resources Act, No. 2 (1931), 21 & 22 Geo. V, c.15(Can.); (1931), 21 Geo. V, c.5(Alta.), the date when the rights of the parties were altered was changed to 1 October 1930.

to reproduce those that are substantially different. Paragraph 1 is identical with paragraph 1, Manitoba agreement. As in the case of the Manitoba agreement it did not originally include the words in square brackets, but these were added by an agreement between Canada and Saskatchewan, dated 5 March 1938, validated by the Natural Resources Transfer (Amendment) Act, 1938, 2 Geo. VI, c.36 (Can.); (1938), 2 Geo. VI, c.14 (Sask.). The provision quoted in *supra* note 4 was also made. Paragraph 2 is identical with paragraph 2, Manitoba agreement, except that it does not contain the words in square brackets; these words were never added. Paragraphs 3 to 6 are substantially the same as paragraphs 3 to 6, Manitoba agreement. Paragraph 7 is identical with the present paragraph 7, Manitoba agreement. Originally the paragraph was identical with the original Manitoba paragraph appearing in *supra* note 6, but by agreement dated 28 May 1948, validated by The Saskatchewan Natural Resources Act, No. 4 (1947–48), 11 & 12 Geo. V, c.69 (Can.); (1949), 13 Geo. VI, c.12 (Sask.), and by agreement dated 29 March 1951, validated 1951, 15 Geo. VI, (1st sess.), c.60 (Can.); (1951), 15 Geo. VI, c.18 (Sask.), it was amended. By agreement dated 13 July 1961, validated by the Natural Resources Transfer (School Lands) Amendment Act, 1961, (1960–61), 9 & 10 Eliz. II, c.62 (Can.); (1962), II Eliz. II, c.33 (Sask.), the paragraph, as amended, was deleted and substituted by the present one. Paragraphs 8 to 15 are substantially the same as paragraphs 9 to 16, Manitoba agreement, respectively. Paragraphs 16 and 17 are reproduced below. Paragraphs 18 to 20 are identical with paragraphs 17 to 19, Manitoba agreement, respectively. By agreement between Canada and Saskatchewan, dated 6 December 1946, validated by The Saskatchewan Natural Resources Act, No. 3, (1947), 11 Geo. VI, c.45 (Can.); (1947), 11 Geo. VI, c.17 (Sask.), a new paragraph 20a, which is substantially the same as paragraph 19a, Alberta agreement, was added. Paragraphs 21, 22, and 24 provide for a subsidy and financial adjustments to put the province in a position of equality with other provinces as of its establishment. Paragraph 23 provides for a reference to the Supreme Court of Canada to determine whether Saskatchewan was entitled to its resources before 1905 and paragraph 24 provides for payment of any sums found to be due the province pursuant to such reference. For a discussion, see pp. 40-1. Paragraphs 25 and 26 are identical with paragraphs 23 and 24, Manitoba agreement. Under paragraph 27 the province retained the right to contest the validity of certain sections of the Saskatchewan Act and the Dominion Lands Act. This reservation was based on the province's view that it was entitled to its natural resources before their transfer in 1930. This view was rejected by the courts. For a discussion, see pp. 28-9. Paragraph 28 was originally identical with paragraph 25, Alberta agreement, but by an agreement between Canada and Saskatchewan, dated 7 August 1930, validated by the Saskatchewan Natural Resources Act, No. 2 (1931), 21 & 22 Geo. V, c.51 (Can.); (1931), 21 Geo. V c.85 (Sask.), the date when the rights of the parties were altered was changed to 1 October 1930.]

16   The Province will not, by works outside the boundaries of the said Park, reduce the flow of water in any of the rivers or streams within the same to less than that which the Minister of the Interior may deem necessary adequately to preserve the scenic beauties of the said park.

17 In the event of its being hereafter agreed by Canada and the Province that any area or areas of land in the Province, in addition to that hereinbefore specified, should be set aside as national parks and be administered by Canada, the foregoing provisions of this agreement on the subject of parks may be applied to such area or areas with such modification as may be agreed upon.

BRITISH COLUMBIA, MEMORANDUM OF AGREEMENT

Made this twentieth day of February, 1930.

Transfer of Railway Belt and Peace River Block Generally

1 Subject as hereinafter provided, all and every interest of Canada in the lands granted by the Province to Canada as hereinbefore recited are hereby re-transferred by Canada to the Province and shall, from and after the date of the coming into force of this agreement, be subject to the laws of the Province then in force relating to the administration of Crown lands therein.

2 Any payment by Canada before the coming into force of this agreement in respect of any interest in the said lands shall continue to belong to Canada, whether paid in advance or otherwise, without any obligation on the part of Canada to account to the Province therefor, and the Province shall be entitled to receive and retain any such payment made after the coming into force of this agreement without accounting to Canada therefor.

3 The Province will carry out in accordance with the terms thereof every contract to purchase or lease any interest in any of the lands hereby transferred and every other arrangement whereby any person has become entitled to any interest therein as against Canada, and will perform every obligation of Canada arising by virtue of the provisions of any statute or order in council or regulation affecting the said lands hereby transferred to any person entitled to a grant of lands by way of subsidy for the construction of railways or otherwise, or to any railway company for grants of land for right of way, roadbed, stations, station grounds, workshops, buildings, yards, ballast pits or other appurtenances.

4 Any power or right which, by any agreement or other arrangement relating to any interest in the lands hereby transferred or by any Act of the Parliament of Canada relating to the said lands, or by any regulation made under any such Act, is reserved to the Governor in Council, or to the Minister of the Interior or any other officer of the Government of Canada, may be exercised by the Lieutenant-Governor of the Province in council or by such officer of the Government of the Province as is authorized to exercise similar powers or rights under the laws of the Province relating to the administration of Crown lands therein.

5 The application to the lands hereby transferred of the laws of the Province relating to the administration of Crown lands therein, as hereinbefore provided, shall not be deemed to affect the terms of any alienation

by Canada of any interest in the said lands or of any agreement made by Canada for such alienation, or the rights to which any person may have become entitled as aforesaid.

Ordnance and Admiralty Lands

6 Nothing in this agreement shall be interpreted as affecting or transferring to the Province any ordnance or admiralty lands included in the Railway Belt which have been or are hereafter transferred or surrendered to Canada by the Government of the United Kingdom of Great Britain and Ireland or of the United Kingdom of Great Britain and Northern Ireland.

7 All ordnance and admiralty lands which were set aside as such before the sixteenth day of May, eighteen hundred and seventy-one, and which have been or are hereafter transferred or surrendered to Canada as aforesaid, whether the same lie within or without the said Railway Belt, shall continue to be vested in and administered by the Government of Canada for the purposes of Canada, provided, however, that Canada shall recognize and confirm any alienation of any part of the said lands heretofore made by the Province and shall perform and execute every obligation of the Province which has arisen with respect to any part of the said lands by virtue of any agreement made by the Province in respect thereof, or by virtue of any Act of the Legislature of the Province or of any Order in Council or regulation made under the authority of any such Act.

8 The location and boundaries of the several parcels of ordnance and admiralty lands aforesaid shall be referred for determination to two persons, one of whom shall be appointed by the Governor General in Council, and one by the Lieutenant-Governor in Council, and in the event of a disagreement between the said two persons, an umpire shall be selected by agreement between the Minister of Justice for Canada and the Attorney-General of British Columbia.

Public Works

9 Notwithstanding anything in the foregoing paragraphs of this agreement, Canada shall retain the wharves and wharf sites situate within the Railway Belt and specified in Schedule One to this agreement, together with the lands adjacent thereto which are required for the convenient use of any such wharf site; the boundaries of the parcels of land reserved to Canada under this clause shall be ascertained and defined by agreement between Canada and the Province as soon as convenient.

10 Forthwith upon any of the said parcels of land ceasing to be required for use as a wharf site, such parcel shall revert to and become the property of the Province.

Harbours

11 Nothing in the foregoing paragraphs of this agreement shall extend to the foreshore or beds of harbours heretofore established within the Railway Belt, but the said foreshores and beds shall continue to be vested

in Canada, and there shall in addition be reserved and retained by
Canada the foreshores and beds of the Fraser River and the Pitt River
lying above the eastern boundaries of New Westminster Harbour and
below lines to be ascertained and defined by agreement at the junction
of Kanaka Creek with the Fraser River and at the point of the exit of the
Pitt River from Pitt Lake.

Sumas Dyking Lands

12 The Province will grant and assure to the Canadian Pacific Railway
Company the lands occupied or required by it for the purpose of the
construction and operation of its railway in that part of the Railway Belt
hereinbefore referred to which is known as the Sumas Dyking Lands, in
such manner that the said Company may obtain a registered title to the
said lands in fee simple from encumbrance.

Indian Reserves

13 Nothing in this agreement shall extend to the lands included within
Indian reserves in the Railway Belt and the Peace River Block, but the
said reserves shall continue to be vested in Canada in trust for the Indians
on the terms and conditions set out in a certain order of the Governor
General of Canada in Council approved on the 3rd day of February,
1930 (P.C. 208).

Parks

14 Nothing in the foregoing clauses of this agreement shall be construed as
re-transferring to the Province any interests of Canada in any of the
lands forming part of the Railway Belt which are included within any
of the national parks described in Schedule Two to this agreement.

15 In order that the said national parks may be administered by Canada as
such, all the rights of the Crown in all the lands, mines and minerals
(precious and base) and the royalties incident thereto within any of the
said parks and hereby vested in Canada, so far as they are not already
so vested.

16 (Paragraph 16 is identical with paragraph 16, Manitoba agreement).

17 On the termination by effluxion of time or surrender or otherwise, of any
interest in any lands included within any of the said areas which is outstanding in any person at the date of the coming into force of this
agreement, the lands in which such interest existed shall vest in and shall
thereafter be administered by Canada as part of the national park within
the outer boundaries of which such lands lie.

18 All rights of the Crown in any waters within the said parks shall be
vested in and administered by Canada, and the Provinces will not by
works outside any such park reduce the flow of water in any of the rivers
or streams within the said park to less than the flow which the Minister
of the Interior may deem necessary adequately to preserve the scenic
beauty of the said park.

19 In the event of the Parliament of Canada at any time declaring that any
of the said areas or any part of any of them are no longer required for

national park purposes, the lands, mines, minerals (precious and base) and the royalties incident thereto specified in any such declaration shall forthwith upon the making thereof belong to the Province and the provisions of paragraphs one to five of this agreement shall apply thereto as from the date of such declaration.

[The remaining provisions of the British Columbia agreement are similar to provisions in the agreements with the other provinces and they are not reproduced. Paragraph 20 is identical with paragraph 17, Saskatchewan agreement. Paragraphs 21, 22, and 23 are identical with paragraphs 14, 19 and 18, Manitoba agreement, respectively. Paragraph 24 provides for the continuation of a subsidy. Paragraphs 25 and 26 are identical with paragraphs 23 and 24, Manitoba agreement, respectively. Paragraph 27 is identical with paragraph 25, Alberta agreement. Unlike the Alberta agreement, the date of coming into force was not altered.]

THE BRITISH NORTH AMERICA ACT, 1949

12–13 George VI, c.22 (Imp.)

1 The Agreement containing Terms of Union between Canada and Newfoundland set out in the Schedule to this Act is hereby confirmed and shall have the force of law notwithstanding anything in the British North America Acts, 1867 to 1946.

SCHEDULE

TERMS OF UNION, NEWFOUNDLAND WITH CANADA

Memorandum of Agreement entered into on the Eleventh Day of December, 1948, between Canada and Newfoundland.

33 The following public works and property of Newfoundland shall become the property of Canada when the service concerned is taken over by Canada, subject to any trusts existing in respect thereof, and to any interest other than that of Newfoundland in the same, namely:

a the Newfoundland Railway, including rights of way, wharves, dry-docks, and other real property, rolling stock, equipment, ships, and other personal property;
b the Newfoundland Airport at Gander; including buildings and equipment, together with any other property used for the operation of the Airport;
c the Newfoundland Hotel and equipment;
d public harbours, wharves, break-waters, and aids to navigation;
e bait depots and the motor vessel *Malakoff*;
f military and naval property, stores, and equipment;
g public dredges and vessels except those used for services that remain the responsibility of Newfoundland and except the nine motor vessels known as the Clarenville boats;
h the public telecommunication system, including rights of way, land lines, cables, telephones, radio stations, and other real and personal property;
i real and personal property of the Broadcasting Corporation of Newfoundland; and
j subject to the provisions of Term thirty-four, customs houses, and post-offices and generally all public works and property, real and personal, used primarily for services taken over by Canada.

34 Where at the date of Union any public buildings of Newfoundland included in paragraph (j) of Term thirty-three are used partly for services taken over by Canada and partly for services of the Province of Newfoundland the following provisions shall apply:

a   where more than half the floor space of a building is used for services taken over by Canada the building shall become the property of Canada and where more than half the floor space of a building is used for services of the Province of Newfoundland the building shall remain the property of the Province of Newfoundland;
b   Canada shall be entitled to rent from the Province of Newfoundland on terms to be mutually agreed such space in the buildings owned by the Province of Newfoundland as is used for the services taken over by Canada and the Province of Newfoundland shall be entitled to rent from Canada on terms to be mutually agreed such space in the buildings owned by Canada as is used for the services of the Province of Newfoundland;
c   the division of buildings for the purposes of this Term shall be made by agreement between the Government of Canada and the Government of the Province of Newfoundland as soon as practicable after the date of Union; and
d   if the division in accordance with the foregoing provisions results in either Canada or the Province of Newfoundland having a total ownership that is substantially out of proportion to the total floor space used for its services an adjustment of the division will be made by mutual agreement between the two Governments.

35 Newfoundland public works and property not transferred to Canada by or under these Terms will remain the property of the Province of Newfoundland.

36 Without prejudice to the legislative authority of the Parliament of Canada under the British North America Acts, 1867 to 1946, any works, property, or services taken over by Canada pursuant to these Terms shall thereupon be subject to the legislative authority of the Parliament of Canada.

37 All lands, mines, minerals, and royalties belonging to Newfoundland at the date of Union, and all sums then due or payable for such lands, mines, minerals, or royalties, shall belong to the Province of Newfoundland, subject to any trusts existing in respect thereof, and to any interest other than that of the Province in the same.

Table of Cases

Index